Özge Sezer
Forming the Modern Turkish Village

D1620482

Özge Sezer, born in 1984, works as a post-doctoral researcher at the DFG Research Training Group 1913 at Brandenburgische Technische Universität Cottbus-Senftenberg. She received her PhD from Technische Universität Berlin with a dissertation on modernist interventions in planning the rural settlements in early republican Turkey. She worked as an architect in preservation projects of historic buildings and archaeological sites, as well as an adjunct lecturer in history and theory of art and architecture. Her research focuses on architectures of rural communities, migration, and state and people relations in different architectural processes.

Özge Sezer

Forming the Modern Turkish Village

Nation Building and Modernization
in Rural Turkey during the Early Republic

[transcript]

Published with the financial support of the ZEIT-Stiftung Ebelin und Gerd Bucerius.

Bibliographic information published by the Deutsche Nationalbibliothek
The Deutsche Nationalbibliothek lists this publication in the Deutsche Nationalbibliografie; detailed bibliographic data are available in the Internet at http://dnb.d-nb.de

© 2023 transcript Verlag, Bielefeld

Cover layout: Maria Arndt, Bielefeld
Cover illustration: Muratli Village, Tekirdag: in »L'Immigration En Turquie«, La Turquie Kemaliste, 23 Janvier (1938), 15-18 (p. 15).
Printed by: Majuskel Medienproduktion GmbH, Wetzlar
https://doi.org/10.14361/9783839461556
Print-ISBN 978-3-8376-6155-2
PDF-ISBN 978-3-8394-6155-6
ISSN of series: 2702-9409
eISSN of series: 2702-9417

Printed on permanent acid-free text paper.

Contents

Abbreviations

RPP   Republican People's Party (*Cumhuriyet Halk Partisi*)

TBMM Grand National Assembly of Turkey (Türkiye Büyük Millet Meclisi)

TCBCA State Archives of Turkey, Republican Archive of Prime Ministry of Turkey (*Türkiye Cumhuriyeti Devlet Arsivleri, Basbakanlik Cumhuriyet Arsivi*)

TCBOA State Archives of Turkey, Ottoman Archive of Prime Ministry of Turkey (*Türkiye Cumhuriyeti Devlet Arsivleri, Basbakanlik Osmanli Arsivi*)

Acknowledgements

This book has been produced from my doctoral thesis I completed with the generous support of my supervisors, colleagues, archivists, librarians, locals in İzmir and Elazığ, friends, and family. I would like to express my sincere gratitude to everyone for being there.

Specifically, I would like to thank Prof. Dr. Gabi Dolff-Bonekämper and Prof. Dr. Zeynep Kuban Tokgöz for their support, motivation they gave me, and immense knowledge on this subject. Their insightful comments and encouragement incanted me to widen my study from various perspectives. I would also like to express my genuine thanks to the residents of the Yeniköy, Havuzbaşı, and Taşkesik villages in Izmir; and the residents of the Kövenk (Güntaşı), Vertetil (Yazıkonak), Etminik (Altınçevre), and Perçenç (Akçakiraz) neighborhoods in Elazığ. I cannot forget their warm hospitality during my travels and fieldwork.

In preparing this book, I owe my thanks to my editor Mirjam Galley for her patience and great work in revisions; to Marcella Christiani for her pleasant cooperation in financial support that I gratefully received from ZEIT-Stiftung Ebelin und Bucerius; and to William Hatherell for improving my manuscript.

I want to note my special appreciation to my friends Vera Egbers, Bilge Gençtürk, and Ayşe Güngör for their loving support, encouragement, motivation, and inspiration whenever I was in need during the realization of this project. Last but not least, I would like to thank my family, who has held my hand and never stopped believing in me in my ongoing journey.

Introduction

In 1936, Turkish architect Zeki Sayar enthusiastically announced the state's program for rural settlements as notable examples of Turkey's internal colonization enterprises.[1] He particularly described the new settlement built in the Harbato village in Diyarbakır, which Kurdish people still populated despite the state-organized deportations that accelerated after enacting the 1934 Settlement Law.[2] The new settlement of Harbato Village was merely an agglomeration of houses on a bare landscape. It contained no school, nursery, or sanctuary like a mosque, but the houses were thoroughly constructed as the state intended. The new settlement's houses with white walls and hipped and tiled roofs radically differed from the adobe plastered walls and earth shelters of the rural houses of Diyarbakır and its surroundings. New village residents were state-supported Turkish-speaking Balkan immigrants who were largely settled in the region during the second half of the 1930s. They were placed in this rough landscape that belonged to the people whose language, customs, and traditions differed entirely from the newcomers. It was one of the remarkable examples of forming the modern Turkish village, which dramatically changed the rural landscape together with the lives of many people in Turkey during the early republic

The period – from the proclamation of the republic on 29 October 1923 under the government of the Republican People's Party to the transition of the

1   Zeki Sayar, "İç Kolonizasyon: Kolonisation Intérieure," *Arkitekt* 62, no. 2 (1936): 46–47.

2   M. Bülent Varlık and Cemil Koçak, eds., *Umumi Müfettişler Konferansı'nda Görüşülen ve Dahiliye Vekâleti'ni İgilendiren İşlere Dair Toplantı Zabıtları ile Rapor ve Hulâsası 1936*, 1. Baskı, Dipnot Yayınları Yakın Tarih, 91 6 (Ankara: Dipnot, 2010).; Uğur Ümit Üngör, *The Making of Modern Turkey: Nation and State in Eastern Anatolia, 1913–1950* (Oxford: Oxford University Press, 2011); Veli Yadirgi, *The Political Economy of the Kurds of Turkey: From the Ottoman Empire to the Turkish Republic*, 2017; Joost Jongerden, *The Settlement Issue in Turkey and the Kurds: An Analysis of Spatical Policies, Modernity and War* (Brill, 2007).

government to the Democrat Party on 14 May 1950 – was defined by state attempts to reform the demographic, economic, and cultural realms of the country in which the majority still inhabited rural regions. During the republic's first years, the lack of urbanization, industrialization, or infrastructure inherited from the Ottoman Empire led the state to focus on rural communities to generate a new structure based on ideals of nationalization and modernization for the whole country. Following social and political reforms intended to construct a nation-state and to distance the country from all imperial aspects of the Ottoman state, the regime of the 1930s legislated a series of policies improving the country towards a "modern" status, as well as reinforcing the central government, not only in developing cities but also in towns and villages.[3] First, the political and economic context of the country, and second the sociocultural picture of Anatolia and East Thrace were reflected in planning and construction interventions for the modern Turkish village in rural society space. In other words, the state ran programs building new rural settlements and reconstructing demolished villages and promoted studies on cultural and social facets of rural life. The idea was to develop the village community to achieve the state's objectives.

Forming the modern Turkish village was a significant field of building practice, closely bound with the realization of the modernized and nationalized rural ideal. The early republican cadre – politicians and elites – mostly followed Eurocentric examples for a developed countryside. German-speaking experts, who participated in architectural and urban planning projects as well as in scientific studies, became influential figures in the exchange of knowledge during the process of shaping the new republican environment, not only in the urban forms but also in the rural.[4] Besides, the modernization and nationalization of the country through the establishing of a genuine "Turkish Village" was repeatedly discussed by Turkish architects and planners

---

3   Niyazi Berkes, *Türkiye'de Çağdaşlaşma*, ed. by Ahmet Kuyaş, Yapı Kredi Yayınları Cogito, 1713 117, 7. baskı (İstanbul: Yapı Kredi Yayınları, 2005), İstanbul; Feroz Ahmad, *From Empire to Republic: Essays on the Late Ottoman Empire and Modern Turkey*, İstanbul Bilgi University Press; History, 218–219. 25–26, 1st ed. (İstanbul: İstanbul Bilgi University Press, 2008), İstanbul; Bernard Lewis, *The Emergence of Modern Turkey* (Oxford University Press, 1961); Erik Jan Zürcher, *Turkey: A Modern History*, New rev. ed (London; New York: I.B. Tauris: Distributed by St. Martin's Press, 1998), London; New York.

4   Eurocentric aspects, early republican state channeled for the welfare and political strength, can be discussed in various cases. Here, the thesis subject reads the state's intentions via village planning and rural program in this period.

who heralded local and regional aspects in architectural concepts to sustain the rural community, culturally and economically.[5]

On the other hand, the state principally founded new rural settlements with sanitary, economical, immediate, and effortless solutions. It integrated demographic programs such as the population exchange between Greece and Turkey in the republic's first years, the deportation of Kurds from Eastern provinces to other regions of the country, and the encouragement of immigration of Turkish-speaking people from Balkan countries into Turkey starting from the early 1930s. The new rural settlements were considered modernized places in terms of space and Turkified places in terms of the nation.[6]

Moreover, planning the rural settlements is not a unique subject in Turkey's cultural history. Considering this act as an expression of nation-building and modernization and a form of general "consequences of modernity," as Anthony Giddens addresses[7], it undoubtedly resembles the radical changes in the rural landscape. Even though they are distinguished by their historical, geographical, and cultural contexts, there are still common impulses to trace and track. Especially the first half of the 20th century was characterized by similar practices in transforming the rural landscape on behalf of the nation-states.[8] These

---

5   For a specific reading on the reactions of Turkish architects to the government's program for village planning, 1930s and 1940s' volumes of magazines such as *Arkitekt* and *Ülkü* provide significant resource.

6   There are significant resources to unveil state's endeavor in Turkification and modernization of rural communities through the new village planning strategies and settlement policies: Varlık and Koçak, *Umumî müfettişler*; Jongerden, *The Settlement Issue in Turkey and the Kurds*; Ramazan Hakkı Öztan, "Settlement Law of 1934: Turkish Nationalism in the Age of Revisionism," *Journal of Migration History* 6, no. 1 (February 17, 2020): 82–103, https://doi.org/10.1163/23519924-00601006; Engin Bulut Çağdaş, "Devletin Taşradaki Eli: Umumi Müfettişlikler," *Cumhuriyet Tarihi Araştırmaları Dergisi* 11, no. 21 (Bahar 2015) (2015): 83–110; Hüseyin Koca, *Yakın Tarihten Günümüze Hükümetlerin Doğu-Güneydoğu Anadolu Politikaları*, Bilimsel Araştırma Dizisi 04 (Konya: Mikro, 1998).

7   Giddens' approach towards the outcomes of modernity, including nation-building and state's modernization attempts is crucial for this study regarding to form a ground for the case of Turkey. Anthony Giddens, *The Consequences of Modernity*, Reprint (Cambridge: Polity Press, 2008).

8   This volume "Governing the Rural in Interwar Europe" generates an outstanding resource to grasp how the rural landscape and people were instrumentalized within several governance methods during the 1920s and 1930s in European context. Liesbeth van de Grift and Amalia Ribi Forclaz, eds., *Governing the Rural in Interwar Europe* (London; New York: Routledge, Taylor & Francis Group, 2018).

examples generate a global vocabulary to translate the patterns and motivations in Turkey during the early republic and better understand the Turkish cases by looking through the transcultural lenses.

Following these points, this book inquiries about how the trajectories of modernization and nation-building shaped Turkey's rural built environment. In so doing, it concentrates on the village as a core of the early republic's cultural, demographic, and economic programs and demonstrates how the politics of these programs formed a new spatial understanding of the rural settlements for a modern Turkish village. This book is produced from the author's Ph.D. thesis[9], which critically scrutinizes early republican tactics for nation-building and modernization of rural Turkey that instrumentalized settlement planning as an idealized practice. Similarly, this volume aims to demonstrate the planned rural settlements as the manufactured forms of rural architecture built within the subtle political atmosphere of the 1930s in Turkey. Finally, it uncovers a sort of disaccord between the foundational theories on the modern Turkish village and the reality of state implementations in the countryside.

Moreover, many scholars have thoroughly examined the architectural historiography of the early republican period of Turkey, engaging the themes of culture, politics, social and economic transformations. Some of these researchers have recently contributed to the presentation of rural architecture and planning, as well as the reformation of the village community within the frame of early republican dynamics.[10] Yet, this volume aims to involve the most

---

9   Özge Sezer, "Idealization of the Land: Forming the New Rural Settlements in the Early Republican Period of Turkey, 1923–1950" (Dissertation, Berlin, Berlin Technical University, 2020), http://dx.doi.org/10.14279/depositonce-9811.

10   Ali Cengizkan presents the motivations for building new rural settlements and reconstructing the pre-existing villages during the time of population exchange, examining the legislative traditions which had been established during the late Ottoman Period at the beginning of the 20th century. Ali Cengizkan, *Mübadele Konut ve Yerleşimleri*, 1. baskı (Ankara: Orta Doğu Teknik Üniversitesi, Mimarlık Fakültesi, 2004); Ali Cengizkan, "Cumhuriyet Döneminde Kırsal Yerleşim Sorunları: Ahi Mes'ud Numune Köyü," *Arredomento Mimarlık*, no. 06 (2004): 110–19. Zeynep Eres opens up the discussion of planned rural settlements built in east Thrace in early republican Turkey by emphasizing their value as crucial subjects of the cultural heritage of Turkey. She also documents the historiography of planned rural settlements from the first years of the republic with a view to the previous practices through integrated archival research. In her field research in the region, she catalogs not only houses, but also other building typologies in the villages. Zeynep Eres, "Türkiye'de Planlı Kırsal Yerleşmelerin Tarihsel Gelişimi ve Erken Cumhuriyet Dönemi Planlı Kırsal Mimarisinin Korunması Sorunu" (Dissertation, İstan-

significant perspectives to demonstrate the layers of village planning and fill in critical blanks in Turkey's architectural culture and history. It weights the 1934 Settlement Law and investigates its nationalization and modernization tones that shaped planning strategies. This angle also utilizes field research in İzmir and Elazığ, where Turkification and modernization were emphasized, and the 1934 Settlement Law was implemented differently in particular ways. Investigating the village planning in the early republic of Turkey manifests the self-legitimation steps of the state. Therefore, looking at examples in İzmir and Elazığ also helps examine these steps while cities' demographic and physical characteristics changed through the state's Turkification and modernization procedures. Namely, the study of this book directs toward an unspoken, new dimension of the theme by showing the genuine bond between 'Forming the Modern Turkish Village' and. 'Nation-Building and Modernization of Rural Turkey during the Early Republic' by introducing the planning examples in İzmir and Elazığ, which have not been specifically and differentially included in the debate before.

The first chapter discusses concepts and analogies linked to the motivations behind the nation-building and modernization in rural Turkey during the early republican period. It is examined in this chapter how nationalism, with its subordinate ideas such as territory, border, and homeland to spatial context, can be used to determine particular interpretations for the definition

---

bul, Istanbul Technical University, 2008); Zeynep Eres, "Erken Cumhuriyet Döneminde Çağdaş Kırsal Kimliğin Örneklenmesi: Planlı Göçmen Köyleri," *Mimarlık*, Cumhuriyet Dönemi Mimarlığı, 375, no. Ocak-Şubat (2014), http://www.mimarlikdergisi.com/in dex.cfm?sayfa=mimarlik&DergiSayi=389&RecID=3306; Zeynep Eres, "Türkiye'de Kırsal Alanda Çağdaşlaşma ve Mübadil Köyleri," in *90. Yılında Türk-Yunan Zorunlu Nüfus Mübadelesi Sempozyumu: Yeni Yaklaşımlar, Yeni Bulgular Sempozyum Bildiri Metinleri, 16–17 Kasım 2013*, ed. Bilge Gönül et al. (İstanbul: Lozan Mübadilleri Vakfı Yayınları, 2016), 174–201. Zeynep Kezer fills a significant gap in Turkey's architectural history with her study on the position of Elazığ in early republican politics, pointing out its strategical development in strengthening governmental power over the people in this region. Her contribution furthers the discussion on forceful state interventions, referring not only to the physical suppression of Kurds but also to the cultural propagation of "Turkishness ."Kezer's study also clearly exemplifies the role of architecture in the state's interventions and top-down decisions during the nation-building processes. Zeynep Kezer, *Building Modern Turkey: State, Space, and Ideology in the Early Republic*, Culture Politics and the Built Environment (Pittsburgh, Pa: University of Pittsburgh Press, 2015); Kezer, "Spatializing Difference."

of the Rural. It first reopens the discussions on the theoretical relationship between nationalist suggestions and modernization processes; then, it continues showing the localization of land as a physical, solid notion in the context of nationalization and modernization programs, and last to the democratization of land. Being a familiar concept to the cases in Turkey, "Internal colonization" is highlighted here, referring to its facets of modernist and nationalist interventions in the rural.

The second chapter presents a priori patterns of the nationalization process in Turkey. It seeks to answer questions about how Anatolia became a reference point in defining Turkish identity and which notions, mediums, and institutions were used for instrumentalizing the nation-building in early republican Turkey. It shows an integrated picture, from establishing nation-building and modernization agendas to implementing them in the Anatolian landscape. The roots of early republican ideology were nourished by nationalist theories of the late 19th century and were crystallized in government activities in rural Turkey. This chapter points explicitly how the nationalist agents were used as powerful tools in the modernization process of the country, and it briefly introduces the methods and conceptions echoed in the rural sphere during the early republican period.

The third chapter introduces approaches in spatial planning in rural Turkey that were integral to the country's modernization process. It underlines the construction activities in the rural space, such as reconstructing small Anatolian cities and towns and building railways, highways, and bridges in the countryside. However, it primarily focuses on conceptualizing the Turkish village through spatial causes. Socio-cultural planning of the Turkish village is detailed with the efforts of the Republican People's Party and their special program of the People's House and its Village Affairs Branch. This was meant to engage local communities with specialists who participated in the socio-cultural reconstruction of the rural community. In this context, newspapers and magazines are examined as tools for rural people's education, and the Village Institutes' establishment is reviewed as a new schooling model for the village children. The economic planning of the Turkish village is illustrated in the economic development concepts during the republic's first years, including statist solutions during the 1930s and country planning grounded in agricultural development and agricultural industry. The architectural conceptualization of the Turkish village is specified within the debates on village architecture and the rural house that were underlined as the origin of national identity, as well as the architectural practice to modernize the countryside by the Turkish architects.

The fourth chapter investigates the legislative scheme of village planning and its implementations in the rural from the early years of the republic. It concentrates on the tradition and progress in the methodology, the legislation, and policies in the architectural practice of the "Turkish village." Firstly, early legislation – the 1924 Village Law and the 1926 Settlement Law – are introduced regarding village construction, and the practices of these organizations are discussed with a focus on the role of population exchange. Secondly, this chapter analyzes the concept of "republican villages," pointing to the state programs that resulted in architectural regulations. After enacting the 1934 Settlement Law, the operations determined this concept and reflected on the changes to the rural landscape. Therefore, government decisions regarding the new demographic program and accompanying the new village construction program are critically examined in this chapter. These practices are investigated by analyzing the official documents and announcements, the regulations, news, and journal articles.

The fifth chapter presents the state operations in constructing new rural settlements in İzmir and Elazığ with a deeper focus on the positions of the two cities in nation-building and modernization projects. Lastly, the historiography of the villages – Yeniköy, Havuzbaşı, and Taskesik in İzmir; Kövenk, Vertetil, Etminik, and Perçenç in Elazığ, in which the field research has been conducted, is introduced with official documents and the results of architectural documentation.

Chapter 1 – Concepts and Analogies

Nationalism: A Repercussion of Modernity

Modernity denotes "to modes of social life or organization which emerged in Europe from about the seventeenth century onwards and which subsequently became more or less worldwide in their influence."[1] It is fully affiliated with "great discoveries in the physical sciences; the industrialization of production; immense demographic upheavals; rapid and often cataclysmic urban growth; increasingly powerful nation states; an ever-expanding, drastically fluctuating capitalist market."[2] The modern society, that encompasses "the subjects as well as the objects of modernization,"[3] is segmented by new policy instruments, and untethered from the tradition in a "radicalized and universalized way."[4] The claims that separate new organizations from conventional social orders in modern society take many forms including, the extreme swiftness and wide scope of change in circumstances, the propagation and connectivity of this social transformation, and their political and economic returns.[5]

Throughout history, the growth of nation-states has served as a political stimulus, especially during the 19th century, altering the foundations of modern life simultaneously with other mechanisms molded modernity. By fostering the notion of nationalism, the nation state also produced an emotional tie between individuals and ideologies which culminated in the feeling that

---

1 Giddens, *The Consequences of Modernity*, 1.
2 Marshall Berman, *All That Is Solid Melts into Air, The Experience of Modernity* (London, UK: Penguin Books, 1988), p. 16.
3 Berman, p. 16.
4 Giddens, p. 3.
5 Giddens, p. 6.

"the supreme loyalty of the individual is [...] due the nation state."[6] Therefore, citizenship became associated with a strong sense of belonging to a national group. As a result of their intertwined relationships, nationalism, and modernity merged into one another during this period of social, economic, and administrative upheaval. An historiographic overview by Hans Kohn depicts this consensus:

> "In the 19th century Europe and America and in the 20th century Asia and Africa have the people identified themselves with the nation, civilization with the national civilization, their life and survival with the life and survival of the nationality. From this time on nationalism has dominated the impulses and attitudes of the masses, and at the same time served as the justification for the authority of the state and the legitimation of its use of force, both against its own citizens and against other states".[7]

Along these lines, the nexus between nationalism and modernity occurs in the process of creating national identity, which has frequently been an assignment for elites. A nationalist credo is typically composed of many key parts referring to a particular culture. During social restorations, the elite views defining these aspects, cultivating a national psyche among the society, and establishing a common identity as critical tasks. Max Weber connects the intelligentsia to the nation's sense of empowerment and dominance over the masses. The concept of country as a collective endeavor[8], which inherently incorporates cultural elements, and executing nation-building advantageously for a group during the self-determination stage are central to the concept of authority. Then, the intelligentsia promotes and/or supports the concept of a nation, "a group of men who by virtue of their peculiarity have special access to certain achievements considered to be 'culture values', and who therefore usurp the leadership of a 'culture community'"[9] while boosting the state's political priority. Additionally, John Breuilly agrees:

> "[Especially in the non-Western World the] intelligentsia can construct a new political identity from nationalist ideology which makes the Western claims

---

6   Hans Kohn, *Nationalism: Its Meaning and History* (Toronto, Canada: Princeton, N.J.: Van Nostrand, 1955), p. 9.

7   Kohn, p.11.

8   Max Weber, *The Nation*, 1948 in: *Nationalism*, ed. by John Hutchinson and Anthony D. Smith, Oxford Readers (Oxford; New York: Oxford University Press, 1994), p. 24.

9   Weber, in: Hutchinson and Smith, 25.

to independence and freedom whilst at the same time relating those claims to a distinct national identity which is asserted to be of equal value with anything to be found in the West. Within this framework this intelligentsia can literally feel itself 'at home' and can, as nationalists, play a leading role in directing the fight for independence and re-creating the national culture in its fullest form".[10]

Ellie Kendorie contributes to this perspective by stating that the elite, particularly in middle- and far-eastern societies, self-identify as a counter-power to the former state while intentionally taking on the responsibility of nation-building. Concurrently, they maintain a contradictory separation from the majority of society.[11]

Hence, the process of developing a nationhood occurs within a faceted environment that promotes diverse dynamics throughout societal structure. This construction also encompasses initiatives to establish the link between the past and the present at a time when society has already undergone a dramatic transformation in terms of political and social life. The difficulty of connectedness, a common manifestation of modernity due to rapid transition, is alleviated by committed nationalism. Subsequently, nationalist movements help modernization by catalyzing an understanding of modernity's heterogeneity.

As noted earlier, nationalism provides a feeling of self and a path onward. It results in a renewed emphasis on education, the economy, and the socio-cultural dimensions of the modern state. The relationship between nationalism, modernity, modernization, and industrialization stems from an imbalanced but unmistakable rupture with previously sanctified social behavior. In other words, the connections exist in the case of "the erosion of the given intimate structures of traditional society, an erosion inherent in the size, mobility, and general ecology and organizations of industrial society, or even of a society moving in this direction."[12] Thus, nationalism as a benign aspect[13] contributes to the current social structure's consolidation. It leverages the force of unfore-

---

10   John Breuilly, *Nationalism and the State*, 2nd ed. (Manchester: Manchester University Press, 1993), p. 415.

11   Ellie Kendouri, *Nationalism and Self-Determination*, in: Hutchinson and Smith, p.55

12   Ernest Gellner, *Thought and Change: The Nature of Human Society* (London, UK: Wiedenfeld and Nicholson, 1964), 157.

13   Gellner, 166.

seen historical occurrences by fusing new ideas with social change for a certain set of people.[14]

Once placed in historical context, nation-building evolved into a dynamic interplay that sparked a variety of reactions in the ethos of the 19th and 20th centuries. Of these was the assumption that nationhood was a rational or necessary phenomenon, as inherent as human existence. Thus, nation-building served as a vehicle for not just designed politics to reform governmental and social life, but also as an interpersonal instrument for uniting society around the ultimate quest for the status quo. One of the first definitions, offered by Ernest Renan in 1882, exemplifies this type of interpersonal understanding by emphasizing the fact that nation was viewed as a shared sacred value owned by people, embracing everyday life as well as the past and future:

> "A nation is therefore a large-scale solidarity, constituted by feeling of the sacrifices that one has made in the past and of those that one is prepared to make in the future. It presupposes a past; it summarized, however, in the present to make a tangible fact, namely, consent, the clearly expressed desire to continue a common life. A nation's existence is, if you will pardon the metaphor, a daily plebiscite, just as an individual's existence is a perpetual affirmation of life. [[...]] The wish of nations is, all in all, the sole legitimate criterion, the one to which one must always return".[15]

Like Ernest Renan noted, the desire for justification also generated a new political agenda for conflicts and national wars and independence became an integral part of national notions. Namely, when self-rule of the people was somehow violated, it was often translated as an invasion of the nation.[16]

Evidently, self-realization is pursued in nation-building mechanisms through cultural, ethnic, and folkloric elements. Thus, legitimization serves a dual goal of identifying the customs, conventional routines, ceremonies, and collective history of a group or society. These manufactured representations

---

14   Geoff Eley and Ronald Grigor Suny, "Introduction: From the Moment of Social History to the Work of Cultural Representation," in *Becoming National: A Reader*, ed. Geoff Eley and Ronald Grigor Suny (New York: Oxford University Press, 1996), 9.

15   Ernest Renan, *What is a Nation?* [Qu'est-ce qu'une nation?], 1882, in: Geoff Eley and Ronald Grigor Suny, eds., *Becoming National: A Reader* (New York: Oxford University Press, 1996), 53.

16   Eley and Suny, 4.

inspire national identity and operate as an emotive foundation for nationalism. National iconography is "something transmitted from the past and secured as a collective belonging, something reproduced in myriad imperceptible ways, grounded in everydayness and mundane experience."[17] Through this principle, national emblems become more understandable to a wider group of people. Similarly, Karl Deutsch claims that nationalism is fostered by "informal social arrangements, pressure of group opinion, and the prestige of national symbols."[18] He stresses the importance of the close relationship between representational conceptions in ordinary and nationalist endeavors as a catalyst for societal dialogue and a guideline for nation building to produce a strong idea of the state.[19] From this point of view, nationalist symbols can be read as replicated facets that aid in the spread of the nation concept via natural and straightforward social interactions in public life, along with representations used as political concepts for political legitimacy of the state. Thus, nationalist symbols encapsulate concepts such as a collective past that fosters a feeling of connectedness, a common language, economic coexistence, and socialization in a designated territory that is communally owned.

Making of the Territory, Border and Homeland

Anthony Giddens describes the modern nation state as a "bordered power-container," adding that, "a nation […] only exists when a state has a unified administrative reach over the territory which its sovereignty is claimed."[20] Thus, the term "territory" relates, not just to the formalization of a particular piece of land, but also to the construct of nation: National territory, as a necessary component of nationalism, is defined by a physical form where the mythos is established via achievement, transmission of history in the present, and aspirations for the future. A national territory, in this sense, is defined by its political, physical, and cultural frontiers. When political assurances are formed, they result in a "particular spatial and social location among other territorial

---

17   Eley and Suny, 22.

18   Karl Deutsch, *Nationalism and Social Communication*, 1966, in: Hutchinson and Smith, p. 28.

19   Karl Deutsch, in: Hutchinson and Smith, pp. 27–28.

20   Anthony Giddens, *The Nation as Power Container*, 1985, in: Hutchinson and Smith, 34.

nations. ... 'Living together' and being 'rooted' in a particular terrain and soil become the criteria for citizenship and the basis of political community."[21]

Throughout the legitimation courses, *national* land serves a "moral geography" for the people entitled to live in and initiated their economic, social, and cultural presence in. Relatedly, as in Anthony D. Smith's words, nations "define social space within which members must live and work and demarcate historic territory that locates a community in time and space."[22] And this is "the place of one's birth and childhood, the extension of hearth and home. It is the place one's ancestors and of the heroes and cultures of one's antiquity."[23] Thus, authorizing nation's borders converts the designated terrain into a romanticized place that serves as a bridge between the country and the state's spatial definitions. Furthermore, the continual tradition, along with the shared practices identify this designated terrain as the "home" of the state's people. The national territory delineates the frontiers specified by "a set of institutional forms of governance"[24] and established for the nation state, "sanctioned by law and direct control of the means of internal and external violence."[25] It becomes a major spatial element portrayed as the sphere which contains the sources of the culture that gave birth to the new state.

Another vein of this formulation develops in the idea of homeland (here *Heimat*), which addresses a sentimentalized geography in the nationalist concept. Its dictionary meaning – "the country, a part of the country or a place in the country where one is born, grown up or one feels home due to his residence"[26] – explains how homeland can be regarded as "being at home." More precisely, it is a structured and reformed setting that fosters a sense of security and a social, cultural, and/or physical realm free of estrangement and othering. It serves as a home, a repository for identity, and a venue for citizens' au-

21   Anthony D. Smith, *National Identity*, Ethnonationalism in Comparative Perspective (Reno: University of Nevada Press, 1991), 117.

22   Smith, 16.

23   Smith, 16.

24   Giddens, 1985, in: Hutchinson and Smith, *Nationalism*, 35.

25   Giddens, 1985, in: Hutchinson and Smith, 35.

26   Original in German: "**Heimat: a)** Land, Landesteil od. Ort, in dem man [geboren u.] aufgewachsen ist od. sich durch ständigen Aufenthalt zu Hause fühlt. Duden, Das große Wörterbuch der deutschen Sprache, Band 3: Fas – Hev, 1993, Duden Verlag, Berlin, Germany, p. 1510.

thorized behaviors within the nation-state.[27] Simultaneously, it refers to "the sentimental demeanor for a harmonic unity which has been lost and sought."[28]

Homeland formerly alluded to a recognized territory for a certain lordship or canton in where they had all rights to residence by birth, marriage and other assets held through money. Since the late 18th century, it however became a subject focused and in its ideological contexts, examined by several disciplines. This sort of consciousness and scientific curiosity towards the topic brought the term as a significant fact to discuss within the transforming political systems.[29] Traditionally, the awareness of homeland was disseminated primarily through linguistic channels such as literature and art, or as a concept straddling between folkloric and scientific aspects. Thereafter, its principles were incorporated (and included) into social and cultural activities.[30]

Moreover, the literary term had been related to the rural life and strongly associated with the countryside, township, and peasants from the late 18th century. During the period of emancipation, which triggered the economic transmission, particularly across Western Europe, the phrase gained highly political implications. One of the most significant facts to develop homeland concept as a political understanding, was the demographical alteration in the rural areas chaining to the new social and economic class definitions both in the countryside and urban centers.[31]

In late 19th century, modern intellectuals began to associate the idea of homeland with a "lost and sought" place. This paired with arising criticisms towards forms of modernization, such as, mechanization, standardization, and professionalization. They claimed that these outcomes created isolating and unfamiliar living environments for the people, and demolished their

---

27   Ina-Maria Greverus, *Der territoriale Mensch: Ein literaturanthropologischer Versuch zum Heimatphänomen* (Frankfurt Am Mein, Germany: Athenäum Verlag, 1972), p. 32.

28   Greverus, 46.

29   Greverus, 28.

30   Greverus, 46.

31   Rudolf Karl Schmidt, 'Zur Heimatideologie', *Das Heft, Zeitschrift für Literatur und Kunst,* 6 (1965), pp. 36–39. Schmidt addresses the industrialization of large, cultivated areas resulting in the disintegration and reorganization of peasant groups and the eradication of small agriculture in the countryside. For such grounds, influx of migrants to industrialized cities generated a class of workers who typically worked in appalling conditions and had to adjust to a new urban lifestyle.

connection with the nature and community.[32] In this line of thought the *rural* emerged as an attribution for a place where people share similar working and crafting environments, preferences, and opportunities in their local social scape that brings a profound connectedness between them.[33] Therefore, grounding the conception of homeland on the rural characteristics occurred in a wide range of political developments; from the rural idyll to robust nationalism. This motivation resulted in facing towards the rural as the sought homeland in the nationalization and modernization processes.

Legitimizing the *Rural*

Another axis towards understanding the conceptualization of the *rural* emerges within the egalitarian practices that gradually paved the way for discourses about utopian society in the late 19th century. However, it later gained a nationalist tone in the 20th century. According to Thomas Spence, who pitched the idea of "land nationalization," defending the equal and common rights on land to live, work, and pass down wealth to future generations, the land existed as a natural heritage of people, which could not be merited. Therefore, everyone should initially have the right to- and freedom of an

---

32   Fritz Pappenheim, *The Alienation of Modern Man: An Interpretation Based on Marx and Tönnies/ Fritz Pappenheim*. (New York: Modern Reader Paperbacks, 1968), 31–32. Seeking the reconnection also emerged in Ferdinand Tönnies' analysis of societal relationships and fastened the links between the conceptions of homeland and rural realm. In his widely discussed theory, Tönnies addresses two defined consents among people: The society (*Gesellschaft*) and the community (*Gemeinschaft*). The society is characterized (*Gesellschaft*) "as a purely mechanical construction, existing in the mind" but the community (*Gemeinschaft*) attributes to "all kinds of social co-existence that are familiar, comfortable and exclusive." Unlike society, serving as "a mechanical aggregate and artifact" community is "a living organism in its own right." The community is therefore grounded on an intentional and volunteer alliance of people, however the society is shaped by the dynamics of a designated realm. Ferdinand Tönnies, *Ferdinand Tönnies: Community and Civil Society*, ed. Jose Harris, trans. Margaret Hollis (Cambridge: Cambridge University Press, 2001), 17–19, https://doi.org/10.1017/CBO9780511816260.

33   Ferdinand Tönnies underlies this sort of societal relationship by arouses in Village Community: He highlights that the organization of community occurs in the village via neighborhood: "the closeness of the dwellings, the common fields, even the way the holdings run alongside each other, cause the people to meet and get used to each other and to develop intimate acquaintance." Tönnies, *Ferdinand Tönnies*, 28.

egalitarian life in the land where they were born.[34] It was a democratic aspect mainly affirmed as the "public primarily have the possession of land".[35] The idea was further interpreted in the rural context, framing it from social and cultural angles. In other words, the Spencean scheme was examined and employed, first, as a romantic approach to the rurality of land;[36] second, it was

---

34   Thomas Spence, *Das Gemeineigentum am Boden*, trans. by F. Eichmann (Leibzig, Germany: Hirschfeld, 1904), p. 23.; T. M. Parssinen, "Thomas Spence and the Origin of English Land Nationalization," Journal of the History of Ideas, 34, no. 1 (1973): 136.

35   Parssinen, "Thomas Spence and the Origin of English Land Nationalization," 138.

36   Spencean discourse emerged, in many senses – and in cultural, social and economic terms, as espousing root of rural idyll and the movement of "back to the land" in England during the next century. Raymond Williams' analysis on rural romanticism in *The Country and the City* demonstrated an "active and continuous history" of relations between the country and the city starting with Industrial Revolution that dominated the metamorphosis of both urban and rural life. Raymond Williams proclaimed that even the urbanization, industrialization in the cities and agrarian capitalism in the country took power over traditional peasantry and this way of life in the country, the idealization of rural life and the rural idyll had the influence on the society. Raymond Williams, *The Country and the City* (New York, USA: Oxford University Press, 1975). As Burchardt explains, Williams underlined that the contrast between country and city that had crucial place in English literature, referring to changes in the agrarian economy and its reflections on social and cultural milieu, and the rurality that became the crucial theme for English nationality during the late 19th and early 20th Centuries. Burchardt, "Agricultural History, Rural History, or Countryside History?", p. 474.
Another significant representation of rurality appears in George Sturt's writings. In *Change in the Village* written in 1912, Sturt observed the economic and social transformation of Bourne with romanticist eyes. He described the changes in the traditional village community due to the capitalist shift in the town. He criticized the collapsing traditional peasant system after the "common land" was priced by private investors. As a result of this, communal life alternated in commercial life in the village where one should have acquainted with three crucial concepts: "a spiritual rebirth, an intellectual expansion and political power". John Burnett, "Introduction", in *Change in the Village* (Dover, N.H: Caliban Books, 1984), pp. xi–xiv. He presented the peasant system in economic terms to point out commercial changes, embraced by private dominancy in the countryside. See George Sturt, *Change in the Village* (Dover, N.H: Caliban Books, 1984), pp. 76–83. Sturt literally emphasized the rural idyll saying that: "in all these ways the parish, if not a true village, seemed quite a country place twenty years ago, and its people were country people. Yet there was another side to the picture. The charm of it was a generalized one – I think an impersonal one; for with the thought of individual persons who might illustrate it there comes too often into my memory a touch of sordidness, if not in connection, then in another; so that I suspect myself, not for the first time, of sentimentality. Was the social atmosphere after all anything but a creation of

altered into "a practical and pressing issue for social reformers"[37] in economic terms on the verge of 20th century. Democratization of the land generated an essential topic in social and political discourse, predominantly concerning to implement reforms in the countryside. It was a common refrain or assumption that "expropriating the landlords and restoring the land to its rightful heirs" would lead the people to freely "trade and manufacture a flourishing agriculture, and complete democracy"[38] on the way to achieving an egalitarian society.

The motivations for land restoration in social and economic areas generated some adaptations in urban and rural areas' spatial planning, especially with the demand for an alternative sphere for the modernizing world. The ideas derived from the democratization of the land can also be rooted in the Garden City Movement that developed with Ebenezer Howard's contribution "Garden Cities of To-morrow," first published in 1898. Howard conceptualized the beneficial aspects of urban and rural qualities of a place. He suggested an alternative model that could function without the significant problems of city and country. Finally, he focused on a scheme to improve the issues of overgrowth, misplacement of industry, disorganization of housing and cultural zones, and degeneration of moral life in the city; together with poverty, lack of infrastructure and social facilities in the country. He formalized a hybrid configuration that would also contribute to social, cultural, and economic progress.[39]

Several interpretations regenerated Howard's suggestion under different cultural and political circumstances during the first half of the 20th century. Most of the time, the approach served as a fundamental scheme for the new town planning by being convenient for such interventions to fulfill urban and rural planning agendas. However, it lost its socialist character through time and evolved into a transcription of housing projects in the state-planned and controlled areas. In other words, the rationality of the scheme allowed it to be adopted in territorial models of politically diverging authorities all over the world. It developed into an effective architectural tool in its spatial character-

---

my own dreams? Was the village life really idyllic? [...] Not for a moment can I pretend that it was." Sturt, 7.

37   Parssinen, "Thomas Spence and the Origin of English Land Nationalization," 138.

38   M. Beer, 'Introduction', in *The Pioneers of Land Reform* (London, UK: G. Bell & Sons, 1920), p. v.

39   Ebenezer Howard, *Garden Cities of To-Morrow*, ed. F. J. Osborn (London, UK: Faber, 1965).

istics during the various nationalization and modernization programs introduced by states in their legitimation politics.[40]

Internal Colonization

Undoubtedly, the 20th century witnessed how the "rural depopulation, anxieties about urbanization and the impact of the agricultural depression"[41] became common issues among the nation-states when legitimizing the *rural*. Most of the time, these common issues were addressed to critically motivate the regeneration of the countryside. However controversially, modernization in agricultural life appeared in social, economic, and cultural discussions. It was believed that education and practice for cultivating a country's land would result in significant improvement that would also help solve other problems like, poverty, rural depopulation, and deviation from the cultural and national agenda of the state.[42] The cultural and national agenda included an investigation of rural tradition, and, at the same time, facets of rural tradition were strongly echoed in the nation-building propaganda. This dynamic initially brought rural idealism to a status that could be justified with pragmatic goals such as: the modernization of the rural areas. Thereafter, it triggered the romanticization of the countryside.

Accordingly, internal colonization occurred as a strong planning strategy applied in nation-states' nationalization and modernization processes. According to Michael Hechter, it is distinct from internal colonialism, which was an administrative model addressing the class differentiations and economic disparities between the core (developed city) and the periphery (underdeveloped country) within the borders of a nation-state. However, internal colonization had a spatial scope as a centralized control mechanism over the people in "the settlement of previously unoccupied (or semi-occupied)

---

40   Stephen V. Ward, ed., *The Garden City: Past, Present, and Future* (London: Routledge, 2011).

41   Jeremy Burchardt, "Editorial: Rurality, Modernity and National Identity between Wars," *Cambridge University Press*, Rural History, 21, no. 2 (2010): 147. Burchardt, "Agricultural History, Rural History, or Countryside History?," 465–81.

42   Burchardt, "Editorial: Rurality, Modernity and National Identity between Wars," 147.

territories within state borders."[43] People, who objected to the internal colonization, were also expected to be "loyal" to the city while establishing security for the state and upholding the economy in the periphery.[44] Therefore, this planning approach was usually conceived as an integration tactic for peripheral groups to manage the people in these regions within the nationalization and modernization schemes. At the beginning of the 20th century, internal colonization became a widespread government intervention as not only an idealistic solution to nationalization, but also a pragmatic way to modernize the rural population to increase the state-beneficial factors in these regions.

The First World War and the economic crisis at the end of the 1920s led states to engage in more governmental involvement in development: Economic plans went hand in hand with the re-formulation of national identity and achieving modernity when widely concentrating on the settlement problem. During the interwar years, these interventions developed into large projects that included an expanded program of planning the land, implementing social and cultural infrastructure, building modern facilities, and settling the people.

Namely, the colonization of internal groups mostly took place intending to cultivate rural areas, to modernize the society in these territories where people of varied national or ethnic origins and modes of life inhabited. Besides its technological aspects, it was a sort of "scientific and social experimentation"[45] that enabled the land as a tool by which national integration and economic progress of underdeveloped rural regions were legitimated. It was a matter of the fact that this idealization became a common topic in the reshaping of the built environment in the countryside, not only in highly urbanized countries, but also in young states. Especially during the interwar years, the practice of internal colonization as cultivating the wastelands and settling the rural population in these areas occurred in the development programs of states to achieve national progress. As Grift accentuates, "democratic, fascist, national socialist

---

43   Michael Hechter, *Internal Colonialism: The Celtic Fringe in British National Development, 1536–1966*, International Library of Sociology (London: Routledge and Kegan Paul, 1975), 34.

44   Liesbeth van de Grift, 'Introduction: Theories and Practices of Internal Colonization, the Cultivation of Lands and People in the Age of Modern Territoriality', International Journal of History, 3.2 (2015), p. 141.

45   Grift, 142–43.

and communist regimes alike perceived of these projects as the exemplifica-
tion if their political values and ideologies."[46]

Between 1928 and 1940, Italy generated a significant program for internal
colonization as a part of the agricultural development program of the National
Fascist Party carried out across the country. The program began with public
works in small Italian towns and villages. Infrastructure in the rural areas was
modernized, and new farmhouses were built. Nevertheless, land reclamation
and new town planning in the Pontine Marshes were primarily placed on the
fascist agenda with a concentration on agricultural productivity and hygiene
in the areas to be reclaimed and building the new rural settlements to house
agriculture workers and peasants.[47] The reclamation started with draining
water in the site, followed by construction of new drainage systems, bridges,
and canals. The network of public roads and the infrastructure for electricity
and telecommunication were built. The land was parceled into family farms,
"equipped with a two-story brick farm-house, stables, a barn, an access road,
irrigation ditches, a well, a small vineyard, fencing, and electricity."[48] In
other words, the fascist government intended to accomplish an "agricultural,
medical, and social utopia"[49] in the region.[50]

The reclamation of the land and the development of the settlements in the
Pontine Marshes demonstrate the concrete plans of Italian Fascism. Although
the principles of the program were declared as realizing agricultural progress
in these areas and improving hygienic conditions for the inhabitants, the new
towns were organized in a scheme through which the state could direct public
activities. These projects also included housing unemployed agricultural workers from all rural regions of Italy in these controlled settlements. Consequently,

46   Liesbeth van de Grift, 'Cultivating Land and People: Internal Colonization in Interwar
     Europe', in *Governing the Rural in Interwar Europe*, ed. by Liesbeth van de Grift and Amalia
     Ribi Forclaz (New York: Routledge/Taylor & Francis Group, 2018), pp. 68–92 (p. 69).

47   Carl Schmidt, "Land Reclamation in Fascist Italy," *The Academy of Political Science* 52
     (1937): 340–63. Ruth Sterling Frost, "The Reclamation of the Pontine Marshes," *Amer-
     ican Geographical Society* 24 (1934): 584–95.

48   Frank Snowden, 'Latina Province, 1944–1950', *Sage Publications*, 43. Relief in the After-
     math of War (2008), 509–26 (p. 510).

49   Snowden, 509.

50   Diane Yvonne Ghirardo, *Building New Communities: New Deal America and Fascist Italy*
     (Princeton: Princeton University Press, 1989). Daniela Spiegel, *Die Città Nuove Des
     Agro Pontino Im Rahmen Der Faschistischen Staatsarchitektur*, Berliner Beiträge Zur Bau-
     forschung Und Denkmalpflege 7 (Petersberg: M. Imhof, 2010).

the new towns emerged as a clear example of the practice of internal colonization, in which the demonstration of fascism occupied a leading prominent position.[51]

Internal colonization in Germany evolved out of changing dynamics of economy, as in the production of agriculture and as a model for Germanizing and developing the rural population economically in specific regions, especially in the Polish borders.[52] During the late 19th century and early 20th century, Prussia, Saxony, and Silesia became important areas to locate the new agricultural colonies through the state organization. Especially in Silesia, which was populated by Germans and Poles to nationalize the area on behalf of each side, the colonization program gained political and economic importance. Right after the First World War, within the Weimar Republic, Silesia was the target of new housing legislation with the goal of Germanizing the region. In 1919, the Silesian government put the new internal colonization program on the agenda and propagated the absorption of the Polish population and Germanization of the land by building model farmhouses for the German workers starting. This accelerated in 1921 with legislation of a rural housing program promoted German farmers, especially on the frontiers. For this program, Ernst May planned the rural settlements and housing typologies for the peasant families by emphasizing a national image as German and Silesian through the vernacular notions.[53]

Together with Great Depression, anti-urbanist and ruralist campaign of National Socialists also lead a series of internal colonization enterprises in Germany. Until the party announced its land reform agricultural plan in 1930, the National Socialists already started to advocate for a land reform, which essentially involved middle class German farmers and workers in the rural areas controlling the enlargement in the states.[54] From the late 1930s to the early 1940s,

---

51   Özge Sezer, "Imagining the Fascist City: A Comparison between Rome and New Towns in the Pontine Marshes during the Fascist Era," in *History Takes Place: Rome: Dynamics of Urban Change*, ed. Anna Hofmann and Martin Zimmermann (Berlin: Jovis Berlin, 2016), 96–107.

52   Dieter Gessner, "Agrarian Protectionism in the Weimar Republic," *Sage Publications* 12, no. 4 (1977): 763.

53   Susan R. Henderson, 'Ernst May and the Campaign to Resettle the Countryside: Rural Housing in Silesia, 1919–1925', *Journal of the Society of Architectural Historians*, 61.2 (2002), 188–211 (pp. 190–92).

54   Johnpeter Horst Grill, "The Nazi Party's Rural Propaganda before 1928," *Central European History* 15, no. 2 (1982): 153–55, http://www.jstor.org/stable/4545955.

they instrumentalized colonization in territorial planning. During the Second World War, the Germans occupied Polish regions partly with the goals of internal colonization, in the form of building new settlements and villages, as well as the reconstruction of old towns. These interventions also included the replacement of non-Germanic people with the German population in these territories.[55] Rural towns and villages built along the eastern border were significant in the realization of National Socialists' ideological aims for the national space. They became places for agricultural experiments that were supposed to improve the country's economy. At the same time, they were territories for replacement of non-Germanic groups on behalf of a *racial* clarity.[56]

Land reclamation, agrarian development, and/or housing people in planned settlements was repeated in different geographical and political contexts by various regimes and state authorities. Nationalization and modernization of a rural populace occurred in several ways. In Sweden, especially after the split from Norway in 1905, the authority encouraged internal colonization models that were grounded in agricultural rural settlements in the northern regions of the country. Within these programs it was similarly aimed to reclaim marsh areas and create plowable land where small farmers and land laborers could live. Likewise, in the 1920s, the Dutch government restored the Zuiderzee and cultivated polders in this region as a central modernizing project. During the 1930s, even post-war, the gained land was developed into cultivable areas where farmers were settled.[57]

In addition to the spatial practices of internal colonization that played a critical role in forming and locating the population, internal colonization also evolved into a powerful engine for developing nation-states in the process of self-determination and establishment of an economic scheme. In this respect, modernizing and nationalizing the rural in Romania occurred as a clear instance of this after the unification of the Romanian kingdoms following the end of the First World War. The new post-war Romanian state, which expanded its territorial land, and had comparably more diversity among the rural population and an agrarian dominated economy. That led to the necessity of poli-

55   Gerhard Wolf, "The East as Historical Imagination and the Germanization Policies of the Third Reich," in *Hitler's Geographies: The Spatialities of the Third Reich*, ed. Paolo Giaccaria and Claudio Minca (Chicago: University of Chicago Press, 2016), 95–105.

56   Gerhard Fehl, "The Nazi Garden City," in *The Garden City: Past, Present and Future* (London: E & FN Spon, 1992), 93–95.

57   Grift, "Cultivating Land and People: Internal Colonization in Interwar Europe."

cymaking regarding the peasantry not only in economic terms, but also social and cultural terms. Therefore, beginning in the 1920s, the Romanian country-side became the subject of social engineering and the transformation of village life guided government implementations in rural planning. This resulted in the emergence of new villages or village parts in which living conditions were improved in healthier and more hygienic ways for the inhabitants.[58] However, at the end of 1930s, the project of socially improving Romanian rural life was transformed under the totalitarian regime of the King Carol II. Some of the model rural settlements built in early 1930s were destroyed and rebuilt according to the new planning ideals of the King's authority.[59]

Starting from the early 20th century, the practices of internal colonization dominated the planning of the rural areas in several cases, and in countries within comparable political perspectives. The methods on every scale – from country planning to the small rural settlements – the ideals were grounded in regulating the movement of the rural populace in their economic, social, and political character. That is to say, the implementations of internal colonization, not only in Europe, but also in the modernization and nation building programs in Russia[60], spatial politics in the American New Deal in the USA, af-

---

58   Raluca Muşat, "'To Cure, Uplift and Ennoble the Village': Militant Sociology in the Romanian Countryside, 1934–1938," *East European Politics and Societies* 27, no. 3 (2012): 353–75. In this article Raluca Muşat discusses the reformist approach of sociologist Dimitri Gusti and the ruralist movement, he generated in Romania during the 1930s.

59   Raluca Muşat, "Lessons for Modern Living: Planned Rural Communities in Interwar Romania, Turkey and Italy," *Journal of Modern European History* 13, no. 4 (2015): 537–41; Raluca Muşat, "The 'Social Museum' of Village Life," in *Governing the Rural in Interwar Europe*, ed. Amalia Ribi Forclaz and Liesbeth van de Grift (New York: Routledge, 2018), 117–41.

60   For agrarian politics under the Tsarist regime, see Hans Rogger, *Russia in the Age of Modernisation and Revolution, 1881–1917*, Longman History of Russia (London; New York: Longman, 1983), 71–99. Gareth Popkins, "Peasant Experiences of the Late Tsarist State: District Congresses of Land Captains, Provincial Boards and the Legal Appeals Process, 1891–1917," *The Slavonic and East European Review* 78, no. 1 (2000): 90–114, http://www.jstor.org/stable/4213009. For the place of peasantry in the 1917 Revolution in Russia see Orlando Figes, "The Russian Revolution of 1917 and Its Language in the Village," *The Russian Review* 56, no. July (1997): 323–45. Amalendu Guha, 'Lenin on the Agrarian Question', *Social Scientist*, 5.9 (1977), 61–80. The projects of Hannes Meyer in the Soviet Union plays crucial role in demonstrating the ideals of planning and also the internal colonization practices in the country. Hannes Meyer was firstly commissioned of reconstruction and development plan of Moscow in 1931–1932. Afterwards he developed several plans for the rural regions within the Soviet territory: Planning of Satellite town

ter the Second World War in the Israeli Kibbutz[61], and so forth, all followed a pattern which impacted and transformed rural life in cultural, social, and economic terms.

In summary, internal colonization – in theory and practice – occurred as another agent of the nation-building and modernization narratives of states in a strong wave during the first half of the 20th century. The implementations usually demonstrated the similarity in the operations across countries and in different socio-cultural and economic circumstances of the peoples. The common ground of the discussion was that the land was idealized in respect to nationalization and the political orientation of the rural people on behalf of the authorities. In addition to this, the rural masses were thoroughly instrumentalized in the development schemes of the countries.

The interrelation between modernity, nationalism, and modernization addressed above, can also characterize the general impulse for *"forming the modern Turkish village."* The spatial concepts for land idealization, such as architectural interventions of internal colonization became significant facets of operations

---

of Nishniy-Kurinsk in 1932, Development Plan of Sozgorod Gorki in 1932, Development Plan of the Capital of Birobidjan State in 1933–1934 and Planning for industrial zone of Perm in 1934; see Claude Schnaidt, *Hannes Meyer: Bauten, Projekte und Schriften; Buildings, Projects and Writings* (Stuttgart: Verlag Gerd Hatje, 1965), pp. 61–76.

61   Here Israeli Kibbutz is considered as a concept in terms of rural community. The concept can be also interpreted as a spatial practice of internal colonization from many angles. For a further reading on this perspective see Paula Rayman, *The Kibbutz Community and Nation Building* (Princeton, N.J.: Princeton University Press, 1981).; Tal Simons and Paul Ingram, "Organization and Ideology: Kibbutzim and Hired Labor, 1951–1965," *Administrative Science Quarterly* 42, no. 4 (1997): 784–813.; C.W. Efroymson, "Collective Agriculture in Israel," *Journal of Political Economy* 58, no. 1 (1950): 30–46.; Amitai Etzioni, "Agrarianism in Israel's Party System," *The Canadian Journal of Economics and Political Science / Revue Canadienne d'Economique et de Science Politique*, 23, no. 3 (1957): 363–75.; Elihu Katz and S. N. Eisenstadt, "Some Sociological Observations on the Response of Israeli Organizations to New Immigrants," *Administrative Science Quarterly* 5, no. 1 (1960): 113–33.; Israel Bartal, "Farming the Land on Three Continents: Bilu, Am Oylom, and Yefe-Nahar," *Jewish History* 21, no. 3/4 (2007): 249–61.; for the reading on the scheme of organizations: Josh van Soer and Michael Marek, *Kibbuzhandbuch: Leben und Arbeiten in Kibbuz und Moshav; Hinweise für Volunteers*, 5. Aufl (Stuttgart: Zündhölzchen Verl, 1985).; Richard Kauffmann's works in Kibbutz and early Israeli rural settlements play a crucial role to grasp the subject in architectural and planning terms. Also, M. Uriel Adiv, 'Richard Kauffmann (1887–1958): Das Architektonische Gesamtwerk' (Dissertation, Technische Universität Berlin: Fachbereich 8 Architektur, 1985).

in Turkey during the early republican period from 1923 to 1950, not only in ideology, but also in terms of active building practice in the countryside. Thus, the review of the topic in the worldwide context builds a bridge between Turkey and the other countries, where these programs served for realization of nation-building and modernization endeavors.

Chapter 2 – *Rural* as the Realm for Turkish Modernism and Nation-Building

Beginning of the Turkish Nationalism and "Anatolia"

Examining the Ottoman Empire at the beginning of the 20th century, in terms of political changes in the region, helps unveil how the ruralism of Anatolia was affected in the process of nation-building and modernization of Turkey. Incidents between the declaration of the Second Constitution after the Young Turk Revolution on the 23rd of July 1908, and the Proclamation of the Republic on the 29th of October 1923, generated the ideological background of the republican regime's land idealization practices in the 1930s. They were culminated by the Republican People's Party (RPP) and Mustafa Kemal Atatürk– who had the strongest political power in Turkey's political history. The theme, "Going towards Anatolia," had become the base of constructing the Turkish nationality; starting from the last years of the Ottoman Empire and lasting through the early republican nation-building operations. Namely, the word, "Anatolia," also expressed a common conception binding the Late Ottoman intelligentsia and Early Republican elites. To grasp the emergence of Turkish nationalism and its relations to the idealization of Anatolian land and its people, it is crucial to review the position of the Ottoman Empire and Ottoman society in the world context (especially in European relations) on the verge of the 20th century.

The 19th century was characterized by rapid cultural and social changes grounded in science and technology, as well as by economic and industrial shifts in Western Countries. This change resulted in the widening of territorial borders and the secession of smaller regions into national unities. The Ottoman Empire, along with the expanding territories of European and Russian powers, ruled over lands from the Balkans to the Arabian Peninsula. To protect this territory, the Ottoman Empire had to adapt its economic and political way of granting privileges of permissive governance. The Ottoman state became rigidly theocratic and coercive for the first time. In the late 19th century, tense conditions, inside and outside of the Ottoman territories, caused the first revolts against the imperial authority of young Ottoman elites. New political groups were organized under several operations at the beginning of the 20th century[1] and "The Young Turk Uprising" took place in an atmosphere that Ottoman Empire declined to resist.[2]

The uprising was instigated by the Party of Union and Progress which was led by groups who were interested in social transformations that had taken place in Paris, Berlin, and Moscow. The Young Turks were also motivated by the Independence Declaration of Bulgaria in 1878. Nevertheless, the work of the uprising cadre consisted of only minor adaptations to popular concepts in European societies. Therefore, the Young Turks and the Party of Union and Progress failed to develop a particular social theory or a lasting ideology. During this period, there was no consensus on achieving cultural and social progress. Only Turkish nationalism, with an emphasis on Ottomanism, acted as a crucial intersection of the political perspectives present during the second constitutional era.[3] According to Uzer, an additional facet explaining the emergence of Turkish nationalism in the late 19th and early 20th centuries was the political strength among non-Turkish Christian and Muslim ethnic groups during this period. These groups gradually gained their independence or left the Ottoman state's political body. Therefore, since the second half of the 19th century, "nationalist movements among Greeks, Serbs, Bulgarians, Albanians,

---

1   Sina Akşin, *Jön Türkler ve İttihat ve Terrakki*, 5. Baskı (İstanbul: İmge Kitabevi, 2014). ŞerifMardin, *Türk Modernleşmesi*, Makaleler, 4, 1. baskı (Cağaloğlu, İstanbul: İletişim Yayınları, 1991), pp. 94–100, Cağaloğlu, İstanbul.

2   Niyazi Berkes, *Türkiye'de Çağdaşlaşma*, ed. by Ahmet Kuyaş, Yapı Kredi Yayınları Cogito, 1713 117, 7. Baskı (İstanbul: Yapı Kredi Yayınları, 2005), pp. 389–390. Stanford Jay Shaw and Ezel Kural Shaw, *Reform, Revolution, and Republic: The Rise of Modern Turkey, 1808 – 1975*, History of the Ottoman Empire and Modern Turkey, Stanford Shaw; Vol. 2, 1. publ. (Cambridge: Cambridge Univ. Press, 1978), pp. 172–272. See also Erik Jan Zürcher, *The Young Turk Legacy and Nation Building: From the Ottoman Empire to Atatürk's Turkey*, Library of Modern Middle East Studies, v. 87 (London; New York: New York: I. B. Tauris; Distributed in the United States exclusively by Palgrave Macmillan, 2010). Stefano Taglia, *Intellectuals and Reform in the Ottoman Empire: The Young Turks on the Challenges of Modernity*, SOAS/Routledge Studies on the Middle East 23 (London: Routledge/Taylor & Francis Group, 2015).

3   Mardin, *Bütün eserleri diszisi*. 1, p. 21.Berkes, *Türkiye'de çağdaşlaşma*, 393–401.

and Arabs downplayed the ideologies of Ottomanism and Islamism, making them irrelevant".[4]

During the second constitutional period, different ethnic and religious groups prominently emerged in the empire's political realm. These emergent groups caused two significant events that dominated the later years. Firstly, the political entities were established separately from the Ottoman Dynasty and other imperial and religious institutions. Secondly, the concept of Turkish nationalism was gradually and strongly spread among the elites. Until the late 19th century, there was no linguistic term that defined Turkish people in Ottoman institutions. However, for the first time during the second constitutional era, the Turkish people were declared a distinct nation alongside other groups in the empire.[5] This was an extension of a crucial maneuver in internal politics that was principally concentrated on the image of Anatolia as homeland since the 1870s. At the end of Abdul Hamid II's reign (from the 31st of August 1876 to the 27th of April 1909), the Ottoman Turks proclaimed Anatolia their homeland.[6]

By the 1860s, the first signs of Turkish nationalism had manifested among Turkic groups under the Tsarist regime in Russia. Specifically, the Tatar population of Tsarist Russia asserted themselves as "Turkish." This influenced the Ottoman elites to pursue a cultural identity.[7] Yusuf Akçura, a Turkish-Tatar intellectual born in Simbirsk in Russian Empire, first gained prominence by establishing the concept of Pan-Turkism during the Young Turks' interventions. Afterward, he participated in the nation-building projects of early republican Turkey.[8]

---

4   Umut Uzer, *An Intellectual History of Turkish Nationalism: Between Turkish Ethnicity and Islamic Identity* (Salt Lake City: The University of Utah Press, 2016), 16.

5   Berkes, *Türkiye'de çağdaşlaşma*, 405. François Georgeon also emphasizes this new perspective. He adds that around 1900s the word "Turk" still referred to an offensive term in the speaking language in Istanbul. It was connoted as coarse-provincial. François Georgeon, *Osmanlı-Türk Modernleşmesi 1900–1930*, trans. Ali Berktay, 2., Tarih 26 (İstanbul: Yapı Kredi Yayınları, 2009), 32.

6   David Kushner, *The Rise of Turkish Nationalism, 1876–1908* (London; Totowa, N.J.: Cass, 1977), pp. 50–55.

7   Sacit Kutlu, *Didâr-ı Hürriyet: Kartpostallarla İkinci Meşrutiyet 1908–1913*, 1. baskı, İstanbul Bilgi Üniversitesi Yayınları 57 (İstanbul: İstanbul Bilgi Üniversitesi, 2004), 333.

8   François Georgeon briefly narrates the biography of Yusuf Akçura: He was born as a son of a Tatar bourgeois family in Russia in the verge of Ottoman-Russian War in 1877–1878. After he studied political science in the Sorbonne in 1900–1903, he settled in Russia and joined the Bolshevik Revolution in 1905. He was banished by tsarist regime. Short after

In 1904, Akçura declared his ideas on Pan-Turkism for the first time in the article, *Üç Tarz-ı Siyaset* (Three Approaches to the Politics), published in Cairo in the journal, *Türk* (Turk). He discussed the Ottoman state's political concepts: Ottomanism, Pan-Islamism, and Pan-Turkism. He advocated that Turkish nationalism should dominate the heterogeneous national patterns of the Ottoman Empire, and Turkic ethnic notions should be emphasized to assert Turkish nationality. He addressed the middle Asian roots and the migration of Turkic folks as a common national myth that could be used as a tool for unification. At the same time, he pointed to Anatolia as the place of the Turkmen nomads and Turkish-origin villagers. He claimed to trace the cultural life of Anatolia to ancient times to assert a Turkish Homeland. His ideas led to a consciousness of the rural people's[9] suffering due to war, underdevelopment, and the (financial) monopoly of privileged foreigners and feudal landlords since the 18th century. However, Akçura offered a narrow perspective by referring only to the Turkish people in Anatolia. Although Anatolia had for many ages been the homeland of various ethnic and religious groups that existed before the Turkish-origin people, he never offered solutions to problems grounded in the claims of the other numerous ethnic populations present across the Ottoman terrain.

As mentioned above, during the Second Constitutional Era, the political realm served as a polyphonic stage for diverse ideas and concepts that dominated cultural life. Political and public organizations developed ideas through several mediums including modernist concepts like the modern state, populist economy, secularism and religion, nationalism, and socialism were discussed. Additionally, political texts were translated into and published in the Ottoman language.[10] It appears to have been a somewhat intellectually stimulating atmosphere that generated a political sensibility that drew attention to the social

---

the Young Turk Revolution in 1908, he was exiled into Istanbul. He was involved in politics during the independence movements of Ottoman states such as Turco-Italian War in 1911–1912, Balkan Wars in 1912–1913. After the First World War, he joined Mustafa Kemal Atatürk and the assembly of Turkey's Independence War. With the proclamation of Turkish Republic Yusuf Akçura served for Kemalist regime during the rest of his life. See François Georgeon, *Türk Milliyetçiliğinin Kökenleri, Yusuf Akçura: (1876–1935)*, Tarih Vakfı Yurt Yayınları, 40, 2. Baskı (İstanbul: Tarih Vakfı Yurt Yayınları, 1996), p. 6.

9   Georgeon, *Türk Milliyetçiliğinin Kökenleri, Yusuf Akçura*, pp. 37–50.

10   Yusuf Akçura, *Yeni Türk Devletinin Öncüleri: 1928 Yılı Yazıları* (Ankara: Kültür Bakanlığı, 1981), p. 188, and Georgeon, *Osmanlı-Türk Modernleşmesi 1900–1930*, 23–37.

and economic needs of the people, and that lasted until the Party of Union and Progress built a government that dominated other ethnic groups.[11]

The associations founded during the Second Constitutional Period, *Türk Derneği* (Turkish Association) in 1908, *Türk Yurdu Cemiyeti* (Association for Turkish Homeland) in 1911, and *Türk Ocağı* (the Turkish Hearths) in 1912, were intended to strengthen Turkish nationalism. Starting from 1912, *Türk Ocağı* (the Turkish Hearths) and its journal, *Türk Yurdu* (Turkish Homeland), aimed to form a theoretical basis for Turkish nationality, and to develop it into a strong ideology.[12]

In 1913, the journal *Halka Doğru* (Towards the People), was founded by the same group associated with the journal, *Türk Yurdu*, with Ziya Gökalp and Yusuf Akçura in the cadre. Both journals, *Halka Doğru* and *Türk Yurdu*, concentrated on the "People" and "Peasantry". They intended to bind the "Turkish elites" to "rural plebeians" by simplifying their language and discussing rural Anatolia's social and economic problems. It was imperative for the authors that the elites direct their attention toward the people to understand and solve their problems. In other words, the elites should glorify the people to glorify the nation. This formula carried over during the early republican period and reflected the powerful bond between Populism and Turkish Nationalism.[13]

This synthesis was echoed in the approach of Ziya Gökalp[14], whose scheme to construct the ideal of Turkish nationalism was clearly apparent in early republican operations. Gökalp introduced an entire program of Turkism in his essays written between 1911 and 1918, and between 1922 and 1924,[15] and he outlined how elites should approach the "people":

---

11   Douglas A. Howard, *The History of Turkey*, The Greenwood Histories of the Modern Nations (Westport, Conn: Greenwood Press, 2001), 76–80.

12   Füsun Üstel, *İmparatorluktan Ulus-Devlete Türk Milliyetçiliği, Türk Ocakları, 1912–1931*, Araştırma-İnceleme Dizisi, 47, 1. Baskı (İstanbul: İletişim, 1997), p. 51.

13   Georgeon, *Türk milliyetçiliğinin kökenleri Yusuf Akçura*, 60–72.

14   François Georgeon briefly outlines the biography of Ziya Gökalp: He was born in the east Anatolian province Diyarbakır as a son of a public servant in the Ottoman Empire. He went to public schools and came to Istanbul for further education. Here, he became interested in literature, philosophy and politics. He was involved in the Young Turks movement in 1908 and he was active in the Party of Union and Progress. His first essays were published in nationalist and populist journals such as *Halka Doğru* and *Türk Yurdu*. Georgeon, *Osmanlı-Türk Modernleşmesi 1900–1930*, 92–93.

15   Niyazi Berkes, "Translator's Introduction," in *Turkish Nationalism and Western Civilization: Selected Essays of Ziya Gökalp*, by Zıya Gökalp (New York: Columbia University Press, 1959), 13. Niyazi Berkes referred for a list on Ziya Gökalp's essays to Uriel Heyd, *Founda-*

"One of the fundamental principles of Turkism is the drive towards 'going to the people' …. What is meant by going to the people? Who are to go to these people?

The intellectuals and the thinkers of a nation constitute its elite. The members of the elite are separated from the masses by their higher education and learning. It is they who ought to go to the people. But why? Some would answer: To carry culture to the mass. But, as we have shown elsewhere, culture is something, which is alive only among the people themselves. The elite are those who lack it. Then, how can the elite, lacking culture, carry culture to the common people who are a living embodiment of culture?

To answer the question, let us first answer the following questions: what do the elite and the people have? The elite are the carriers of civilization and the people the holders of culture. Therefore, the elite's approach to the people should only have following two purposes: to receive a training in culture from the people and to carry the civilization to them. Yes, it is only with these two purposes that the elite should go to the people. The elite will find culture only there and nowhere else…"[16]

And he continued:

"To reach the people in a real sense, they [the elite] must live amongst the people and get the national culture from the people. The only way to do this is for the nationalist youth to go to the villages as schoolteachers. Those who are not young should at least go to the towns in Anatolia. The Ottoman elite will become a national elite only by completely assimilating the folk culture. The second aim of going towards the people is to carry civilization to the people. The people lack civilization and the elite have its keys. But the civilization that they should carry to the people as a precious contribution will not be Oriental civilization or its offshoot, Ottoman civilization, but Western civilization…"[17]

The fundamental principles of Turkish Nationalism in Gökalp's texts were more concerned with cultural self-assertion and language than with race and

---

tions of Turkish Nationalism: The Life and Teachings of Ziya Gökalp (Westport, Conn: Hyperion Press, 1979), 174.

16   Zıya Gökalp, Turkish Nationalism and Western Civilization: Selected Essays of Ziya Gökalp, trans. by Niyazi Berkes (New York: Columbia University Press, 1959), p. 259.

17   Gökalp, 261–62.

ethnic origins.[18] Gökalp distinguished between the people and the elite, but no normative definitions were used to delineate classes or ethnicities. He mainly underlined concepts of *Hars ve Medeniyet*[19] (Culture and Civilization) and aimed to apply these concepts by "going towards the people".

Here, populism differed in meaning and practice from European (and Russian) contexts. Both Ziya Gökalp and Yusuf Akçura interpreted the term in association with Ottoman societal patterns. The class conflict in modernized societies that brought about radical changes in cultural, economic, and public life emerged as a completely different case than had occurred during the Ottoman reign. The empire did not consist of a class grounded on society—it included several communities where differences and definitions were ambiguous. According to Yusuf Akçura's description, Ottoman-Turkish societyembodied two classes: the people's class which comprised smallholding farmers and villagers, agricultural laborers, artisans, and small traders, and the (economically) ruling class including civil servants, merchants, landlords.[20]

Yusuf Akçura categorized communities according to their economic positions in Ottoman society, while Ziya Gökalp identified the people in terms of their status in the construction of culture and civilization. Although they approached the problem via different paths, they both focused on the Turkish population in rural Anatolia. Yusuf Akçura and Ziya Gökalp provoked a perception of Turkish villagers, smallholders, and agriculture laborers whose living conditions were claimed to be improved and, at the same time, whose cultural origins were appropriated to affirm Turkism in Anatolia.

Turkish Anatolia as the Homeland

In 1913, Hungarian scholar Béla Horváth led a research trip in Anatolia, from Istanbul to Konya. It was a significant study that thereafter motivated Turkish intelligentsia. During his excursion, Horváth observed the living conditions and daily habits of Anatolian Turks, Turkmen nomads, and settlers in the

---

18   Taha Parla, Füsun Üstel, and Sabir Yücesoy, *Ziya Gökalp, Kemalizm ve Türkiye'de korporatizm*, 3. baskı, İletişim Yayınları Araştırma İnceleme Dizisi, 76 9 (İstanbul: İletişim Yayınları, 1999), 31.

19   Gökalp, *Turkish Nationalism and Western Civilization*, 89–109.

20   (Georgeon, 1996, pp. 90–91) Here Georgeon referred to Yusuf Akçura's writings in *Halka Doğru* in 1930. Yusuf Akçura, "Halka," *Halka Doğru* I (1930): 22–23, 25, 27, 30.

villages. It was not only an ethnographical collection of data— the narratives Horvath introduced generally illustrated the social and economic conditions of rural life in Anatolia. He described Anatolia as a place for "a composition of peoples" who, surprisingly, amalgamated their diverse characteristics.[21]

Horváth's observations of the region from Istanbul to Konya included details on rural architecture and building traditions that reflected the living conditions of rural populations. He introduced the Tatarian village, organized according to a central plan consisting of a square in the heart of the village with small single houses arranged around the square, and the Circassian village organized according to the central axis on which small single houses were built. Horváth further described another architectural element that he observed in every village he visited: *Köy Odası* (The Village Room). He described these buildings as simple one-room houses where the villagers gathered.[22]

Horváth's excursion was crucial in its observation of Anatolian rural life right before (immediately prior to) the First World War. He described the environments of villages and small rural towns which illuminated disparate social and economic circumstances. For the first time, he brought the daily life of the rural population, within its cultural context, to light. He exposed their poverty and lack of awareness of a social and economic class conflict.

Moreover, during the First War, the nostalgia for Anatolia as the Turkish Homeland suddenly appeared among Turkish elites, politicians, and military officers, continuing with the Turkish War of Independence between 1919 and 1923. The seizure of Ottoman terrain, especially the majority of Anatolia and Eastern Thrace, united Anatolian populations in building a counterattack against the occupation forces. It developed into a collective defense that consolidated communities, political parties, ethnic and religious groups, and peoples.[23]

---

21   Béla Horváth, *Anadolu 1913*, trans. Tarık Demirkan, Tarih Vakfı Yurt Yayınları 36 (İstanbul: Tarih Vakfı, 1996), V–VI.

22   Horváth, 8.

23   Howard, *The History of Turkey*, 80–84. Berkes, *Türkiye'de Çağdaşlaşma*, pp. 468–69. For further reading on the political circumstances of Anatolian terrain in the Ottoman Empire during the First World War, see also *The Gallipoli Campaign: The Turkish Perspective*, ed. by Metin Gürcan and Robert Johnson, Routledge Studies in First World War History (London: Routledge/Taylor & Francis Group, 2016), Haluk Oral, *Gallipoli 1915: Through Turkish Eyes*, 1st ed (Beyoğlu, İstanbul: Türkiye İş Bankası Kültür Yayınları, 2007), Mustafa Aksakal, *The Ottoman Road to War in 1914: The Ottoman Empire and the*

The organization against the occupation forces and the Ottoman Dynasty was led by military officers discharged from the Ottoman Army and Mustafa Kemal Atatürk. They guided this group, starting with congresses in the north and north-eastern Anatolia, and declared that they rejected the dynasty to conduct the state, calling on the politicians, elites, merchants, and landlords to unite against the occupation.[24] They expected to create a consciousness of a struggle for an independent state, firstly among ruling groups, and then the people. The establishment of the Grand National Assembly in Ankara, on the 23rd of April 1920, strengthened the political and administrational dimension of the war in Anatolia and the Thrace Region, which emerged from army operations supported by several civil movements.[25] The First World War and, immediately afterward, the War of Independence, created a collective myth, considered the most robust tool for the emerging nation by the republican intelligentsia and politicians.

Starting from the second half of the 19th century, the desire for a Turkish Anatolia developed from various political changes. The transformation from a multi-national Ottoman Empire to the nation-state of Turkey did not emerge as only a regime change in the political context. It also had strong veins altering the society to form the nationhood. Bernard Lewis interpreted that although the War of Independence and the creation of Turkish state were impulses of the First World War, they were also reactions against the Ottoman authorities. The accomplishments of civil organizations in Anatolia during the war and the establishment of a new parliament in Ankara caused a shift in focus from the European provinces of Ottoman Empire to Anatolia during the negotiation of the borders for the Republic of Turkey.[26] This was a significant reflection of the fact that Anatolia not only became the administrative center of Turkey, but it constituted the emotional center of the new Turkish nation.[27] The situation of

First World War, Cambridge Military Histories (Cambridge, UK; New York: Cambridge University Press, 2008).

24   M. Kemal Atatürk, *Atatürk'ün Söylev ve Demeçleri: Açıklamalı Dizin İle* (Ankara: Atatürk Araştırma Merkezi, 2006), pp. 1–6.

25   Howard, *The History of Turkey*, 84–90.

26   For further reading on peace conferences between 1919–1923; Andrew Mango, *From the Sultan to Atatürk: Turkey*, Haus Histories (London: Haus Publishing, 2009). For the correspondences during the peace conferences in Lausanne Treaty, see also Mustafa Kemal Atatürk, *Nutuk, 1919–1927: Tam Metin*, ed. Mustafa Bayram Mısır (Ankara: Palme Yayınları;, 2010), 674–712.

27   Lewis, *The Emergence of Modern Turkey*, 478–79.

the empire from the late 19ᵗʰ century to the early 20ᵗʰ century assisted in creating the fundament for the nation as the Turkish people and its idealized land, Anatolia. Nevertheless, constructing rural Anatolia with systematic programs to reshape the rural society and the built environment did not occur until the early republican years. It developed into a complete concentration on the whole land and the new definition of Turkey's Anatolia.[28]

The social processes following the First World War led the country towards becoming the nation-state of Turkey. In fact, without national awareness, The War of Independence against the occupation forces of the First World War in the several locations of Anatolia and the eastern Thrace, and later the Greco-Turkish War in the western Anatolia created a collective memory of victory which united the people who fought. The determination of Turkey's borders defined a national territory, which included Anatolia and the east of the Thrace Region. Turkey's map after the negotiation of the Lausanne Treaty on the 23ʳᵈ of July 1923 showed the Turkish state and the land that was to be thoroughly nationalized, namely – Turkified. The nationalization approach of early republican Turkey cemented the idea that the nation consisted of an imagined community that would have the will to build its national state. This approach guided state campaigns to affirm Turkey's land as a whole nation. The concept of Turkish Anatolia was legitimated during the dramatic and didactic nation-building process of early republican Turkey.[29]

The new regime constructed a national historicism, which unconditionally rejected the Ottoman Empire. Turkish Anatolia culturally referred to the people rooted in ancient central Asian Turkic tribes who migrated to Anatolia and Thrace and blended with the ancient peoples. Shared cultural habits and common language as Turkish resulted from living closely for centuries under the

---

28   Here I use the term 'Turkey's Anatolia' to include in the geographical reference of eastern Thrace, remained within the Republic of Turkey's border after the Treaty of Lausanne.

29   Anthony D. Smith, *The Ethnic Origins of Nations*, 17. [reprint] (Malden, Mass.: Blackwell, 2008), 75–84. Anthony Smith explains the 'dramatic' and 'didactic' patterns in the nation-building process. He introduced the Pan-Turkism and Turanism in the late Ottoman period as an exemplary idea for dramatic and didactic practices. He claimed that both Pan-Turkism and Turanism pointed to roots and the homeland to the central Asia. The migration from central Asia and settling in the Anatolia and Balkans became a collective history and myth among the idea. And this conception demonstrated the dramatic narrative in historical context, and the didactic narrative to pass through to the future generations.

Turkish-speaking authority. This historical reading was used as a tool to cement the idea of a Turkified Anatolia. The formula was clearly declared in the speech of Mustafa Kemal Atatürk in 1930: "The Turkish Nation is Turkey's People who established the Republic of Turkey."[30] Here the Republic of Turkey was meant in terms of the national territory. The people who settled in this terrain, and could speak the Turkish language, were considered Turkish; irrespective of their ethnic, cultural, or social differences.

The early republican approach to Turkish nationalism shaped itself in the new pursuit to melt the ethnic and cultural differences in the pot of Turkification. İsmail Hakkı Baltacıoğlu, who was another early republican intellectual supporting Turkish nationalism during the 1930s and 1940s, sought a solution for the definition of Turkish nationalism in his texts published in several mouthpieces of the Kemalist regime. He declared, "The idea of a nation emerged from the idea of history, the idea of genesis, and the idea of evolution."[31] He believed the nation was the foundation of a bridge to connect the past, present, and future with a dynamic structure, and there was no other nation in the world without a shared memory and history and a promising future.[32] He added that "the culture and tradition belonged to the nation; however, the civilization belonged to all nations,"[33] an international goal to achieve.

Similar to Ziya Gökalp's "Culture and Civilization," İsmail Hakkı Baltacıoğlu endeavored to construct a national ideology, including cultural aspects and its development towards a higher civilization. Again, he theorized that civilization occurred as an empirical process, but culture emerged and was nourished by the de facto habits of peoples, and therefore, culture demonstrated the essential character of a nation. To be acquainted with the essence of a nation – the culture, which one could discover by "going towards the people," ought to be the most important movement. The ideal folk consisted of the shared cultural values between the people, who preserved the fundamental elements of culture, and élites, who transmitted civilization.[34]

---

30   Ayse Afet Inan, *Medeni bilgiler ve M. Kemal Atatürk'ün el yazıları* (Ankara: Türk Tarih Kurumu Basimevi, 1998), p. 18, Ankara.

31   İsmail Hakkı Baltacıoğlu, *Millet Nedir?*, *Türk'e Doğru* (Ankara: Atatürk Kültür, Dil, Tarih Yüksek Kurumu, 1994), 369.

32   Baltacıoğlu, 369–70.

33   İsmail Hakkı Baltacıoğlu, *Milleti Anla!*, *Türk'e Doğru* (Ankara: Atatürk Kültür, Dil, Tarih Yüksek Kurumu, 1994), 247.

34   İsmail Hakkı Baltacıoğlu, *Problemler*, *Türk'e Doğru* (Ankara: Atatürk Kültür, Dil, Tarih Yüksek Kurumu, 1994), 23.

The Turkification and modernization of Anatolia occurred in several ways following this approach. This method accomplished the agenda of the new state and justified the regime's interventions by observing, displaying, reconstructing, and improving rural Anatolian people and their living conditions. At the same time, the common perspective saw the new regime's ideology as a synthesis of nationalism and populism. According to Şerif Mardin, early republican objectives existed in a realm where the self-recognition of a nation had not wholly arisen and where the forms of social classes did not exist as they had in western societies. However, early republican ideology, as in Kemalism[35] – systematically blended nationalism and a form of populism that would not develop into class differentiation in the Western sense.[36]

The program in the 1935 fourth congress of the Republican People's Party (RPP), established in 1919 and the political face of the new regime, generated the crystallized relationship between the party, state, and Kemalism with this statement: "The main lines of our intentions, not only for a few years but for the future as well, are here put together in a compact form. All these principles, which are the fundamentals of the party, constitute Kemalism." Party principles were declared repeatedly and emphatically: the homeland, the nation, the constitution of the state, and public rights:

"Fatherland is the sacred country within our present political boundaries, where the Turkish nation lives with its ancient and illustrious history, and with its past glories still living in the depths of its soil. Fatherland is a Unity, which does not accept separation under any circumstance.

The Nation is political composed of citizens bound together with the bonds of language, culture and ideal.

[Statement for the constitution of the state:] Turkey is a nationalist, populist[37], state socialist, secular, and revolutionary Republic.

[Statement for the public rights:] It is one of the important principles of our Party to safeguard the individual and social rights of liberty, of equality, of

---

35   The principles of Kemalism which dominated the early republican years, were embodied in six precepts: Republicanism, Nationalism, Populism, Secularism, Statism and Reformism. (Munis) Tekinalp, *Kemalizm* (İstanbul: Cumhuriyet Gazete ve Matbaası, 1936).

36   Şerif Mardin, *Bütün eserleri diszisi. 3: İdeoloji*, İletişim yayınları, 191, 3. baskı (Cağaloğlu, İstanbul: İletişim Yayınları, 1995), p. 98, Cağaloğlu, İstanbul.

37   Translators' note: "i.e. dependent upon popular sovereignty".

inviolability, and of property. These rights are with the bounds of the State's authority".[38]

It is significant to note that during the first period – from the establishment in 1919 to the one-party regime of the RPP in 1930 – Kemalist ideology had a populist character, and with the plurality in parliament, unified diverse folks under the Republic of Turkey.[39] After 1930, the ideology slightly shifted from one of populism to that of nationalism. It strengthened the idea of a Turkish Anatolia that idealized Anatolian land on behalf of the "Turkish" population and the Kemalist state.

Institutionalization to Legitimize the Turkish Anatolia

The efforts of the intelligentsia and the politicians to determine a Turkish Anatolia starting in the late Ottoman period gained momentum in the early republican ideology. These attempts occurred principally in institutional forms, as well as in the construction operations of the state. Proof of Turkishness was first pursued in the historical and linguistic roots of the existing Turkish population. With the establishment of the Archaeological Museum in the republican capital city Ankara in 1921, the Turkish Historical Society in 1931, and the Turkish Language Association in 1932, state institutions sought to prove a form of

---

38   John Parker and Charles Smith, trans., 'Appendix: Program of Republican People's Party', in *Modern Turkey*, 1. ed. (London: George Routledge & Sons, Ltd., 1940), pp. 235–251 (pp. 235–236).
      Another resource which points to the strong bond between Kemalism, the RPP and the Turkish state was written by Malik Evrenol in 1936. In his book "Revolutionary Turkey", Evrenol introduced the party program, state reforms, the economic, industrial and cultural developments and the role of Mustafa Kemal Atatürk to the English-speaking public. Malik Evrenol, *Revolutionary Turkey* (Ankara: Istanbul: Librairie Hachette, 1936), Ankara: Istanbul.

39   Nazan Maksudyan emphasizes the period, the authoritarianism started to appear, in terms of emergence of Turkish nationalism. She pointed to the Law on the Maintance of Order – *Takrir-i Sükun Kanunu* in 1925 which restricted opposition in parliament. In 1927, in the second Party Congress of RPP, Mustafa Kemal Atatürk read the *Nutuk* (the Speech on the incidents from the beginning of Independence War in 1919 to the proclamation of Turkish Republic in 1923). This paved the way for the authoritarian regime emphasizing Atatürk's competence and Kemalism, that ruled the following years. See Nazan Maksudyan, *Türklüğü Ölçmek: Bilimkurgusal Antropoloji ve Türk Milliyetçiliğinin Irkçı Çehresi, 1925–1939*, İlk basım (Beyoğlu, İstanbul: Metis, 2005), 40–42.

Turkism that had been blended with other civilizations and cultivated in Anatolia for ages.

One of the earliest institutions for research on Anatolian cultures was the Ankara Archaeological Museum[40], founded in 1921, which aimed to narrate an ancient storyline of the Anatolian people. The primary purpose emerged from the idea to create a museum for the Hittite Civilization in Ankara. At this time, the intelligentsia was moving from Istanbul to Ankara to be involved in establishing the new state and following the new parliament.[41] In the first years, the Hittite monuments around Ankara were placed in the museum. Afterward, the collection expanded to the monuments of ancient civilizations from all over the country.[42]

The priority placed on Hittite studies by the Ankara Archaeological Museum represented another intention of early republican nationalist ideology: showcasing Ankara and its surrounding region as the geographical center of Hittite civilization. In this respect, the capital city of the new Turkey in the heart of this ancient civilization would support the testimony that the Anatolian people inherited the land, the culture, and the tradition from past civilizations. Now they would carry this heritage into the future.[43] The Ankara Archaeological Museum is early evidence of the state's intention to connect to-

---

40   The museum later renamed as "Museum for Anatolian Civilizations".

41   Hittite research started in 1905 by Theodor Makridi, who was in charge of the Royal Museum in Istanbul, and German philologist Hugo Winckler, an Assyriologist and Associate Professor of Semitic Languages in Berlin. Makridi and Winckler studied in Bogazkoy. In 1907, the German Archaeological Institute participated in the excavations on the site. The team – Otto Puchstein, Heinrich Kohl, Daniel Krencker, Ludwig Curtius, and Erich Puchstein – studied the temples, city walls and city gates until 1912. Jürgen Seeher and Deutsches Archäologisches Institut, eds., 'Hattuşa'da 106 Yıl': Hitit Kazılarının Fotoğraflarla Öyküsü = '106 Years in Hattusha': Photographs Tell the Story of the Excavations in the Hittite Capital, Yapı Kredi yayınları, 3712, 1. baskı (Beyoğlu, İstanbul: Yapı Kredi Yayınları: DAI, 2012), pp. 23–71, Beyoğlu, İstanbul. The excavation started again in 1931 with a team of Dr. Kurt Bittel and the support of the German Archaeological Institute and the Deutsche Orient Gesellschaft until 1939. During this period the Hittite Palace buildings and fortification walls were excavated. Seeher and Deutsches Archäologisches Institut, 72–89. The excavations were discontinued due to the Second World War and restarted in 1952 by Kurt Bittel. The research was extended by Peter Neve between 1978 and 1993 and by Jürgen Seeher between 1994 and 2005. The studies on site are continued by Andreas Schachner since 2005.

42   Raci Temizer, Ankara Arkeoloji Müzesi (Ankara: Türk Tarih Kurumu Yayınları, 1966), 1.

43   Bozdoğan states that: "it was postulated that the first indigenous people of Anatolia, the Hittites, were in fact ancestors of Turks." Sibel Bozdoğan, Modernism and Nation

day's people to the cultural roots of Anatolia in ancient civilizations by erasing the memory of Ottoman history and underlining the archaic one. At the same time, archaeological research undertaken by the state aimed to construct a substantial bond between the people and western culture; since the 18th century, archaeology arose as a vigorous tool for self-determination of national identity among European societies.[44]

Since the 18th century, Antiquity was idealized as the roots of European culture. Excavations directed by German and English scholars in the Ottoman territories showed Ottoman intelligentsia that fields like archaeology, anthropology, and ethnography serve to justify nationalist theories in the West. Following this tradition, early republican intelligentsia aspired to construct another bridge between the European civilizations and Turkey's people who were one of the first inhabitants of Anatolia due to the discourse in the early republic.[45] Anatolia, considered the origin of Western society, was also affirmed by this discourse as a shared element between Turkey and Europe. According to Can Bilsel, this approach demonstrated the desire of the nation, which rooted itself in archaic ancestors in Anatolia and central Asia, to seek a connection to European civilizations.[46]

Relatedly, in 1930, the Ethnography Museum of Ankara was founded to present components of the Anatolian culture studied in empirical research across the country. In 1933, the Ankara Archaeological Museum and the

---

Building: Turkish Architectural Culture in the Early Republic, Studies in Modernity and National Identity (Seattle: University of Washington Press, 2001), p. 243.

44   For a reading on archaeology as a tool for nationalism, see Bruce G. Trigger, "Alternative Archaeologies: Nationalist, Colonialist, Imperialist", *Man*, 19 (1984), 355 <doi:10.2307/2802176>. For further reading on how archaeology was instrumentalized in early republican Turkey's nation building program, see Tuğba Tanyeri-Erdemir, "Archaeology as a Source of National Pride in the Early Years of the Turkish Republic", *Journal of Field Archaeology*, 31 (2006), 381–393. See also Serpil Akkaya, *Sumerer, Hethiter und Trojaner – Urahnen der anatolischen Türken? Eine rezeptionsgeschichtliche Betrachtung der Rolle antiker Kulturen in den Identitätskonzeptionen der Atatürk'schen Reformpolitik*, 1. Aufl, Thesis series (Innsbruck: Innsbruck Univ. Press, 2012).

45   Hamit Sadi, *İktisadi Türkiye: Tabii, Beşeri ve Mevzii Coğrafya Tetkikleri*, Yüksek İktisat ve Ticaret Mektebi 14 (İstanbul: Ahmet Sait Matbaası, 1932), 51.

46   S. M. Can Bilsel, "'Our Anatolia': Organicism And The Making Of Humanist Culture In Turkey', in *Muqarnas, Volume 24 Muqarnas, Volume 24 History and Ideology: Architectural Heritage of the 'Lands of Rum'*, ed. by Gülru Necipoglu Bozdoğan (Brill Academic Publishers, 2007), pp. 223–242 (p. 224) <doi:10.1163/ej.9789004163201.i-310.39>.

Ethnography Museum of Ankara joined under the publication *Türk Tarih, Arke-ologya ve Etnografya Dergisi* (The Journal for Turkish History, Archaeology, and Ethnography). Reşit Galip (Mustafa Reşit Baydur), the minister of education, announced the journal's primary goal in the first issue. "This journal targets to disclose archaeological studies, create a communication tool between local and foreigner scholars, record historical, archaeological and ethnographical news about Anatolia which contains a great, untouched treasure, and report them abroad."[47]

Moreover, Turkish history research was maintained by the *Türkocağı Türk Tarihi Tetkik Encümeni* (Turkish Hearths Research Committee for Turkish History) from 1930. This committee consisted of historians and politicians such as Yusuf Akçura, Halil Ethem Eldem, Ayşe Afet Inan, Reşit Galip (Mustafa Reşit Baydur), Samih Rifat and İsmail Hakkı Uzunçarşılı. In 1931, they released the first stage of the study of Turkish history called *Türk Tarihinin Anahatları* (Outline of Turkish History)[48]. In the same year, the committee founded the Turkish Historical Society focusing on research about Turkish history.[49]

Reşit Galip (Mustafa Reşit Baydur) presented the fundamental Turkish history hypothesis. The direction of relationship dynamics between Europe and Asia was hitherto introduced as a flow from the West to the East. However, on the contrary, a flow from the East to the West was historically more prevalent. During the archaic ages, Turkic tribes had moved from Central Asia to the West, where they settled and took on new cultural qualities due to the conditions they confronted in different environments. Anatolia emerged as a region where the majority of migrated tribes were settled since it was geographically midway on the path of migration. Therefore, the Turkification of Anatolia began in the Paleolithic ages, and the masses had gradually Turkified for centuries, turning Anatolia into a land purely representing Turks. As a result of

---

47   Reşit Galip, "Tarih, Arkeologya ve Etnografya Dergisi Niçin Çıkıyor?," *Türk Tarih, Arkeol-ogya ve Etnografya Dergisi* Temmuz, no. 1 (1933): 4.

48   The Turkish histoty hypothesis was presented in publication by Ayşe Afetinan in 1931, with the title of Prolegomena to an Outline of Turkish History – Türk Tarihinin Ana Hat-ları, Methal Kısmı. See (Ayşe) Afetinan, "Afet İnan: Prolegomena to an Outline of Turk-ish History", in *Discourses of Collective Identity in Central and Southeast Europe (1770–1945): Texts and Commentaries*, ed. by Ahmet Ersoy, Maciej Górny, and Vangelis Kechriotis, trans. by Ahmet Ersoy (Budapest; New York: Central European University Press, 2010), pp. 54–61.

49   Büşra Ersanlı, *İktidar ve Tarih*, İletişim Yayınları 880, Araştırma İnceleme Dizisi 139 (İs-tanbul, Turkey: İletişim Yayınları, 2003), 139–80.

that fact, Anatolia exhibited a Turkish history as early as central Asia.[50] Following this argument, the Turkish Historical Society crystallized the idea of the "Roots of Turkism in Anatolia" enormously depending on the hypothesis. Then the Turkish scholars focused on folklore and ethnography studies as well as archaeological and historical research to testify to a parallel history belonging to Turkic folks in Anatolia.

The establishment of the *Türk Dili Tetkik Cemiyeti* (Turkish Language Association) in July 1932 was another endeavor of the Turkish Historical Society to create a testimony to Turkish Anatolia. The Alphabet Reform in 1928[51] created a new language theory related to the Turkish history hypothesis. Changing lettering from the Arab alphabet to the Latin-origin alphabet emerged as a step in continuing the process of language reform, which also included replacing Arab-origin words with Turkish-origin words.[52]

In October 1932, the First Turkish Language Congress was assembled. During the conferences, the committee concentrated on discussions about the history of the Turkish language, strategies for its development, and systematic research that would elevate the Turkish language to a prestigious place among other languages worldwide. First, differences between written and spoken language should be reconciled. Then, with the help of a thorough analysis of dialects and articulations of idioms seen in different parts of the country, the Turkish language should be reformed into a more populist and nationalist adaptation.[53] The committee of the First Language Congress developed a theory on the Turkish language – The Sun Language Theory following the Turkish history hypothesis. Hereafter, the Turkish language contained features belonging to Indo-European and Semitic languages; in fact, the origin of Turkish arose as the genesis of these languages. In other words, scholars proposed that the first Turkic languages appeared as the ancestors of all human

---

50   Reşit Galip, 'Türk Tarih Tarih İnkılabı ve Yabancı Tezler', Birinci Teşrin. Sayı 9 (1933), pp. 167–168, and Maksudyan, *Türklüğü Ölçmek*, 56–62.

51   Yeşim Bayar introduces the Alphabet Reform from the perspective in which Language politics were instrumentalized in the nation-building projects.: Yeşim Bayar, *Formation of the Turkish Nation-State, 1920–1938* (New York, NY: Palgrave Macmillan, 2014), 54–58.

52   İsa Öztürk, *Harf Devrimi ve Sonuçları: Deneme* (İstanbul: Adam, 2004), and *Harf İnkılabı, 1928–1938: Tarih, Tahlil, Tasvir*, C.H.P. Beşiktaş Halkevi Yayınları, Sayı 1 (İstanbul: İstanbul: Kader Basımevi, 1938), İstanbul.

53   Samih Rifat (Yalnızgil), "Birinci Gün, 26 Eylül 1932 Pazartesi, Türk Dili Tetkik Cemiyeti Reisi Samih Rifat Beyin Açma Nutku" (İstanbul Devlet Matbaası, 1933), 1–10.

languages.[54] The Sun Language Theory represented early republican ideology in forming well-established nationhood, which roots referred to essences of other cultures, especially Western civilizations.[55]

Between 1932 and 1934, the Turkish Language Association conducted research on the dictionary, grammar, syntax, and etymology of spoken and written language in Anatolia. At the same time, the association established a committee that collected the words in spoken Turkish and sought replacements for foreign expressions in the language. They believed that the essence of Turkish was being spoken among Turkoman nomads or Turkic-origin villagers in the country. Therefore, the research team traveled across the country to discover new dialects, accents, and vocabulary. The scholars lived with the villagers to grasp the language's authenticity and categorized and compiled materials by region.[56] This approach ushered in a physical connection between the intelligentsia and rural people that was realized in theory and practice.

Language studies and research on archaeology, ethnography, and history were not the only fields in which scholars focused projects on rural Anatolia. Various institutional programs of the one-party government of RPP from 1930[57] to 1945 ultimately defined the acts of the state. Among them the People's House – Halkevi was introduced in the third congress of RPP in 1931 as a significant program to approach the masses and serve the political and ideological endeavors of the RPP, and hence the state, not only in cities, but also in small towns all over the country:

"The principles which summarize the essentials of the Turkish state, and the revolutions of Atatürk are to discard deleterious and negative facts from the

---

54   Hüseyin Sadoğlu, *Türkiye'de Ulusçuluk ve Dil Politikaları*, 1. baskı, İstanbul Bilgi Üniversitesi Yayınları 44 (İstanbul: İstanbul Bilgi Üniversitesi Yayınları, 2003), 246–63.

55   Can Bilsel also comments on the Sun Language Theory: Can Bilsel, "Our Anatolia," 225.

56   Ahmet Caferoğlu, *Anadolu Dialektolojisi Üzerine Malzeme I: Balıkesir, Manisa, Afyonkarahisar, Isparta, Aydın, İzmir, Burdur, Antalya, Muğla, Denizli, Kütahya Vilayetleri Ağızları*, Edebiyat Fakültesi Dil Seminerleri 105 (İstanbul: İstanbul Üniversitesi Yayınları, 1940), VII–XI.

57   Free Republican Party (or Liberal Republican Party) – *Serbest Cumhuriyet Fırkası* was established by Fethi Okyar. in August 1930. However, it was dissolved after four months due to their strong opposition to Kemalist reforms. For the reading on the multi-party experience in early republican Turkey, see Ahmet Ağaoğlu, *Serbest Fırka Hatıraları*, İletişim Yayınları Anı Dizisi, 253 15, 3. bs (İstanbul: İletişim, 1994), İstanbul.Osman Okyar and Mehmet Seyitdanlıoğlu, *Fethi Okyar'ın Anıları: Atatürk-Okyar ve Çok Partili Türkiye* (İstanbul: Türkiye İş Bankası Kültür yayınları, 1999).

country and the people, to operate positive science and modern technology in all fields, to preserve the national character of the country and the people, to raise Turkish people up to the greatest civilization that they've merited, to increase the population and enrich it to a higher wealth level.

It was necessary that the great revolution of Atatürk approach to the hearth of People. The revolution was leading us to a new life and in a new direction. It was our duty to unite the People in ideology and its process, to inspire them in development and to display their unique qualities in their essence by inducing a new perspective on life.

According to RPP, it was crucial to step our people up through the public education except from the state education, having adopted the particular ways of our people. Therefore, it was thought that the new perspectives in the social and cultural sphere will be nourished by a new and national institution which will emerge from the elements of our own society. This idea resulted in the regulations for the People's House in the third congress of the Party in 1931. After a long examination, the instruction of organization was gridded. According to this guide the People's House establish in nine branches: 1. Language, Literature, History; 2. Fine Arts; 3. Performance Arts; 4. Sport; 5. Social Assistance; 6. Public Training Schools and Courses; 7. Library and Publication; 8. Village Affairs (*Köycüler*); 9. Museum and Exhibition. All of these branches have the missions to widen and develop the essence of the society".[58]

The organization, officially established in 1932 in 14 city centers, emerged from a program based on Kemalist reforms directed towards the people, especially in rural areas. Based on a short-term multi-party experience in 1930, it was believed that the people could not adopt the principles of Kemalism. At first, the People's House was meant to realize Kemalist Revolutions in big cities and small towns and villages by providing adult education. To make scientific observations about this kind of organization and learn how to improve the national model, scholars were sent to Germany and Central European countries, where state houses became a substantial place for public schooling during the 1930s.[59] Although the organization was defined as a Public Education Center, it was de facto aimed to develop it into the state's local agent to govern, hence

---

58   *Cumhuriyet Halk Partisi Onbeşinci Yıl Kitabı* (Ankara: TBMM, 1938), 15. Author's translation.

59   M. Asim Karaömerlioğlu, 'The People's Houses and the Cult of the Peasant in Turkey', *Middle Eastern Studies*, 34 (1998), 67–91 (p. 69).

controlling the population in the countryside. On the other hand, the People's House provided a platform for Turkish intelligentsia to reach the villagers, provincials, and their culture. In other words, besides the political and ideological aims, the organization intended to bridge the differentiated groups of society. Moreover, it resulted in the founding of 379 People's Houses[60] in the cities and towns and equipping education programs by the peasantist discourse of the early republic.[61]

The People's House provided a physical space to spread the ideology of state – the ideology of RPP, and to construct the bond between the people and elites. When reemphasizing early republican nationalist discourse, it was believed that the national culture was rooted in rurality while the elites held the keys to improving in a modernized landscape. Here the People's House was perceived as a shared place to bring these two essences of the society together. The People's House generated an awakening for Anatolia to artists, academics, and officials who left the big cities such as Istanbul and Ankara to participate in particular programs in rural Turkey. The mobilization of intelligentsia caused the idealization of Anatolian land and, at the same time, initiated the discussion on the social and economic problems of Anatolian people.

Institutional organizations of the republican state occurred in several fields in addition to academic research and adult education programs in the countryside. One of the crucial examples of these interventions was the Gazi Educational Institute, founded in 1929 in Ankara, which prepared students for teacher training in the countryside. After graduation, young teachers worked in secondary schools in small towns and elementary schools in the villages and small rural towns of Anatolian cities. In 1932 the Art Department of the Gazi Educational Institute was founded by educationist İsmail Hakkı Tonguç, who aimed to generate a new art movement that emphasized Anatolia. The educators in this department concentrated on the Anatolian people, their living conditions, built environment, and the landscape. Malik Aksel worked

---

60   Asım Karaömerlioğlu, *Orada Bir Köy Var Uzakta: Erken Cumhuriyet Döneminde Köycü Söylem*, 1. baskı, Araştırma-İnceleme Dizisi 200 (Cağaloğlu, İstanbul: İletişim, 2006), 56. Referring to: Ilhan Başgöz, *Türkiye'nin eğitim çıkmazı ve Atatürk* (Istanbul: Pan, 2005), 198.

61   İlhan Tekeli and Gencay Şaylan, "Türkiye'de Halkçılık İdeolojisinin Evrimi," *Toplum ve Bilim Dergisi* 6–7, no. Yaz-Güz (1978): 83.; Karaömerlioğlu, *Orada Bir Köy Var Uzakta*, 56–60. For further reading on the establishment and function of People's House during early republican years, see Nurcan Toksoy, *Halkevleri: Bir Kültürel Kalkınma Modeli Olarak* (Kavaklıdere, Ankara: Orion Yayınevi, 2007).

in the institute as a painter and an art historian and pioneered the movement of "Anatolia in Turkish Art". In 1934, Malik Aksel and his students organized an exhibition in the People's House in Ankara under the theme of the Anatolian landscape and people. After this performance, several artists looked to "Anatolia" for thematic material in art.[62]

The RPP and People's House initiated a program between 1938 and 1944 called *Yurt Gezileri* (Homeland Excursions). The artists were encouraged to travel to the country to include folkloric elements and cultural and national motifs in their art. It was aimed that artists' observations reflected on the canvas would result from empirical research about the land. They were supported and awarded by the state.[63] The first excursion started after the legal decision of RPP on the 27th of July 1938. According to the act, the goal was an organization for artistic research about homeland focusing on confirming the "beauty" of Anatolia in ten different cities. The artists who participated in the excursions were chosen by a committee of the Fine Arts Academy in Istanbul. Each of them was sent to different cities and returned with a considerable amount of artwork about landscape and cultural/local symbols of the cities and towns.[64]

Homeland Excursions attracted the attention of artists in that, on the one hand, they could participate in the nation-building project of the state by becoming acquainted with the daily lives and customs of Anatolian people. However, on the other hand, they were glad to get the state's support. Either artist involved supported the ideological facet of RPP's program, or they considered the Homeland Excursions as a point of access to a prestigious position in their field. In both cases, this enterprise made an acquaintance between artists and the people. Painter Refik Epikman stressed this fact in *Ülkü*, the journal that served as a mouthpiece for the RPP during the 1930s:

"This program [Homeland Excursions] which connects the people to art and artists, will, no doubt, generate a new movement in [Turkish] art. The party

---

62   Kaya Özsezgin, *Cumhuriyetin 75 Yılında Türk Resmi*, Türkiye İş Bankası, Kültür Yayınları; Cumhuriyet Dizisi, Genel yayın no. 436. 20 (İstanbul: Türkiye İş Bankası Kültür Yayınları, 1999), 43; Sezer Tansuğ, *Çağdaş Türk sanatı*, 3. basım (İstanbul: Remzi Kitabevi, 1993), 171; İsmail Hakkı (Tonguç), "Malik Bey ve Talebesinin Resim Sergisi," *Ülkü* 16, no. Haziran (1934): 297.

63   Tansuğ, *Çağdaş Türk sanatı*, 216.

64   Kıymet Giray, "Yurdu Gezen Türk Ressamları-1: 1939–1944 Yurt Gezileri," *Türkiye'de Sanat* 18, no. Mart-Nisan (1995): 34–35.

[RPP] places the importance of art with supportive and incentive attitude that leaves very positive impact on the people. A growing amount of comments from people demonstrating their will to be enlightened by art, appears to be the greatest evidence of this impact".[65]

Homeland Excursions were not the only enterprise concentrating on Anatolia in art. Art and sculpture exhibitions organized by the People's House between 1936 and 1938 motivated artists to travel to Anatolian cities, small towns, and villages, live with locals, and exchange cultural notions.[66] Artists pictured and hence documented rural Turkey, exhibiting the locality and variety of culture in different parts of the country. This led to the need for a consciousness of a relationship between the elites and people. Besides, this connection echoed in art movements in the 1930s and 1940s in Turkey. The artists first sought the synthesis of folkloric materials of Anatolian culture and coded them using the cubist abstraction.[67] Later this approach transformed into a political criticism by introducing the rural life from a realistic perspective rather than an idealized image. Finally, they emphasized an aesthetical version of socio-realism; the group took a more critical position towards the state by illustrating the problems in the countryside.[68]

Another dimension in the idealization of Anatolian Land emerged in Turkish literature beginning in the republic's first years following the nationalist wave. The nationalist and populist approach, formed during the last years of the Ottoman Empire, and advocated by Ziya Gökalp, shaped this dimension in literature during the early republican period.[69] As in the field of art, the theme of Anatolia was placed at the center of literature. In Rural Anatolia, small towns and villages emerged as the scenery for bringing the people's living circumstances and issues to light in a realistic way. The facts of peasantry and village life, their cultural, societal, and moral transformation on the verge of evolution from feudalism to capitalism, and the practices pursued during this pro-

---

65   Refik Epikman, "Türk Ressamlarının Yurt Gezisi," *Ülkü* 21, no. Temmuz (1939): 461. Author's translation.

66   Kıymet Giray, "Örneklerle Cumhuriyet Dönemi Türk Resim Sanatı," in *Cumhuriyet Dönemi Türk Resim Sanatından Örnekler: 22 Ekim – 03 Aralık 2003 Ankara Devlet Resim ve Heykel Müzesi Sergi Kataloğu* (Ankara: TC Merkez Bankası – Kültür Bakanlığı, 2003), 7.

67   Tansuğ, *Çağdaş Türk sanatı*, 181.

68   Kaya Özsezgin, *Cumhuriyetin Elli Yılında Plastik Sanatlar* (Tunca Sanat, 2010), 111.

69   Ramazan Kaplan, *Cumhuriyet Dönemi Türk Romanında Köy*, 3. baskı, Kaynak Eserler 32 (Kızılay, Ankara: Akçağ, 1997), 43.

cess were portrayed particularly after 1950. However, early republican litera-ture also projected rural life to demonstrate its transformation and, at the same time, its position in nation-building and modernization enterprises.[70] Liter-ature on rurality referred to the concept, "towards the People" and the other mediums. Texts on Anatolian people and their way of living had another value, in addition to depicting circumstances in the rural realm and as populist en-lightenment among elites. The authors, who portrayed rural life, believed that their texts were crucial tools for the people to guide their own lives.

According to İsmail Hakkı Baltacıoğlu early republican literature, like the art in other disciplines based on rural narratives, provided a critical function in society. In his writings *Edebiyatta Türk'e Doğru* (Towards Turk in the Literature), he stressed the idea of "Art for the People":

"The assignment of literature is a genuine duty in the society. ... Like econ-omy and technics, literature is a beneficial discipline for the society. ... The masses, literature addressed, is the People. The people, themselves, are the entity, which is not influenced by the separation related to wealth, status, and education. Thus, the literature work, addressed the large masses, re-mains forever".[71]

The theme of Anatolia and Anatolian people in early republican literature ap-peared in different ways, such as, in the representation of Kemalist approaches and criticism of intelligentsia, social, economic, and political inequality, and realistic perspective toward the social life of rural people.[72]

Asım Karaömerlioğlu categorized the peasantry theme related to Anato-lia in Turkish literature under these three authors: Yakup Kadri Karaosman-oğlu represented the Kemalist perspective; Sabahattin Ali introduced a social-ist point of view, and Memduh Şevket Esendal thematically addressed the pop-ulist approach. In his 1932 novel, *Yaban* (The Stranger), Yakup Kadri Karaos-manoğlu portrayed the conflict between intellectuals and rural people for the first time. He pointed to the problems of the Anatolian peasant and aimed

---

70   Ahmet Oktay, *Cumhuriyet Dönemi Edebiyatı*, Kültür Bakanlığı Yayınları; Sanat-Edebiyat Dizisi / Yayımlar Dairesi Başkanlığı, 1562. 69–6 (Ankara: Kültür Bakanlığı, 1993), p. 129, Ankara.

71   İsmail Hakkı Baltacıoğlu, *Edebiyatta Türk'e Doğru*, *Türk'e Doğru* (Ankara: Atatürk Kültür, Dil, Tarih Yüksek Kurumu, 1994), 82. Author's translation.

72   Carole Leslie Rathbun, "The Village in the Turkish Novel and Short Story 1920 to 1955" (unpublished Thesis (Ph. D.), Princeton University, 1968), pp. 21–22.

to convince the early republican elites of the significance of peasantry. At the same time, he backed the operations of the Kemalist Revolution and ideology in the countryside. As a result of this, he drew the attention of Kemalist intelligentsia during the 1930s.[73]

In *Yaban*, the author writes a storyline around the main character, Ahmet Cemal, a well-educated military officer who fought in the First World War and afterward participated in the Turkish War of Independence. Ahmet Cemal decides to settle in one of his soldier's villages in the center of Anatolia. He describes the village as "a frozen part of the earth" and "an ancient Hittite ruin," and criticizes the relations between the officers and the villagers:

> "The reason for this, young Turkish intellectual, is you! What did you ever do for this devastated realm and this mass of deprived humanity? For years you sucked his blood and threw him back to the hard earth like pulp, and now you come and find in yourself the right to loathe him.[74]
>
> Anatolian people had a soul; you couldn't touch it. They had a mind you couldn't enlighten. They had a body you couldn't nourish. They had land to live on; you couldn't cultivate. You gave them up to the hands of ignorance, poverty, and drought. They grew like a weed between hard earth and dry sky. Now, you came here with a hook to harvest. What did you ever plant to harvest, these nettles or dry hawthorns? Then, of course, they prick to your feet! Look, you are bleeding, and you are wincing with pain. You are boiling with rage. This thing, grates you, is all your fault, it is all your fault!"[75]

Emphasis on the ignorance towards the Turkish peasant and rural people engendered the idea that the distance between elites and people must be broken to begin the populist enlightenment in all layers of society. Elites should engage the people intelligently by considering facts and providing development instead of simply idealizing them. This point of view spread further with the idea that continued progress in society and building the new Turkish nation were completely dependent on the circumstances of the Turkish peasantry.[76]

---

73   Karaömerlioğlu, *Orada Bir Köy Var Uzakta*, 153–55.

74   Carole Leslie Rathbun translated this part in her Ph. D. thesis. See Rathbun, "The Village in the Turkish Novel and Short Story 1920 to 1955," 38. Yakup Kadri Karaosmanoğlu, *Yaban*, 34. baskı, Y. Kadri Karaosmanoğlu Bütün Eserleri Dizisi 1 (İstanbul: İletişim, 1999), 100.

75   Karaosmanoğlu, *Yaban*, 100. Author's translation.

76   Karaömerlioğlu, *Orada Bir Köy Var Uzakta*, 160–61.

The critical position of the relationship between the intelligentsia and the rural population also appeared in Sabahattin Ali's works. In contrast to Yakup Kadri Karaosmanoğlu's acceptance of Kemalist ideology, which directed the rural population to a community without any social class, Sabahattin Ali did not support this idea or romanticize the rural life. Instead, he addressed the realities among the rural people in a bitter sense. He addressed to the social and economic struggle of the Turkish peasant. According to Rathbun, he "concentrated more on a portrayal of political and social injustice suffered by a passive and uninformed peasantry."[77] His novel, *Kuyucaklı Yusuf*, written in 1937, was considered one of the earliest works issued about the Turkish village, rural people, and, again, their relationships with Turkish elites from a socio-realistic perspective. This criticism of the circumstances of peasants and villagers was also addressed in *İnce Memed* (Memed, My Hawk), written by Yaşar Kemal in 1955. Similar to Ali's approach, he conveyed a bitter relationship and struggle between the state, villagers, bandits, and landlords.[78]

Another artistic vein for the theme of Anatolia emerged in studies of Turkish music during the early republic. While the attempts of Turkish scholars sought to foster authenticity in folkloric elements and lyrics, the state supported the Western forms; especially classical music. They invited several German and Central European musicologists to the country to produce a Western-Turkish synthesis in music.[79]

Comprehensive research on Turkish folk music was conducted by Turkish scholar, Adnan Saygun, and Hungarian scholar, Béla Bartók, who arrived in the country in 1936. On several excursions throughout the country, Saygun and Bartók collected local motifs and generated an archive of Turkish folk music in the Ankara State Conservatory. This study motivated Turkish musicians who were willingly forming a national art. Béla Bartók analyzed the folkloric melodies and sought to create a synthesis between them and Western music.[80]

---

77   Rathbun, "The Village in the Turkish Novel and Short Story 1920 to 1955," 22.

78   Yaşar Kemal, *Memed, My Hawk*, trans. Edouard Roditi, New York Review Books Classics (New York: New York Review Books, 2005).

79   During the early republican years, Turkish music was forbidden in the state radio. The state policy was ambiguous, since the studies on folkloric music was carried out by scholars all over the country. Fethiye Erbay and Mutlu Erbay, *Cumhuriyet Dönemi (1923–1938), Atatürk'ün Sanat Politikası*, 1. basım (İstanbul: Boğaziçi Üniversitesi, 2006), 150.

80   Tansuğ, *Çağdaş Türk sanatı*, 216.

His analysis of local melodies referred not only to ethnomusicological vocabulary. He also noted the cultural and social status of the people and the characteristics of the villages, and he collected the information in terms of literature, linguistics, history, and folklore. He sought to display the cultural characteristics by studying the layers of Anatolian melodies.[81]

Adnan Saygun and Béla Bartók's approach to national music fulfilled early republican aims. He believed it was essential to collect folkloric themes from Anatolian villages where the real authentic tunes were rendered to generate Turkish national music. Researching these motifs and exhibiting them would foster national awareness. According to Bartók, this was the reason why the melodies in a village had the most outstanding artistic quality, and they would become the "classical" pieces of Turkish culture. Following his concept, in 1936, the People's House organized another excursion, *Kültür Gezileri* (Culture Excursions), into small towns and villages to understand folkloric melodies with a sense of cultural archaeology.[82] However, the compilation of Turkish folk music did not reach the public until musician and folklorist Muzaffer Sarısözen accessed the archived songs that Saygun and B Bartók collected. Sarısözen started a new choir, *Yurttan Sesler Korosu* (Choir of the Sounds from the Homeland), in the Ankara State Conservatory in 1947. The choir was broadcasted on the state radio and carried Turkish folk music to a more considerable amount of publicity for the first time.[83]

During the 1930s and 1940s, the theme of Anatolia, which appeared prominently in state politics, projects, institutional organizations, and studies, was considered the most significant subject matter. Typically, early republican intelligentsia, politicians, and artists collected narratives that either supported the Kemalist ideology and its actions, or not. In any case they learned about the Anatolian people. Their study grounded the nation on the Anatolian cultural landscape by observing the rural people and their livelihoods. Indeed, these organizational, artistic, and scientific interventions also paved the way for operations modernizing the land and influencing the rural population on behalf of the republican regime.

---

81   Béla Bartók, *Küçük asya'dan türk halk musıkisi*, trans. by Bülent Aksoy, Pan Yayıncılık, 16 (İstanbul: Pan Yayıncılık, 1991), p. 8, İstanbul.

82   Bartók, 9.

83   Niyazi Yılmaz, *Türk Halk Müziğinin Kurucu Hocası Muzaffer Sarısözen* (Ankara: Ocak Yayınları, 1996), 16–20.

Chapter 3 – Spatial Agents of Rural Development and Conceptualization of the Village

Transportation in the *Rural*

The symbolism of reconstructing *Rural* was generated in various ways, with an emphasis on architectural transformation and planning of the towns and small cities during the early republican era. As the major territory of the country, Anatolia was selected as the place to re-build and to house the people, and as a large site for state intervention in the name of modernization. In other words, Anatolian towns were taken into the republican agenda in the context of country planning, including modern transportation based on railway construction that took place up until the late 1940s. Railway construction represented progress in techniques that connected the whole land, not only transporting goods, infrastructures, and people, but also culture and development among the Turkish people in the cities and the villages.

Relatedly, in 1931 Mustafa Kemal Atatürk announced the primary transportation program of the RPP:

> "Within the projects, Turkish government ordained, all terrains of the homeland will be connected by the railways in a certain period. The whole homeland will become an iron mass. Railways are a much more significant weapon for our country than the rifle and cannon. ... [They] are the roads to the welfare and civilization of the Turkish people."[1]

The theme of transportation firmly addressed the transformation of rural areas in the pursuit of modernism; in other words, the industrial and agricultural

---

[1] Mustafa Kemal Atatürk, *Hâkimiyeti Milliye* (Ankara, 15 Şubat 1931). Also in: Mustafa Kemal Atatürk, *Atatürk'ün Söylev ve Demeçleri: I-III* (Ankara: Atatürk Araştırma Merkezi, 2006), p. 394. Author's translation.

development of the country in areas where the rural populace was in the majority. Therefore, a functional conveyance network, based on a railway system reaching all parts of the country, was prioritized in country planning and architectonic enhancement of urban and rural areas.

Early republican operations in road construction took over the late-Ottoman enterprises which had been dominated by foreign companies and discontinued due to the First World War, the War of Independence, and the Greco-Turkish War of the early 1920s. These operations had two aims. The first was to address the urgent need for a transportation network, which appeared to be in line with military goals, and later fundamentally associated with the national economic development plan. Secondly, the transportation network played a crucial role in urbanizing rural Anatolia by bridging the villages and small towns to larger cities in each region, and those cities to the capital Ankara. Therefore, an effective transportation structure would blur the cultural and social contrasts between regions and cities, and help to unite and control the people, who differed in their ethnic, economic, and socio-cultural characteristics.[2]

Between 1922 and 1948, the early republican state concentrated on the construction of railroads as part of the cultivation of land for agricultural production, industrial manufacturing, and the development program for Anatolia. The program also included mining activities, and socio-cultural engineering in the countryside. After 1933 the government introduced a new policy in railway projects that monopolized and nationalized the lines built and operated by foreigners, and also favored Turkish construction firms for the building of new lines. Starting from the early 1930s, the republican state controlled railway operations and considered the transportation program as an inseparable

---

2   Özge Sezer, 'Railways and Bridges as Expression of Rural in Early Republican Period, 1930–1945 (Erken Cumhuriyet Döneminde Kırsalın İfadesi Bağlamında Demiryolları ve Köprüler)' (unpublished Master Thesis, Istanbul Technical University, 2010), pp. 128–47; Özge Sezer, 'Modernizasyon Düşleri; Erken Cumhuriyet Dönemi Türkiyesi'nde Anadolu Kırsalında İstasyon Yapıları ve Köprüler', in *International Symposium on Theories of Art / Design and Aesthetics, 19–21 October 2011 Faculty of Fine Arts Antalya University Turkey, Papers* (Antalya: Akdeniz Üniversitesi Güzel Sanatlar Fakültesi Dekanlığı, 2012), pp. 278–85.

part of the statist agenda. In 1948,[3] 60 lines connected towns and cities to the harbors on the west, north, and south coasts of Turkey.[4]

Figure 3.1. *Two illustrations showing railway construction in the country.*[5]

In the architectonic sense, transportation objects – the railroads, bridges, and stations – especially in the small Anatolian towns and cities became analogical figures of technology, engineering, and progress in the context of national modernization. These elements were considered signatures of the transformative hands of republican ideology in rural Turkey, where no type of modern infrastructure had previously existed.[6] **(Figure 3.1.)** Therefore railroads,

---

3   In 1948 Turkey obtained Marshall Plan aid, leading to another epoch in the transportation politics that shifted from railroads to highways. For further reading on the operations of Marshall Plan in Turkey from 1948 to 1952, see Senem Üstün, 'Turkey and the Marshall Plan: Strive for Aid', *The Turkish Yearbook of International Relations (Milletlerarası Münasebetler Türk Yıllığı)*, 27.0 (1997), 31–52.

4   İlhan Tekeli and Selim İlkin, *Cumhuriyetin Harcı III: Modernitenin Altyapısı Oluşurken*, İstanbul Bilgi Üniversitesi Yayınları; Siyaset Bilimi, 39 4, 1. baskı (İstanbul: İstanbul Bilgi Üniversitesi, 2003), pp. 288–92. And S. C. Wyatt, 'Turkey: The Economic Situation and Five Years Plan', *International Affairs*, 13.6 (1934), 826–44 (p. 832).

5   *Demiryollar Mecmuası*, 85. İkinci Teşrin (1932), 78, 92.

6   It must be noted here that at the beginning of the 20th century some projects, such as the incomplete Anatolia-Bagdad Railway in the eastern regions of the Ottoman state, were seen as political acts against the ethnic groups in that region. On the other hand, starting from the late 19th century in west Anatolia, in the hinterland of İzmir (includ-

bridges, tunnels and terminals in the towns and cities were celebrated by the Turkish intelligentsia and early republican authorities as material examples of the regime's achievements in rural Turkey.

The representative meaning of modern transportation was echoed in the urbanization of Anatolia, and in aesthetic changes in the countryside. Road construction and bridges represented a sort of modernist fabrication by romanticizing the technology and craftsmanship. Additionally, the terminal buildings in Anatolian cities and towns emerged as the architectonic structures of this production and agents of republican ideology in the countryside. Especially in 1930s, when the statist economy dominated architectural and urban changes, station buildings arose in a particular aesthetic form, referencing an early central European modernism that highlighted the arrangement of clear rectangular volumes, minimal repetition on the façade, plain coating on the external surfaces, and functional organization of the interior. The new railway stations developed into a unique urban element in the countryside since their function was to connect the country to the city. The railway route and terminal buildings in Anatolian cities and towns emerged as the core of planning, centering transportation in the project of urbanization.

Urbanization in the *Rural*

Reconstruction of the cities and towns in rural Anatolia followed the republican regime's strategy of legitimating itself via building activities in the countryside as well as implementing the interventions of the development plan in cultural, social and economic terms. In 1930, with law number 1580, municipalities were defined as local administrations formed in accordance with public needs in the cities and towns. The same law held all municipalities responsible for setting a budget with the Bank of Municipalities (*Belediyeler Bankası*) that promoted the funding of various urbanization projects. Later, the law (number 2290), enacted in 1933, organized the municipal establishment principles

---

ing the cities Manisa and Aydın) – the most significant harbour after Istanbul – the railway network had been constructed by British and French companies. This network contained the rural areas to control the production and transfer of agricultural and mining goods from the region to the mainland. The Ottoman state was allowed to use this railway network only for military purposes. Peter H. Christensen, *Germany and the Ottoman Railways: Art, Empire, and Infrastructure* (New Haven: Yale University Press, 2017).

of towns and cities, including legislation for roads and public buildings. The law also obliged the municipalities to establish a city plan consisting of future development schemes. With the law (number 2497), enacted in 1934, the municipalities had the right of eminent domain for infrastructure and public projects in their districts, such as vehicle roads and pedestrian ways, electricity and water mains, hospitals and health clinics, railway stations, schools, public education centers, parks, and bazaar areas.[7]

After the establishment of the Urbanism Department in the Ministry of Public Works in 1935,[8] projects in the Anatolian towns were carried out in accordance with country planning and announced in journals promoted by the state. *Belediyeler Dergisi (The Journal of Municipalities)* and *Bayındırlık İşleri Dergisi (The Journal of Public Works)* became the mouthpieces that introduced new laws and regulations and presented the current debates on urbanity and projects completed as part of the statist program. Architects and planners in the Ministry of Public Works published articles about modern planning principles, alternative schemes, and urbanization issues in the country as well as ongoing construction works and concept projects for the towns and cities.

Relatedly, in 1939 Celal Ulusan – city and town planner in the Ministry of Public Works – announced the principles of modern city planning, concentrating on completed and planned projects by Turkish and foreign professionals.[9] He described the basic guidelines of town planning in the countryside, such as the goals of town planning, the growth of towns, and industrial and agricultural targets. He elaborated that a useful and pragmatic plan should include detailed research on various elements that should also be shown in the drafts:

"1. Topographic setup of the town, 2. Population of the town (increase, density and division), 3. Field of the town (land use and land value), 4. Designation of the industrial area, 5. Designation of the area for public buildings and schools, 6. Condition of existing dwellings, 7. Condition of existing transportation system, 8. Condition of existing roads, 9. Advantageous areas for the shipment, 10. Harbours and their particulars, 11. Railroads, gateways and terminals, 12. Stations for aerial transportation, 13. Parks and recreational areas, 14. Historical and new monuments, 15. Lighting, decoration and arbor of

---

7   'Geçen 4 Yılda Yapılan İşler', *Belediyeler Dergisi*, 1.6 (1936), 30–36 (pp. 30–32).

8   Celal Ulusan, "Şehir İmar Planları Nasıl Tanzim Edilmelidir," *Belediyeler Dergisi* 32 (1939): 41.

9   Ibid, pp. 42–44.

the streets, 16. Condition of houses, their facades and gardens, 17. Mains water and electricity, 18. Canalization system and sewage discharge stations, 19. Waste, its transportation and disposal stations."[10]

In addition to the fundamental components of the town planning, Ulusan advocated for affordable housing and small settlements for new quarters of the town and emphasized the importance of construction field research. He outlined the principles for the location of garden settlements that workers and public officers would inhabit. At the same time, Ulusan suggested various housing and settlement typologies in accordance with the inhabitant profiles, not only describing garden settlements but also apartment blocks within the arrangement of gardens, playgrounds, and recreational areas. He laid out three typologies for new housing quarters in the towns that reflected the needs of dwellers: group or detached houses and blocks, single houses and blocks, and garden houses.[11]

Following the publication of Ulusan's text, a significant proportion of plans for Anatolian provinces and towns[12] followed the planning categories that he articulated. These categories included the local components of the site, the economic and cultural potential of the area, and "modernist", utilitarian proposals for the architectonic form. Most of the drawings included a "republican" center where the major public buildings – the governorship, municipal building, the People's House, and school – the square and the park, including a memorial statue, were to be placed. It was also determined that the "republican" center of town should be located along the axis of main boulevards connected to the railway station. Garden settlements in which the inhabitants could engage in small-scale agricultural activity were promoted as dwelling models, especially in the planning of small towns.

On the other hand, the urban development schemes of the Anatolian provinces were envisioned to include modern planning concepts such as functional zoning, defining the location of industrial utilities and separating that area from the city center, as well as various dwelling types to fit the inhabitant profiles. But similarly to the concept followed in the new rural towns, Anatolian cities also contained a recognizable center where republican symbolism

---

10   Ibid, p. 38. Author's translation.
11   Ibid, pp. 45–46, 52, 54.
12   Celal Ulusan announced that plans of 18 cities and 44 towns had been accomplished by the end of 1939.

dominated the design with particular landmarks such as buildings for the governorship, the People House, and the republican square and park.

Here, one can interpret that the main objective of the state was to urbanize the agriculturally dependent rural Anatolian provinces. Therefore, each province was included in a regional development program that outlined industrial enterprises, and mining and agricultural activities. No doubt the well-connected transportation system developed the cities into centers for their rural districts and villages, and not only in cultural, societal, and economic terms. Anatolian cities served as the centers and the urban apparatus with which the state strengthened its position of control over the rural areas. Similar to the cities, the new towns were also planned as stable urban forms that allowed the state to remain the people in the controlled rural realm.

Conceptualization of the Village

Socio-Cultural Planning

Following the motivations for rural development in the country, "village" was defined in the early republican vocabulary in terms of two dimensions of state operations. On the one hand, the village, together with all its spatial significance, was considered to be the cultural and societal center of the nation-building agenda. On the other hand, it referred to the core of the statist economy that was grounded in agricultural growth and sufficiency, supported by the agrarian industry, as well as mining activities, to achieve the modernization goals of the regime. From this point of view, the village was instrumentalized as the space for rurality and characterized by the culture of Turkish Anatolia that formed the basis for national determination and unity. At the same time, the village became a site for economic and social interventions by the state. The village – as the core of Anatolian rural space during the early republican period – was designated to form the rural realm, not only architecturally but also in socio-cultural, economic, and demographic terms.

It is crucial to repeat here that the establishment of the People's House in 1932 brought state operations to rural Anatolia and facilitated an immediate consideration of the Turkish village, its existing condition, and its eventual socio-cultural improvement. The People's House was organized into nine branches, including the *Köycüler Kolu* (Village Affairs Branch), with a mission to bridge the peasant population in the Anatolian countryside and the Turkish intelligentsia and to carry through the program of the Republican People's Party and the state. This branch would also organize the platform that brought people from the city closer to those in the villages. Relatedly, in 1932 a formula – the Village Camps – was introduced to develop the cultural and social interaction between people in the city and the country:

> "Can't we start a campaign and send people, who camp next to the city, who get bored by idleness, or drowse away their time in the coffee shops, to the villages?
>
> We let them camp in the villages, we require each educated person to teach one villager how to read and write. And we let them consider this duty as an ideal one.
>
> In this way, the youth of the city will get to know the village and the villagers, and the villagers will warm to the youth of the city. And this will bridge the village and the city.
>
> The youth of the city will internalize the [republican] revolution by taking this social responsibility. In the villages they will organize programs involving performances, conferences, plays, sport festivals, and bring cultural instruments such as gramophone, radio, photography, and cinema that will foster village development and speed it like a great engine.
>
> If there are teachers, agricultural experts, and doctors in the village camps, then they will not only transform the village in [socio-cultural] conditions, but also in sanitation and agriculture.
>
> In short, the Village Camps will be the "camps of revolution".[13]

With this objective in mind, Village Affairs Branch of the People's Houses supported peasantry studies as an extension of state organization in the countryside, concentrating on the improvement of rural culture by bringing art and craftsmanship to the village, with the participants consisting of villagers and city people. Village Affairs also focused on the problems in the village to bring about modern change and the development of the rural built environment. For that purpose, the Village Affairs departments of the People's Houses organized excursions that were intended to establish connections between urbanites and rural people, who were culturally and socially distant from each other.[14]

---

13   V. N., 'Köy Kampları', *Kadro*, 1.1 (1932), 42–43. Author's translation.
14   Anıl Çeçen, *Atatürk'ün Kültür Kurumu Halkevleri* (Cağaloğlu, İstanbul: Cumhuriyet Kitapları, 2000), p. 127.

The results of the excursions were enthusiastically introduced in the publication series called *Köy Tetkikleri* (Village Surveys) contributed by the RPP and the institution. The scholars particularly concentrated on the geographic and historic characteristics of the villages, including an analysis of the economic and socio-cultural circumstances of the inhabitants. Along with customs and daily habits, the ceremonies and rituals of the villagers were a significant focus of the research to understand rural life and the social structures of rural communities. It was believed that "a survey in the village might not be followed with methods such as wandering around the village, talking with the villagers, and spending pleasant time in the coffee house as a guest. But one should earn the confidence and trust of the villagers."[15] Rather, the researcher–observer, who most of the time was the school principal or teacher, should participate in village life with the inhabitants.

In 1936 the Village Affairs Branch of the Ankara People's House published research on Küçükyozgat village in Ankara province. The survey report consisted of the overall situation (location, population, geographic characteristics), culture (educational background, operations of the People's House in the village, and folkloric elements), sanitary conditions, socio-economic status (customs and daily life, subsistence level, consumption patterns and landownership), and the agricultural and craftsmanship activities (forestry, corn cultivation, weaving as well as forging, blacksmithing, carpentry and shoe-making). The architecture of dwellings and settlement organization were described, including the sanitary conditions of the village. The roads were regular, and there was no canalization system, but each house had a lavatory. The houses were made of clay brick and stone. They were usually one-storey earth-sheltered structures consisting of two rooms and an entrance hall, open to the barn and the toilet.[16]

In another report about villages in Kırşehir – an Anatolian city in the south of Ankara – the village principal Hulusi Özen promoted a modernizing social program for the village and the people:

"In both villages people are spending spare time and holidays gathering in the coffee houses and having idle talks. Against all the odds, the Village Affairs Branch of the People's House organizes conferences and some perfor-

---

15   Ankara Halkevi, 'Birkaç Söz', in *Küçükyozgat Köyü: Köy Tetkiki*, Ankara Halkevi Neşriyatı Köycüler Şubesi, 17/2 (Ankara: Ankara Halkevi, 1936), pp. 3–4 (p. 3). Author's translation.
16   Alaettin Güleç, *Küçükyozgat Köyü: Köy Tetkiki*, Ankara Halkevi Neşriyatı Köycüler Şubesi, 17/2 (Ankara: Ankara Halkevi, 1936).

mances two to three times in a year to awaken a cultural awareness among the villagers. Yet, the municipality should [also] get involved in building a library and a reading room where the [up to date] newspapers, magazines, brochures, and books are served for the villagers, and seminars and plays are held by the village's teachers and students. In this way, people grow accustomed to the innovation and modern viewpoints."[17]

In addition to the village surveys, organized by the Village Affair's Branch, the mouthpiece of the People's House – the journal *Ülkü* – featured village development through materials such as articles, reports, drawings, and images about the circumstances of Turkish villages and proposals for their ideal future forms. Architect Abdullah Ziya Kozanoğlu made one of the most significant contributions to this work. In his early writings in *Ülkü*, Kozanoğlu presented the village, addressed the cultural roots of Turkish people, and advocated for ethnic, social, and economic changes through the republican reforms. He called on the Turkish elite to uplift the modern rural populace by reconstructing the Turkish village:

"[In our villages] there are brothers who have forgotten their own language and speak another one. There are citizens who consider, indeed, it an insult to be called Turkish. We must reconstruct our villages, we must make our brothers speak [Turkish], dress [modern] and make them live [in better conditions] like us."[18]

What Abdullah Ziya Kozanoğlu presented was a generic approach, advocating that the early republican intelligentsia should plan the village as an inclusive socio-cultural form, separate from the cities and towns. In other words, the villager should continue to live in his own settlement – in the village – in order not to invade the cities and towns: "[in] all circumstances, the villager connected to his settlement, should remain in the village, otherwise the villager thrusts into the cities and towns to seek these conditions."[19] The village was defined in cultural, social, ethnic and economic terms by elites who considered it an entirely distinct system, different from any other urban orders. Therefore, most of the time village planning and the urbanization of Anatolian cities were linked together only in a very limited field of practice.

---

17   Hulusi Özen, *Köy Tetkikleri: Genezin ve Göynük*, Kırşehir Halkevi Neşriyatından, 7–8 (Kırşehir: Köy Basımevi, 1941), p. 6. Author's translation.

18   Abdullah Ziya (Kozanoğlu), 'Köy Mimarisi', *Ülkü*, 7. Ağustos (1933), 37–41 (p. 40).

19   Ibid, p. 38.

Nusret Kemal Köymen, village sociologist and the editor of the village affairs section in *Ülkü*, described the principles of rural planning with a focus on the building of the Turkish village. In his articles and books Köymen often introduced a concept of the village grounded in republican ideology and emphasizing a sort of socio-cultural populist realm. He became one of the most enthusiastic supporters of the village campaign, starting from the early 1930s. In 1933 he called for the social and cultural mobilization of rural Anatolia:

> "41.000 villages are spread out on almost 800.000 km² (of the country). There are neither schools, nor post office and markets in 37.000 of them. In these 41.000 villages live 12 million people. Only two per cent of them can read and write. The most intelligent ones use only 500 words to think and talk. Only those who came back from military service know the country and are aware of the circumstances around it. There are some who have never been out of their village. Since the social capabilities are too low, the economic situation of the village is also unsatisfactory. Here it is the general view of our country and the village puzzle.[20]

His solution to the "village puzzle" was to organize the socio-cultural and economic aspects of the village: "The socio-cultural and economic conditions of the village should be strengthened to achieve a democratic society with no unequal division of classes, unlike in Western societies and where democracy is firmly established. In this way, the peasantry would also foster Turkish democracy."[21] Educational improvement of the rural people therefore played the most significant role in resolving problems in the countryside, and hence in nationalizing and modernizing the Anatolian village. Moreover, Köymen drew up the aims of operation:

> "to increase the income of the villager, to point each villager to a consciousness of their place in the national economy; to improve the social standards of the villager (in terms of morality, community life, ideals, cooperation, entertainment, eagerness to work, customs, and so on); to educate the villagers in grasping the republican revolutions and regime, and in being an independent citizen; to educate the villager in being a rational, secular, open-minded and "civilized" individual; to discipline the villager in being conventional and

---

20   Nusret Kemal (Köymen), *Halkçılık ve Köycülük* (Ankara: Tarık Edip Kütüphanesi, 1934), 46. Author's translation.

21   Ibid, p. 48.

a "faithful Turk" to his nation and tradition; to discipline the villager in learning his physical and intellectual skills".[22]

Köymen focused on efforts "to discipline" the village and villager in different ways, using the tools of adult education strongly associated with the Village Affairs Branch in the People's House. In addition to school-oriented education, he suggested educating the village people through specific journals, newspapers and radio programs, associations for villager–journalists, travelling theatres, libraries, exhibitions, and conferences providing informing about agriculture, domestic economy, sanitation and hygiene, village fairs demonstrating local productions and model farms, and religious books written to offer moral guidance. Köymen emphasized the need for public health maintained by travelling dentists, nurses and doctors and the necessity of a market, café and post office in each village.[23]

Furthermore, Köymen announced the creation of a new profession – the village mentors (*Köy Rehberleri*) – to fulfil these duties in the village. A village mentor should be well informed about culture, tradition, and civilization so that he could successfully act as a transmitter between the under-developed and developed parts of the society. In this capacity, the mentors would gather the villagers to give lectures in topics including literature, history, geography, agriculture, and public health. Although the mentors would focus on cultural improvement in the village, they would also be involved in the economic activities of the village. They would support and control the ateliers in which villagers produced local goods, as well as the products the villager would buy from the village shop and from markets outside of his village. In this regard, they would assist in sustaining and growing culture and the economy.[24]

To educate the village mentors, Köymen proposed establishing an institute where they would be trained in themes such as science and sanitation, social and physical geography, the history of civilizations, Turkey and Turkish folk culture, agriculture and village economy, morality and religious philosophy, secular morality, sociality and state philosophy, principles of village education, examples from other countries, and the Village Act and judicial instructions.[25]

---

22   Ibid, p. 50.
23   Ibid, pp. 55–56.
24   Ibid, pp. 59–62.
25   Villagers' education had been examined for a particular purpose since the first years of the Turkish republic. In 1924 John Dewey was invited to the country to prepare a report about Turkey's educational plan in which Dewey suggested that village educa-

Students would also train in the villages of Anatolia, and successful ones would be sent to Mexico,[26] Denmark, the Soviet Union and the United States for further education.[27] In other words, Köymen addressed the village campaign as the crucial operation, which included not only the republican regime's interventions and regulations, but which was also a populist project, undertaken by the rural and urban populace together. Köymen developed a method for solving the obstacles of the underdeveloped countryside by placing the "village" at the center.

In his book *The Principles of Village Affairs* (*Köycülük Esasları*, 1934), Köymen presented the village as a rural extension of the modern city, the development of which had been studied since the end of 19th century. However, Köymen's definitions of city and village were quite different in social, cultural, and economic terms. He centered the modern village in the urbanization discourse as part of sustainable and well-controlled country planning. According to Köymen, the village is the core of the country, and the city is a complex central form in which these cores are concentrated:

"The difference between the village and the city is the life and operations, namely their functions: the village is a self-contained and bordered home-

---

tion should be organized in accordance with regional circumstances, and that schools should not only be where lectures took place but also centres of village cultural and social life. Schools should include healthcare services in which doctors would take care of the village inhabitants and educate them in sanitation. John Dewey, *Türkiye Maarifi Hakkında Rapor*, ed. by Hasan Ali Yücel, T.C. aarif Vekilliği, Ana Programa Hazırlıklar, B.1 (Istanbul: Devlet Basımevi, 1939), pp. 2–20 <http://hdl.handle.net/11543/928>. Dewey saw the village school and the village teacher as the generating factors in rural society. Following Dewey's ideas, the Ministry of Education regulated [amended or introduced?] law numbered 789 in 03.04.1926 that allowed for the establishment of Schools for Village Teacher Training. TBMM, *Maarif Teşkilâtına Dair Kanun*, 1926 <https://www.tbmm.gov.tr/tutanaklar/KANUNLAR_KARARLAR/kanuntbm mc004/kanuntbmmc004/kanuntbmmc00400789.pdf>.

26   Nusret Kemal Köymen published a book – *Village Affairs in Mexico* (*Meksika'da Köycülük*) – in 1934 chronicling the development of the peasantry and rural revolution in Mexico. He recounted state operations after 1910 and the state program between 1920 and 1933 and presented the community life of the village in socio-cultural terms, public education in the village, and the significant role of the village school and village teachers in the economic development of the village. He advocated for the Mexican model of rural modernization, and sought to adapt and translate it into the early republican project. Nusret Kemal (Köymen), *Meksika'da Köycülük* (Ankara: Tarık Edip Kütüphanesi, 1934).

27   (Köymen), *Halkçılık ve Köycülük*, 64–67.

land–nucleus considering the production, consumption, and labor relations in cultural, social, economic, industrial, and administrative fields. However, the city is an administrative, cultural, social, economic, financial, and industrial center and a geographical country-piece consisting of villages, which are related to each other geographically, culturally, socially, and economically. In this respect, many communication functions are concentrated in the city, which exists not only for itself but also for the surrounding area."[28]

He added that the village had existed as an essential form of community life, with varying structures such as a smaller village with a smaller community and a larger village with a bigger population in a more complex administrative and social apparatus. From this point of view, Köymen represented the village as "the oldest, fundamental and native society".[29] He believed that urban growth had been concentrated in the cities since the last century, resulting in a disorganized economic and socio-cultural environment in the village. However, in the preceding decades nationalist, populist and self-sufficient approaches had emerged grounded on the improvement of the village structure.[30] The aim of Village Affairs, Köymen argued, was to center the village in country planning in a way that furthered the various development objectives of the republican agenda.

According to this idea, the village was not only an agricultural sphere in which the raw materials or local goods were produced, but also a complete unit

---

28   Nusret Kemal (Köymen), *Köycülük Esasları* (Ankara: Tarık Edip Kütüphanesi, 1934), 12. Author's translation.

29   Ibid, p. 10.

30   Ibid, pp. 12–13. Nusret Köymen discussed the conception of village in terms of peasants' movements starting from the mid-19th century. He exemplified the peasants' movement in Denmark in 1849 and he stated that the movement resulted in social and cultural improvement. Another significant incident was the revolt of Mexican peasants in 1910 and its effect on the agricultural development program in 1912. Köymen also addressed the 1917 revolution as a crucial threshold for the Russian peasantry but considered that the movement started among the Russian peasants and shifted to the worker class and therefore was transformed into a revolution in the cities rather than in the villages. On the other hand, the urbanization of the European cities held the peasantry backwards in the political and economic frame, and European states, nowadays, concentrated on cities more than rural areas since the infrastructure in the cities had already been prepared for country development. Thus he suggested that the new improved peasant civilization emerged in the West in Mexico and in the East in Turkey. Ibid, pp. 15–16.

in which commodities were produced to serve the essential needs of people. With the rest of production and labor, the village contributed to the national economy in its geographical scope. The village would be furnished with all the equipment needed for its own local circumstances, resulting in an enduring system resistant to social and economic obstacles.[31]

Another crucial point, Köymen emphasized, was that in this sort of system, the villager would have his own property. With land and a house, he was independent and responsible for his economic and social situation. Moreover, in this scheme the villager did not require the assistance of the state with cultural, social, economic, administrative, and municipal affairs. The state was involved only in the infrastructure of the village and in providing transportation, security, health, and educational services to the village. In exchange for this work of the state, the villager paid taxes and undertook military service. In this formula the city served to provide the equipment and professionals for the state's services to the village. And industry, concentrated in the city, cooperated with agriculture and manufacture in surrounding villages.[32]

At the same time Köymen advocated for an industrial production model in the villages. He suggested a smaller scale industry, taking place in houses and on farms where the villagers would labor with their family. Unlike the city where the worker class arose due to industry, this method would create a strong Turkish peasant class and develop culture and society. In other words, in the city the worker relied on the factory for day wages, but in the village people were committed to their work because work was also a part of custom and daily habits. Agricultural small industry could therefore prosper in the village and also help form cultural values in the countryside.[33]

In addition to characterizing the village as more or less the opposite of urbanity, Köymen sought solutions for the rural population who arrived in the cities in several instances. He introduced the "Villager's Hostel" (*Köylü Hanı*), a particular type of house in cities where villagers were accommodated for short periods for activities such as selling their products, legal and administrative affairs, hospital services, and seeking work. He believed that "villagers, visiting the city, were more skilled, civilized, and open-eyed people"; they were capable of grasping republican ideals and practicing good manners during their sojourn. He addressed the Village Affairs Branch of the People's House about the

---

31   Ibid, p. 22.
32   Ibid, pp. 22–24.
33   Ibid, pp. 25–26.

rural populace in the urban sphere. Köymen proposed building the "Villager's Hostels" as "a laboratory and a communication center" for village affairs similar to the programs operated by the People's Houses all over the country.[34]

An ideal "Villager's Hostel" should be constructed with natural building materials and local methods used in the villages, so that it would be a representative modern, standardized building built with modest, traditional techniques. The house would also contain a library, reading room and space for cultural events such as agricultural exhibitions, educational films and conferences, shadow plays and theatre performances. Moreover, the Villager's Hostel would be administered by a director, who would manage an adult education program (particularly for rural people) and organize hygienic living conditions for the visitors.[35]

Köymen promoted the Villager's Hostel as a crucial communication bridge between rural people and the intelligentsia. The cultural program and living circumstances would acquaint these two groups with each other, and the villager would be exposed to the educational programs in the villages managed by the republican regime and its agents. In this way, the villager, who had experience in the village house, would volunteer for socio-cultural activities, brought by the elites from the city to the countryside.[36]

However, Köymen's approach supported, once again, the control mechanism of the republican cadre towards the Turkish peasantry and village society to coerce their participation in the "achievement of a more civilized and modernized populace". It was provocative that he proposed for the villager and the urbanite a sterilized sphere in which they congregated together and came up with the governing tactics for the villager. He tenaciously supported this idea to keep the villager away from "recklessly" wandering in the streets of the city, limiting his actions and urban activities to one particular place.

In addition to practical interventions, research, and conceptual approaches to forming the Turkish village during the early republican period, village newspapers and magazines arose as an additional mouthpiece for public education in rural society, promoting and demonstrating republican accomplishments and ideals for the Turkish peasantry, villages, and rural people. Starting from the alphabet reform in 1928, Turkish elites were inspired to create publications for the villagers. The new media would include issues

---

34   (Köymen), *Halkçılık ve Köycülük*, 86–87.
35   Ibid, pp. 87–88.
36   Ibid, p. 88.

about village life and the villagers' problems to communicate with the rural people. Therefore, *Köylünün Gazetesi*, first published in 1929, and *Yurt*, first published in 1933, were distributed free of charge to the villages by the state.[37]

Later, periodicals such as *Karınca*, *Köy Dergisi* and *Köy Postası*, which informed the people and the elites at the same time, included articles, reports and observations about conditions in the villages, the obstacles that the rural populace encountered, development methods for the agricultural realm in the countryside, and methods for the socio-cultural improvement of the peasants with a remarkable tone of statist politics.

In 1934 the Turkish Cooperatives' Association published the magazine *Karınca*, which introduced state operations in the countryside, aiming to answer problems of the Turkish peasantry and bridging the elites with the rural people. It was underlined that the authority – elites and the republican state – should approach Turkish peasants by seeking to speak "the same language". For example, scholars promoted discussing agricultural labor and challenges in the countryside with the peasants themselves to examine and consider their needs. Moreover, republican intellectuals proposed bringing up the subjects that peasants had not yet demanded. It was believed that only this way would it be possible to comprehend the obstacles posed by rural life in socio-cultural terms, to develop and modernize the Turkish village, and to implement statist reforms in rural Anatolia. Like the village surveys organized by the Village Affair's Branch of People's Houses all over the country, these articles and reports also portrayed social and cultural life in rural Anatolia and promoted a sort of "village journalism". The "village journalists" were republican intelligentsia sent to the countryside not only to make an observation on the site. But they were pioneers to enhance a "civilized" life in the countryside.[38]

The idea that the village economy controlled the socio-cultural sphere dominated the discourse, especially after the first programs in the Anatolian countryside in the 1930s. During the late 1930s and early 1940s, magazines and newspapers addressed to the Turkish village and villager concentrated

---

37   Türkan Çetin, 'Cumhuriyet Döneminde Köycülük Politikaları: Köye Doğru Hareketi', in *75 Yılda Köylerden Şehirlere*, Bilanço' 98 Yayın Dizisi (Istanbul: Türkiye Ekonomik ve Toplumsal Tarih Vakfı, 1999), pp. 213–30, (p.215).

38   Dr. Savran approvingly narrated his visit to Katranci Village in central Anatolia and participation in the village committee of RPP. Cevdet Nasuhi Savran, 'Yurdun Bucaklarından: Kantrancı Köyü', *Karınca: Türk Kooperatifçilik Cemiyetinin Aylık Mecmuası*, 14.Haziran (1935), 5–6.

on news about modernization projects in rural Anatolia, new agricultural methods and production, and small agrarian industry models in the countryside. *Köy Dergisi*, first published in 1939, and *Köy Postası*, first published in 1944, became the major media outlets informing the villagers (and the elites who were engaged with the village) about village affairs and operations by the state. They also educated about topics such as hygiene, health, home economy, childcare, and social and cultural activities in the village.

In the first issue of *Köy Dergisi*, founders Kadri Kemal Kop, Murat Sertoğlu and Necaettin Atasagon announced that the doctrines and aims of the journal were to serve the village, villager, and the intelligentsia according to the major principles of the RPP:

> "The village is an administrative unit of a country, but it is the general configuration of Turkey. Seeing and analyzing the village and learning from it means learning [understanding] the whole country.
> With this magazine, we will introduce the village of yesterday and today, and the model villages which the republican regime will create from now on."[39]

Accordingly, the periodical included reports about agricultural projects in particular regions, and articles about current circumstances, progress and future programs in small towns and villages in Anatolia. In the late 1940s, the connection between the socio-cultural atmosphere and economic circumstances in the Turkish village was more effectively established, and generally echoed in these mediums. In that respect, in addition to the news, informative commentaries for villagers, and literary columns for short stories, poems and myths about village culture and village life, *Köy Postası* introduced a program of travelling village courses to import professional knowledge and build a cultural and economic bridge between the city and country. It was announced that women were to train in needlecraft, and men were to train in carpentry and forging within the program maintained by the Ministry of Education. By presenting practical information about craftsmanship, the goal was to create opportunities for the villager away from agrarian fields, and to sustain the village in its terrain.[40]

Up until the 1940s the village was at the center of discussion about the development of rural Anatolia, using tools such as analysis of the social and eco-

---

39   Kadri Kop Kemal, Murad Sertoğlu, and Necaettin Atasagon, 'Köy Dergisi'nin Prensip ve Gayesi', *Köy Dergisi*, 1.1 (1939), p. 2. Author's translation.

40   İsmet Hulusi İmset, 'Köye Gidelim', *Köy Postası*, 52.09 (1948), p.13.

nomic structure of village life and cultural narratives in the village. Therefore, the early republican intelligentsia and regime focused on the reconstruction of rural patterns in the framework of nationalization and modernization programs and sought to realize these changes by linking the social, economic, and architectural infrastructure to the village. The 1930s therefore witnessed various empiric operations, including the education program for villagers to bolster the Turkish village. In the 1930s climate, the consensus was that villagers should be promoted and instructed in accordance with the daily needs of their villages. And, starting from the second half of the 1930s, the theme of education played a crucial role in village planning.

Between 1935 and 1937, İsmail Hakkı Tonguç, General Director of Elementary Education, and Saffet Arıkan, Minister of National Education, prepared the program for the village schools. A report about the concept of the schools and the qualification of teachers and trainers in the village schools was released: the schools would be organized according to provincial circumstances to serve the children in the region. The schools would be equipped with fields for agricultural training, laboratories, and ateliers, in addition to rooms for seminars, lectures and artistic activities, as well as dormitories. The teacher–candidates should be chosen from the village youth and were to be educated in an atmosphere similar to village life. In this way the teachers would serve as role models for not only the children but also the adults in the village.[41]

This report formulated the law (number 3238) – The Village Educators Law of 11 June 1937.[42] From 1937 to 1939, the first educator schools were established in the villages of İzmir, Eskişehir, Kirklareli and Kastamonu to train candidates who had finished their military service and were inclined to engage in agricultural work in their villages. After three years, the project became law on

---

41   Bekir Semerci, 'Yeni Arayışlar', in *Köy Enstitüleri: Amaçlar İlkeler Uygulamalar*, ed. by Mustafa Aydoğan, Tanıtım Dizisi, 1 (İstanbul: Köy Enstitüleri ve Çağdaş Eğitim Vakfı Yayınları, 1997), pp. 18–27 (pp. 23–25).

42   The Village Educators Law, numbered 3238. TBMM, *Köy Eğitmenleri Kanunu*, 1937 <http s://www.tbmm.gov.tr/tutanaklar/KANUNLAR_KARARLAR/kanuntbmmc017/kanuntb mmc017/kanuntbmmc01703238.pdf>.

17 April 1940 with law 3803,[43] and the Village Institutes officially started up in rural Anatolia and Trace region.[44]

The aim of the institutes was to train village teachers and the other professionals in issues related to village affairs. The education lasted five years, and the students would be directed into different fields according to their relevant skills. The teachers who graduated from the institutes would be responsible for all educational activities in the village where they worked. They would not only lecture in the village schools, but also instruct the villagers in the technical procedures and practices of agrarian production in the provided fields, orchards, and ateliers.[45]

Until the state closed the institutes in 1954, it was intended to establish a substantial education network by separating the country into four regions and organizing the village institutes as the pioneering units in each district. According to İsmail Hakkı Tonguç, the institutes' program was grounded in teaching the students particular practices related to the region. Additionally, the training also addressed social and natural sciences, agriculture, art and sport, introductory excursions for learning about the country, and especially methods for the improvement of literacy in the villages.[46] In other words, the program provided the education to regenerate the Turkish village and transform its social and economic dynamics. In this way, the village institutes were the centers of "learning by doing" for the villagers and included the rural populace in the development plan in a pragmatic manner that was carried on by the Turkish elite.[47]

In particular, from 1935 (the first drafts of the organization) to 1946 (the first multi-party elections) the project basically promoted teaching the villagers to

---

43   The Village Institutes Law, numbered 3803. TBMM, *Köy Enstitüleri Kanunu*, 1940, pp. 233–237 <https://www.tbmm.gov.tr/tutanaklar/KANUNLAR_KARARLAR/kanuntbmm c021/kanuntbmmc021/kanuntbmmc02103803.pdf>.

44   Seval Kocak and Gulsun Atanur Baskan, 'Village Institutes and Life-Long Learning', *Procedia – Social and Behavioral Sciences*, 46 (2012), 5937–40 <https://doi.org/10.1016/j.sbsp ro.2012.08.009>.

45   TBMM, Köy Enstitüleri Kanunu, 233.

46   İsmail Hakkı Tonguç, *Eğitim Yolu ile Canlandırılacak Köy*, 2. Baskı (İstanbul: Remzi Kitabevi, 1947), p. 506.

47   For the comment: M. Asim Karaömerlioğlu, "The Village Institutes Experience in Turkey," *British Journal of Middle Eastern Studies* 25, no. 1 (May 1998): 47–73, http://ww w.jstor.org/stable/195847.

sustain rural life with mottos such as "controlling and exploiting nature", "increasing productivity", "developing technology", "being rational", and directly addressing the connection between the backwardness and ignorance of the rural populace socio-cultural terms with "the incompetence of the peasants in their struggle against the rural environment".[48] Fay Kirby summarizes this process, pointing to the pragmatic and empirical methods led by the institutes, but also highlighting the genuine goals underlining the concept of "developing modern values in the Turkish society", "generating the national culture", "professionalizing in the economic life", and "improving the country's economy" by positioning the village at the center of all courses of action.[49]

The dynamism brought by the village institutes to rural Turkey helped to improve both socio-cultural and economic conditions. The operation paved the way for analyzing the layers of rural society from an insider perspective. In this respect, one of the most important figures was Mahmut Makal, who published his book *Bizim Köy (Our Village)* in 1950, and two years later *Köyümden (From My Village)*, portraying the village in several dimensions. He pointed out that the Turkish village appeared to be neither a socio-cultural project nor an economic nucleus in rural Anatolia. Makal demonstrated that the village was a holistic organism consisting of cultural, social, economic, and ethnic themes. For the first time the village was narrated by the insider, particularly when Makal presented Demirci village, where he was born, and Nürgüz village, where he worked as a teacher after he graduated from Ivriz Village Institute in Konya. At the end of 1940s, Makal's works also gained political significance due to his critical reading of early republican programs for the emerging Turkish peasantry.[50] Makal clearly discussed the obstacles in the statist program from the villagers' perspective. His work consisted of several chapters about the social, cultural, and economic details of village life and the political positions of the villagers.[51]

---

48   Ibid, p. 63.
49   Fay Kirby, *Türkiye'de Köy Enstitüleri*, trans. by Niyazi Berkes, 3. Baskı (İstanbul: Tarihçi Kitabevi, 2010), p. 269.
50   He was accused by the Turkish government of "communist propaganda" in 1950 and jailed for two months. See Lewis Thomas J., 'Foreword', in *A Village in Anatolia* (London: Vallentine, Mitchell & Co. Ltd., 1954), pp. ix–xii (p. xi).
51   In 1954 Mahmut Makal's books *Our Village (Bizim Köy)* and *From My Village (Köyümden)* were compiled and translated into English as one book, *A Village in Anatolia,*, with contributions by Lewis V. Thomas and social anthropologist Paul Stirling. Mahmut Makal,

The village institutes and the progress they brought about in the Turkish countryside established a bridge between many actors such as the politicians, urban intelligentsia, villagers, and feudal landowners. The village institutes created the potential for a bottom-up rise instead of the top-down implementations of the Kemalist regime. Within the political climate of 1950s, however, the existence of the institutes and their power in the countryside were considered as a threat to governmental prepotency. Although the impact of the project was echoed in the later years, the institutes continued to be a romanticized ideal in rural Turkey.

Economic Planning

Government economic policy contemplated the reformation of rural Turkey from the early years of the republic. During the 1930s economic planning for the Turkish village was framed in terms of keeping the village community in its socio-cultural sphere and improving production activities locally by developing modern infrastructure in the rural areas. According to Caglar Keyder, in the 1940s the village was still traditionally organized in its social and economic aspects. The exceptions were minor regions in Anatolia where rural households engaged in local trade. These areas had been included in the market since the late 19th century by foreign merchandise groups, and non-Muslim citizens had been deported since the years of the First World War.[52]

Considering that the rural populace was the majority of the country,[53] the populist approach to economic policy at the time implied another significant dimension of village planning in the 1920s. On 1 March 1922, Mustafa Kemal Atatürk, the first republican president of Turkey, gave a speech that became a motto in reference to the Turkish villager and was used as a significant propaganda statement by many politicians in the following years:

A Village in Anatolia, ed. by Paul Stirling, trans. by Sir Wyndham Deedes, (London: Vallentine, Mitchell & Co. Ltd., 1954).

52   Caglar Keyder, "Genesis of Petty Commodity Production in Agriculture: The Case of Turkey," in *Culture and Economy: Changes in Turkish Villages*, ed. Paul Stirling (Huntingdon: Eothen, 1993), 171–72.

53   Around 1923 the populace of Turkey largely consisted of landowners, small agriculture holders and non-landowner villagers, especially after the Armenians and Greeks, who traditionally dominated trade and capital networks, were forced to leave during the wars.

"The real warden and governor of Turkey is the villager, who is the real producer. Then the villager deserves prosperity and wealth more than anyone else. Therefore, the government of Grand National Assembly of Turkey directs economic policy to construct the foundations of this aim."[54]

The first attempt to improve the conditions of "the real warden and governor of Turkey" was the First Economy Congress in İzmir from 17 February to 4 March 1923, before the official proclamation of the Republic of Turkey on 23 October 1923. The congress was focused on determining the economic principles of the new Turkish state, of which the majority were living in villages and towns, laboring in small agricultural households, craftsmanship or small manufacturing.[55] In 1923, 10.3 million of Turkey's total population of 13.6 million were agricultural holders, small landowners or landless peasants, and living in the small rural towns or villages.[56]

Although the program to restore industry emerged as the larger theme during the meetings, the foodstock via agrarian activities formed an important part of the congress. This directed topics of discussion to rural areas, particularly to the strategies for regenerating economic life in the villages. With the

---

54   Atatürk, *Atatürk'ün söylev ve demeçleri*, 2006, 239. Ayse Afeinan introduced her book, published for the 50th anniversary of the proclamation of Turkish Republic with the title *Our Villages* – Köylerimiz, with the same quotation. Ayşe Afetinan, *Cumhuriyet'in Ellinci Yılı İçin: Köylerimiz*, vol. XVI, 36 (Ankara: Türk Tarih Kurumu Basımevi, 1978), VII. Author's translation.

55   'İktisat Esaslarımız: 17 Şubat 339 – 4 Mart 339 Tarihine Kadar İzmir'de Toplanan İlk Türk İktisat Kongresinde Kabul Olunan Esaslar ve İrat Olunan Nutuklar', in *İzmir İktisat Kongresi, 17 Şubat – 4 Mart 1923*, ed. by Ayşe Afetinan, Türk Tarih Kurumu Yayınları XVI. Dizi, 46 (Ankara: Türk Tarih Kurumu Basımevi, 1982), pp. 17–90.

56   *İstatistik Göstergeler – Statistical Indicators, 1923–1992*, 1682 (Ankara: T.C. Başbakanlık Devlet İstatistik Enstitüsü, 1994), p. 8. See also, Oya Köymen, "Cumhuriyet Döneminde Tarımsal Yapı ve Tarım Politikaları," in *75 Yılda Köylerden Şehirlere*, Bilanço' 98 Yayın Dizisi (İstanbul: Türkiye Ekonomik ve Toplumsal Tarih Vakfı, 1999), 1. According to a 1932 report, in 1927 the population was 13.65 million living in only 40 locations, with the higher density in the west Anatolia, east Thrace. There were 13 cities with the population of over 30,000 people, which was 12% of the whole population. The big cities in which industry and trade relatively dominated the regions, were İstanbul, Bursa, İzmir, Ankara, Konya and Adana. Among the whole population, 5.8 million people were considered as belonging to an occupational group, and 4.3 million of this group worked in agriculture. The other 8.2 million people were villagers who labored in agrarian fields and households. *İktisadi Türkiye: Tabii, Beşeri ve Mevzii Coğrafya Tetkikleri*, 38, 42–49.

initial operations, the aim was to bring about economic recovery in the country, addressing obstacles such as reforming and consolidating the network and resources of the national economy, and providing a sustainable market for local and regional producers.[57] Thus the state gradually planned to construct better infrastructure to boost the economic life and sustain this improvement. The government passed laws pertaining to the conditions for agricultural laborers, including legal agreements between the landowners and agrarian workers, and it took a step towards new regulations for landownership reform.[58]

In this respect, the first regularization occurred in the Village Law (number 442) on 18 March 1924, declaring the village a legal entity for the first time.[59] In addition to this, to revive production in the villages, on 21 April 1924, through another law (number 498), the government encouraged farmers and smallholders from the same region to cooperate in the agrarian fields.[60] And, in the law (number 1470) of 28 May 1929, the Agricultural Credit Cooperatives was

---

57   The state primarily focused on industrial growth in the agenda; nevertheless, there were several attempts to increase the quality and quantity of agricultural production. First of all, the Agriculture Ministry operated stations for seed improvement in 1926 in Eskişehir, Adana, Adapazari, Edirne and Ankara. From 1927, the new seeds were exported and studied in these stations. In addition, starting from 1925, the Agriculture Ministry established exemplar farms in order to demonstrate the new techniques and methods in agriculture and become a model in their regions. *Birinci Köy ve Ziraat Kalkınma Kongresi Yayını: Türk Ziraat Tarihine Bir Bakış* (İstanbul: Devlet Basımevi, 1938), 282., and İlhan Tekeli and Selim İlkin, 'Devletçilik Dönemi Tarım Politikalari (Modernleşme Çabaları)', in *75 Yılda Köylerden Şehirlere* (Istanbul: Türkiye Ekonomik ve Toplumsal Tarih Vakfı, 1999), pp. 43–56 (p. 47–49).

58   Ayşe Afet Inan. Caglar Keyder introduces the İzmir Economy Congress as the step for the "encouragement of industry", pointing out that the congress echoed the 1913 Law for the Encouragement of Industry, which was still kept on the agenda during the first years of the republic. See also Çağlar Keyder, *The Definition of a Peripheral Economy: Turkey, 1923–1929*, Studies in Modern Capitalism = Etudes Sur Le Capitalisme Moderne (Cambridge [Cambridgeshire]; New Yorkand Paris: Cambridge University Press; Editions de la maison des sciences de l'homme, 1981), pp. 25, 57–58.

59   "Köy Kanunu," Pub. L. No. 442, 237 (1924), http://www.mevzuat.gov.tr/MevzuatMetin/1.3.442.pdf.; Gafur Soylu, *Köy Nedir ve Nasıl İdare Edilir*, 2. Basılış (İstanbul: Marifet Basımevi, 1940), 7–27.

60   TBMM, *İtibarı Zirai Birliği Kanunu*, 1924, pp. 396–97 (p. 396) <https://www.tbmm.gov.tr/tutanaklar/KANUNLAR_KARARLAR/kanuntbmmc002/kanuntbmmc002/kanuntbmmc00200498.pdf>.

enacted by the state to maintain the production of farmers and villagers who held arable lands.[61]

During the first years of the republic, village development dealt with obstacles stemming from the economic depression that lasted until the beginning of the 1930s. The economic policy of the state tended to concentrate on industry, promoting the manufacture of industrial raw material for internal and external markets instead of supporting agriculture-based production, the occupation of the majority of the population.[62] The villagers, who were smallholders and laborers in agrarian farms, confronted severe circumstances that prompted the government to seek solutions for underdeveloped areas. On 5 January 1931, the first Agricultural Congress was assembled in Ankara with representatives of councils of several agricultural regions, the Ministry of Economy, and the state banks. The congress concentrated on finding answers to topics such as technical backwardness in agrarian activities, new economic resources for farmers and villagers, transportation of agrarian goods, improvement of the market, enhancement of the quality of agricultural production, promotion of agricultural education and professions, engagement with foreign markets, and difficulties in the living conditions of villagers.[63] The deci-

---

61 *Zirai Kredi Kooperatifleri Kanunu*, 1929 <http://www.resmigazete.gov.tr/arsiv/1208.p df>. On 21 October 1935, the law for Agricultural Credit Cooperatives established within the new law number 2836 included larger state control of the credits and partnerships. See TBMM, *Tarım Kredi Kooperatifleri Kanunu*, 1935, pp. 764–69 <https://www.tbmm.gov.tr/tutanaklar/KANUNLAR_KARARLAR/kanuntbmm c015/kanuntbmmc015/kanuntbmmc01502836.pdf>. For further reading on the structure of agricultural cooperatives in Turkey's history, see also Özlem Kocabaş Yıldırır, *Türkiye'de Tarımsal Kooperatifçilik Düşüncesinin Gelişimi*, Libra Kitap, 35, 1. baskı (Osmanbey, İstanbul: Libra Kitap, 2010).

62 Until early 1930s, the government focused on judicial arrangements for the production of industrial raw materials such as tobacco, sugar, and cotton which were produced by the landowners and smallholders in particular areas. Especially during the years of economic depression, the aim was to adjust the production of agricultural material and industrial raw material, and to strengthen the statist tone in the economy with new regulations. See Hamit Bey, *Devlet İnhisarlarına Müteallik Mevzuat*, İnhisarlar Umum Müdürlüğü Hukuk Müşavirliği, I, II (İstanbul: İnhisarlar Matbaası, 1932).; Oya Köymen, "Cumhuriyet Döneminde Tarımsal Yapı ve Tarım Politikaları," 10–12.

63 *İhtisas Raporları: 1931 Birinci Türkiye Ziraat Kongresi* (Ankara: Milli İktisat ve Tasarruf Cemiyeti, 1931), I. During the First Agriculture Congress, the National Economy and Appropriations Association organized an international exhibition for agricultural technology, inviting foreign allies such as Russia and Hungary. See Türkan Çetin, '1929 Dünya Ekonomik Bunalimi Sonrası Türkiye'nin Tarım Politikasında Arayışlar: Birinci

sions made in the congress are seen in the first and second industrial plans of 1933 and 1936,[64] and directed the policy for economic planning of Turkish villages during the 1930s.

In addition to the governmental interventions in the rural economy, a group of intellectuals gathered under the journal *Kadro* (*Cadre*), which was published from 1932 to 1935 and supported the populist and statist operations for improvement in rural Turkey. İsmail Hüsrev Tökin, Şevket Süreyya Aydemir, Vedat Nedim Tör, Burhan Asaf Belge and the novelist Yakup Kadri Karaosmanoğlu concentrated on the village economy from statist and populist perspectives, promoting the RPP's, and hence the state's, policy interventions. From this point of view, the group associated with *Kadro* represented the economic dimension of republican ideology by introducing the village as the center of the development plan and the core of social categorization in Turkey.[65]

The group pointed to the legitimatized definition of republican ideals in theory and practice. Building a new country during the depression could not be considered only a political matter, but also involved the economic circumstances in the formation of state structures. The statist perspective would resolve the actual and future problems and achieve prosperity and socio-cultural reinforcement. According to Şevket Süreyya Aydemir:

> "The first duty of the state should be to intervene [and control] the national economy in the frame of (and in accordance with) the national and international status, not promoting only one limited class [referring to the privileged classes in Ottoman State as an example]. The state would be the organization that represented and regulated the people at the same time;

Türkiye Ziraat Kongresi', *DEÜ Atatürk İlkeleri ve İnkılap Tarihi Enstitüsü Çağdaş Türkiye Tarihi Araştırmaları Dergisi*, 2.6–7 (1996), 213–26 (p. 214).

64   According to Ayse Afet İnan, Turkey's first industry plan formed in 1933 for a period of five years and focused on the program for statist operations in industrial fields related to agriculture. The second industry plan, formed in 1936, intended to apply to a larger area than the agriculture-based improvement, but it concentrated on government enterprises and the encouragement of private associations in industry as well as it aimed to maintain the adjustments in agrarian economy. *Türkiye Cumhuriyetinin İkinci Sanayi Planı 1936*, XVI (Ankara: Türk Tarih Kurumu Basımevi, 1973), XXI, pp. VII–X.

65   İlhan Tekeli and Gencay Şaylan, 'Türkiye'de Halkçılık İdeolojisinin Evrimi', *Toplum ve Bilim Dergisi*, 6–7. Yaz-Güz (1978), 111–56.

namely it would emerge from the people but conduct the public life, build the economic accumulations, and adopt them on behalf of the people."[66]

Within a series of articles in *Kadro*, İsmail Hüsrev Tökin specifically analyzed the national economy with the village as the core theme, and detailed the village economy in terms of several topics such as ground rent and land ownership in rural areas,[67] feudalism and its impacts in rural Turkey,[68] economic changes in village life,[69] land reform and land provision for villagers,[70] and cooperatives[71] and other forms of agricultural enterprises in Anatolia.[72] In these articles Tökin presented the fundamental problem that the national funds had remained in the cities instead of the villages. Thus, the Turkish village, even though it was the key form of settlement for most of the population, was underdeveloped, with economic problems and difficulties in the socio-cultural sphere. He advocated statist reforms in the village economy, beginning with the land and landowners, in addition to the re-organization of agricultural labor in the villages and the class definition of the village population.[73]

İsmail Hüsrev Tökin highlighted that statist reforms should begin with land provision for villagers who did not hold cultivated land already. The aim was to rationalize agrarian production by connecting the villager to the land and thus to increase national income. It was also believed that an ideal land reform would extinguish every aspect of social polarization, which prevented

66   Şevket Süreyya (Aydemir), *İnkılâp ve Kadro: İnkılâbın İdeolojisi* (Ankara: Muallim Ahmet Halit Kitaphanesi, 1932), p. 109. Author's translation.

67   İsmail Hüsrev (Tökin), 'Türkiye Köy İktisadiyatında Toprak Rantı', *Kadro*, 4. Nisan (1932), 10–14.

68   İsmail Hüsrev (Tökin), 'Milli İktisat Tetkikleri: Türkiye'de Toprak Ağalığı', *Kadro*, 9.Eylül (1932), 23–29., and İsmail Hüsrev (Tökin), 'Milli İktisat Tetkikleri: Şark Vilayetlerinde Derebeylik', *Kadro*, 11.İkinci Teşrin (1932), 22–29.

69   İsmail Hüsrev (Tökin), 'Milli İktisat Tetkikleri: Anadolu Köyünde Bünye Tahavvülü', *Kadro*, 14. Şubat (1933), 18–24.

70   İsmail Hüsrev (Tökin), 'Milli İktisat Tetkikleri: Türk Köylüsü Bir Toprak Reformu Bekliyor', *Kadro*, 21.Eylül (1933), 21–24., and İsmail Hüsrev (Tökin), 'Milli İktisat Tetkikleri: Türk Köylüsünü Topraklandırmalı. Fakat Nasıl?', *Kadro*, 23. İkinci Teşrin (1933), 33–39.

71   Vedat Nedim (Tör), 'Millet İktisadiyatı: Köylü Kazanmalıdır', *Kadro*, 33. Eylül (1934), 11–15. According to Vedat Nedim Tör agricultural cooperatives, encouraged by the state, assisted small producers not only in connecting them with the market, but the cooperatives also provided modern agrarian technical equipment and methods.

72   İsmail Hüsrev (Tökin), 'Milli İktisat Tetkikleri: Anadolu'da Zirai İşletme Şekilleri', *Kadro*, 24. Birinci Kanun (1933), 25–32.

73   İsmail Hüsrev (Tökin), 'Millet İçinde Sınıf Meselesi II', *Kadro*, 26. Şubat (1934), 20–26.

the emergence of national integrity. Statist land reform would provide land to villagers and forge national cooperation in agricultural labor.[74] Tökin argued that the state should encourage villagers and farmers in technical and organizational matters such as quality improvement in agricultural production, affordable credit, and profitable marketing advantages. However, landownership remained a problem in social and economic stratification, and a large scope of legislative reorganization was needed to consolidate the economy in rural areas.[75]

In the early 1930s landowners in Turkey had varying profiles depending on their location. First, in the eastern regions, the feudal structure was still maintained and dominated by the aghas – landowners who held the villages and the surrounding cultivated land. Second, in the western and middle regions of Anatolia especially, sharecroppers who did not own agrarian land worked together with the landowners. Third, in the industrially developed areas such as Adana, İzmir and Istanbul, agricultural producers who were also landowners ran farms equipped with modernized technology and employed the villagers. Fourth, throughout Anatolia, there were self-contained smallholdings, run by families with a limited amount of cultivated land such as vineyards and orchards. Considering these circumstances, scholars pointed to the potential for technical and legislative reforms in rural Turkey. They principally advocated for state intervention to modernize agricultural production and the education of villagers. They also argued for the provision of land for all villagers to remove the privileges of feudalism in particular regions and to fix the economic balance between the different social groups in the country.[76]

The *Kadro* group urged republican reforms. At the same time, they campaigned for a realistic path in rural development, highlighting the village as the economic center of the country. The group's discussions inspired efforts to advance Turkey's peasant class and fulfil their social and economic potential, as had already occurred in Europe and Russia but not previously in Turkey.

Starting from the mid-1930s, contributions from republican intellectuals on the planning of the Turkish village and seeking solutions for the economic disadvantages of the villager resulted in an acceleration of regulations. Indeed, the legislative proceedings started with two early acts. First, the government

---

74   (Tökin), "Milli İktisat Tetkikleri: Türk Köylüsünü Topraklandırmalı. Fakat Nasıl?," 33.
75   Ibid, p. 21.
76   Ibid, pp. 22, 24.

declared on 2 June 1929 in law number 1505 that the agricultural lands belonging to people displaced from eastern provinces to the west, were to be provided to villagers, migrants, and refugees. On 13 March 1930, the recorder of deeds announced the new ordinance that the government would distribute ownerless lands seized after the deportation of the Greek populace to the local and exchanged people.[77] But these developments were not sufficient to bring economic advancement to the countryside.

On 14 June 1934, the Settlement Law number 2510 was enacted for organizing housing in the rural areas as well as regulating cultivated land distribution for the exchanged population, encouraging residents to move to areas where the Kurdish populace dominated.[78] The goal of the law and its regulations enacted in 1936 was to ease the ethnic conflict that had emerged between the republican authority and the people in the eastern regions since the late 1920s.[79] Moreover, the settlement law condemned property in order to provide agricultural fields for people who agreed to settle in the places chosen by the governors. This became one of the first examples of state expropriation of private lands in the eastern provinces.[80]

Nevertheless, legal interventions in the economic planning of the village were implemented parallel to land reform and scientific analysis for the benefit of development and sustainability in agriculture. Within the law (number 2291), enacted on 10 June 1933, the Higher Institute of Agriculture was founded in Ankara with professor of agriculture Friedrich Falke (1871–1948) as its first president and the objective of educating students in the fields of agriculture, veterinary science, natural science, agricultural craftsmanship, and forestry.[81]

The institute focused on technology and methods in agrarian production that could be easily transmitted to farmers and agricultural workers by the

---

77   Tapu Kadastro Umum Müdürlüğü, 'Mübadil ve Yerli Ahaliye Tevzi Edilen Arazi Kayıtları Hakkında Tamim', *Resmi Gazete* (Ankara, 13 March 1930), section 1444, p. 8765.

78   TBMM, *İskan Kanunu*, 1934 <http://www.resmigazete.gov.tr/arsiv/2733.pdf>., and "İskan Kanunu," *Resmi Gazete*, 04 1934, sec. 2733, http://www.resmigazete.gov.tr/arsiv/2733.pdf.

79   Uğur Ümit Üngör points out that the settlement law, enacted in 1934, allowed for the deportation of the Kurdish population and also the polarization of the country into two parts: Turkish west and Kurdish east. Üngör, pp. 153–54.

80   For this comment: Karaömerlioğlu, *Orada Bir Köy Var Uzakta*, 120–21.

81   Kerim Çağlar Ömer, *Yüksek Ziraat Enstitüsü: Kanunlar, Kararnameler, Bütçe ve Talimatnameler*, T.C. Yüksek Ziraat Enstitüsü Neşriyatı 101 (Ankara: Yüksek Ziraat Enstitüsü Basımevi, 1940), 11–13.

students who would train in the farms and villages during their education.[82] In addition, the institute promulgated research and practical instruction programs for agrarian people. Starting from 1934, under the directorship of Otto Gerngross who was the head of Faculty of Agricultural Technology, the institute published a series of instructional books known as *Çiftçiye Öğütler* (Guides to the Farmer) for farmers and agricultural producers.[83]

In 1935 Friedrich Falke announced that the institute was to play a critical role in the development of an academic organization for scientific applications to agriculture. He advocated that Turkish science should follow two significant directions. First, scholars should concentrate on the land, the people, and their particular problems in order to develop the national scientific perspective on agricultural growth. Second, they should get acquainted with relevant global debates, technology, and methodology to achieve recognition in the scientific world. Friedrich Falke pointed to these two objectives as the fundamental principles of the institute and its program.[84]

The Higher Institute of Agriculture, the Bank of Agriculture and the cooperatives collaborated to found the Agriculture Associations[85] in order to respond to problems in the countryside and to organize villagers and farmers in each village in accordance with local circumstances. It was believed that the associations in the villages would serve to instruct the people in more sufficient methods and techniques in agriculture, provide the equipment for more profitable production, and assist them with handling their goods in the market.[86]

Since the first years of the republic the state had been seeking to advance agriculture by building seed improvement stations, organizing the distribution of developed seeds to the peasants, funding animal farms to revive stock-

---

82   Çağlar, 37, 61–62.

83   Otto Gerngross, *Şarap Kurulması: Bağbozumundan İçkiyi Elde Edinceye Kadar Şarap İçin Yapılacak İşler Hakkında Çiftçiye Öğütler – Weinbereitung: Ratgeber für den praktischen Landwirt zur richtigen Behandlung des Weines von der Traubenlese bis zum fertigen Getränk*, trans. by Turgut Küşat, Çiftçiye Öğütler, 1 (Ankara: Yüksek Ziraat Enstitüsü Basımevi, 1934).

84   Friedrich Falke, 'Die Landwirtschaftliche Hochschule Ankara am Schluss ihres zweiten Studienjahres', *La Turquie Kemaliste*, 9.Octobre (1935), 2–9 (pp. 2–3).

85   Agriculture Associations was founded on 15 May 1957 with law numbered 6964. TBMM, *Ziraat Odaları ve Ziraat Odaları Birliği Kanunu*, 1957, pp. 3119–35 <http://www.mevzuat.gov.tr/MevzuatMetin/1.3.6964.pdf>.

86   Alaettin Topçubaşı Cemil, 'Köy Tarım Odaları ve Tarımsal Kredi Kooperatifleri', *Karınca: Türk Kooperatifçilik Cemiyetinin Aylık Mecmuası*, 15. Temmuz (1935), 16–19.

breeding, fighting against agricultural diseases, and organizing forestry affairs and plantations.[87] However, in 1934 there were only 63.936 members from 2550 villages in agriculture cooperatives, through which the state and institutional organizations provided assistance to the producers.[88] Nevertheless, these endeavors paved the way for the first Village and Agricultural Development Congress in 1938. On 29 December 1938 the commissions reported on topics such as vineyard and orchard agriculture, field agriculture, animal breeding and forage, forestry, agricultural handicraft, marketing, and agricultural education.[89] A consensus emerged during the congress that the country's economy was fundamentally based on the peasantry and depended on the development of the village community. In addition to strengthening the relationship between agricultural production and industry, the congress explored options to increase the quality of production, to rationalize and modernize agrarian activities, and to integrate local goods into foreign markets. To this end, delegates presented the organizational structures of agricultural cooperatives in the USA, Latin America, Germany, Switzerland, and Italy. In particular, they pointed to peasant associations in Switzerland as a model for Turkey.[90]

The commission reports illustrated the condition of the Turkish peasantry, methods for increasing agrarian production, adjustments and necessary regulations in governmental organizations and initiatives in agriculture, and state support for farmers and agricultural craftsmen. The decisions highlighted some crucial points for village planning. First, it stressed the urgency of land provision for landless peasants, following the cadastral planning of cultivated fields in and around the villages. The delegates then decided on programs for improving the physical condition of villages, such as land reclamation around rural areas, and the rehabilitation and restoration of hygiene and sanitation in village houses. In addition, a proposal was put forward to provide more radios in the villages, and to broadcast for and about village life in the national media.[91]

The congress had a significant impact on village life, creating a much more realistic agenda for country planning in rural Turkey by concentrating on the

---

87   *Birinci Köy ve Ziraat Kalkınma Kongresi Yayını: Türk Ziraat Tarihine Bir Bakış*, 300.

88   Topçubaşı, "Köy Tarım Odaları ve Tarımsal Kredi Kooperatifleri," 17.

89   *Birinci Köy Kalkınma Kongresi Komisyonlar Mazbatası* (Ankara: TBMM, 1938), p. 2, TBMM Kütüphanesi, 75–920.

90   *Birinci Köy ve Ziraat Kalkınma Kongresi: Belgeler* (Ankara: T.C. Ziraat Vekaleti, 1938), 69–91.

91   Ibid, pp. 337–40.

village community in the economic realm. Furthermore, the studies presented at the conference at the end of the 1930s offered a holistic perspective, displaying not only the village's socio-cultural aspects and capacities, but also its place in the economic development and modernization of the country.

At the end of 1930s the republican authorities re-emphasized rural planning and reformation targets for the Turkish village and Turkish peasantry. State politics focused on comprehensive land reform, interventions in the village economy enabling peasants to participate in the agricultural industry, management of sustainable, sufficient life in the villages to prevent unrestrained rural depopulation, and the political pacification and control of rural population in the villages. Government operations were still a major force in rural areas and were promoted by scholars who presented their ideas for the improvement of the village economy.

Among these scholars, Nusret Kemal Köymen again presented the argument that industrialization in rural areas and its organization in villages would induce progress in the countryside. He proposed to provide work for industrial laborers in rural areas instead of establishing industry around the cities. In this way, the village would prosper and be integrated with the country's economy:

> "Turkey, with about 80 per cent of her population living in villages, only few little industrialized cities and with all the lessons she is learning from costly and painful experiences of the Western World and the new technical possibilities, is building her new industries away from big cities.
>
> As there are but few big cities in Turkey to lure away the more enterprising, leaving villages as living cemeteries where old people eke out a meagre living from depleted soil, the question of "rural exodus" is unknown in Turkey. And the new rising tide of rural industrialization is promising a better future to village and agriculture.
>
> The motto of the Turkish Revolution is not "Back to the land" but "Forward to the progressive village".[92]

Köymen also published his book *Türk Köyünü Yükseltme Çareleri* (Solutions for the Rise of the Turkish Village) in 1939, highlighting the fundamental problems of the village community in achieving "modern facilities and circumstances, production, consumption, participation in the state economy, welfare and

---

92   Nusret Kemal Köymen, 'Forward to the Progressive Village', *La Turquie Kemaliste*, 32.Avril (1939), 15–18 (p. 18).

knowledge".[93] Repeatedly in the book he proposed supporting industrialization in rural areas and organizing the village in accordance with the industrial enterprises, which would be built to provide the villagers another occupation outside agriculture. In this way, more of the country's population in the villages would benefit from better living conditions. He also pointed to industrial towns in Europe, the USA and Mexico that had been built since the late 19th century. With these as examples, he suggested similar town models fitted to the community of the Turkish village and adapted to their industrial activities.[94]

However, in the 1940s the reality in Turkish villages did not meet this expectation, and the economic and socio-cultural conditions were still severe. As Çağlar Keyder explains: "The village was often the only life-world, and all national and world concerns were filtered through its structure; market transactions were few and infrequent; most of the output was for household's own consumption or for local exchange; hardly any of the productive inputs required for a technology of wooden plough and a team of oxen were purchased from outside the domestic sphere."[95] Undoubtedly the common ground for the state, republican intelligentsia, farmers, producers and villagers was the land reform besides other programs.

There had been a few steps made towards land provision regulations when the village was formed as an administrative legal entity,[96] but the political and economic instability of the war years had the result that the Turkish government regularly shelved legislation for effective land reform. The place of landless villagers among the rural populace was still a crucial theme until 1945. In addition, in the mid-1940s the RPP recognized their declining political domination, and with land reform the party aimed to regain the support of the rural masses. Relatedly, on 11 June 1945 law number 4753 (Land Provision for Farmers) was enacted in the parliament, becoming the greatest propaganda tool for the RPP in the 1945 election. This legislation aimed to cultivate the agriculture-based economy and support peasant families in the country. According to the law, land would be provided by the state to villagers who were only agrarian

---

93   Nusret Kemal Köymen, *Türk Köyünü Yükseltme Çareleri* (Ankara: Çankaya Matbaası, 1939), 8.

94   Ibid, pp. 14–21.

95   Keyder, "Genesis of Petty Commodity Production in Agriculture: The Case of Turkey," 171–72.

96   Soylu, *Köy Nedir ve Nasıl İdare Edilir*, 52–53.

workers, renters or sharecroppers, farmers who did not own sufficient fields for financial viability, graduate students from the Higher Institute of Agriculture who did not own arable fields, nomads, and immigrants.[97]

According to Asım Karaömerlioğlu, the land reform passed in 1945 was not truly politically radical in its impact in rural Turkey, but rather a strictly conventional program to keep villagers in their villages and to reinforce the importance of this group through landownership for the benefit of the regime. Moreover, the land reform availed to prevent the rise of potential leftist and radical political oppositions, and to secure the privilege of the state in a country in which people had not been urbanized, or culturally and socially diversified.[98]

The date of the law corresponded to another significant point at the beginning of the post-war period. Especially from 1945 to 1960, the economic dynamics surrounding Turkey appeared in two forms: the socialist formula of the Soviet Union, and the capitalist formula of the Western countries. As Turkey decided to step up to Western Europe and the USA, the economic structure promptly constrained major adjustments. Sinan Yıldırmaz highlights that this period resonated very dramatically throughout the Turkish peasantry, and hence in the Turkish village. Right after the statist land reform, the 1947 Economic Development Plan of Turkey adapted private enterprise instead of domestic capital to make inroads for Turkish industry and commerce within the international market economy.[99]

The law for land provision introduced statist approaches to the economic planning of the Turkish village in terms of agricultural development. However, less than a decade after the implementation of this reform, the state adopted capitalist solutions, resulting in a concentration on cities and urbanization. In other words, the transformation of the state's economic mentality because of alternatives and preferences in the post-war period is reflected in the village society as an impediment to improvement for the majority of the population. On a larger scale, the decisions taken after 1945 caused the depopulation of rural Turkey and centralization of labor in the cities.

---

97   *Çiftçiyi Topraklandırma Kanunu*, 1945 <http://www.resmigazete.gov.tr/arsiv/6032.pdf>.

98   Karaömerlioğlu, *Orada Bir Köy Var Uzakta*, 143.

99   Sinan Yıldırmaz, *Politics and the Peasantry in Post-War Turkey: Social History, Culture and Modernization*, Library of Ottoman Studies, 46 (London New York: I.B. Tauris, 2017), pp. 53, 55.

Architectural Planning

Starting from the early years of the republic, the socio-cultural and economic programs led to the regeneration of rural life and improvement of the village community. In addition, the village was considered the spatial core of the countryside and the improvement of its architecture became a government objective. Thus, during the 1930s, Turkish architects introduced various ideas about rural settlements and rural dwellings, considering architecture a powerful agent for the development program in the rural Anatolia.

The village discourse in architecture had several inputs, but in early 1930s, among Turkish architects, it evolved into a criticism of the state's interventions, arguing that the spatial organization of new villages was alien and conflicted with the needs of villagers.[100] Indeed some scholars advocated for a new profession – village architect – who would concentrate on this theme. Abdullah Ziya Kozanoğlu presented the "village architect", who would follow contemporary developments in design and construction and conform to the expectations of peasants to a national subtlety. He believed that village architecture arose from inside, and thus the architect should be acquainted with the village environment: "The village is constructed with its own stone, soil and wood."[101] He presented a scheme for an ideal settlement with descriptions of the state's new building program.

The site plan consisted of rectangular parts that formed a square. In the center, there was a public square, coffee house, and a school, with the village houses arranged around the center. These houses were larger and much more articulated than existing village houses and had direct access to the agricultural fields. The public square served for social organizations such as touring theatres and cinemas. In the center of the square the coffee house, which included a library, became a gathering space for the villagers. According to Abdullah Ziya Kozanoğlu, the coffee house emerged as the "modern temple of the villager".[102]

The architect proposed the local materials and building methods for the construction of the village. Thus, he believed that the "national" component of the village would be accomplished. He also advocated delivering modern living

---

100   Sıdıka Çetin, 'Erken Cumhuriyet Döneminde Köyün Modernizasyonu, Örnek Köyler Üzerinden Okuma', *Arredomento Mimarlık*, 2003, 99–105 (pp. 101–2).

101   Abdullah Ziya (Kozanoğlu), 'Köy Mimarisi', *Ülkü*, 5. Haziran (1933), 370–74 (p. 370).

102   Ibid, p. 38.

standards to the village. The villager would then participate in a modernization project in his own territory, apart from city-dwellers. In other words, Abdullah Ziya Kozanoğlu was suggesting a built environment produced with tactics adapted to rural Turkey.

The village proposals comprised components of the republican development program. Yet religious institutions, which still had a large impact on village communities, were intentionally not represented in models for the projects. Strongly affirming the secular agenda of Kemalist regime, most of the ideal village planning did not emphasize a spatial organization that could take the place of sacred space. Not only the religious image of a mosque, but also its social impact on the Islamic community were considered a threat to authority. No doubt the mosque was a provocative symbol against modernization, and the aim was that villagers would ideally be attached to the social activities defined by governmental program to civilize the community in a modern sense.[103]

Gülsüm Baydar discusses these conceptual projects grounded in national and regional research. She points out that these approaches were incomparable and different to the existing villages in Anatolia. Scenarios, under the theme of "ideal villages", were schematic adaptations of the "Ideal City" concept introduced in Europe from the end the 19th century.[104] Likewise, the "Ideal Republican Village" (İdeal Cumhuriyet Köyü)[105] presented in the early 1930s by Kazım Dirik, the governor of İzmir, was a blueprint of Ebenezer Howard's "Garden City" diagram, adapted to the concept of the republican village. The proposal was developed from the center with a monumental emphasis on the periphery. The first segment included public places such as the school, hospital, mosque, guesthouse and village hotel, village bar, the village association, and the agriculture office, and the RPP's house. The village houses were located in the second segment. The third segment consisted of the market area, factories, sports fields, fairground, coppice, and medical center. A cemetery and village rubbish dump were located outside of the circular organization. All segments had axial connections with each other. **(Figure 3.2.)**

---

103   Bozdoğan, *Modernism and Nation Building*, 116.

104   Gülsüm Baydar (Nalbantoğlu), 'Silent Interruptions: Urban Encounters with Rural Turkey', in *Rethinking Modernity and National Identity in Turkey*, ed. by Sibel Bozdoğan and Reşat Kasaba, Publications on the Near East, 3 (Seattle: London: University of Washington Press, 1997), pp. 192–210 (p. 153).

105   Dirik, TCBCA, 30.1.0.0/111.705.8.

Figure 3.2. *"The Ideal Republican Village" proposed by Kazim Dirik.* [106]

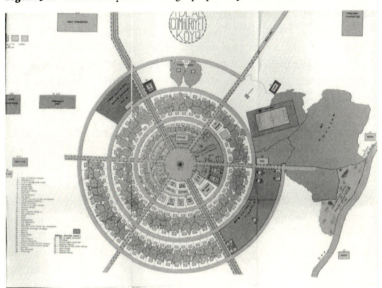

Another diagram of ideal village planning was proposed by Burhan Arif Ongun in 1935. In the project, the housing area was organized parallel to the village center, which introduced the public program along an axis. Two symmetrical public squares were located in the center, and in between were the bazaar, village association, schools, gendarmerie, village club, museum and a fountain. Another architect, Abidin Mortaş, described Burhan Arif Ongun's project within the framework of an organic relationship with Western industrial city concepts: "Cities which are settled according to feasible and science-based state plans, can have a mechanism to control residential and industrial demand of population in a cultural and sustainable context. Village planning, grounded on this formation, is substantial."[107]

However, neither cities nor villages were able to develop in accordance with European models. Also, the social structure presented with the building program contrasted with the real circumstances in the country. The formula

---

106   Ayşe Afet Inan, *Cumhuriyet'in Ellinci Yılı İçin: Köylerimiz*, 36 (Ankara: Türk Tarih Kurumu Basımevi, 1978), XVI.

107   Abidin Mortaş, "Köy Projesi: Mimar Burhan Arif," *Arkitekt* 59–60, no. 11–12 (1935): 320.

was ambiguous: the architects, on the one hand, emphasized the sustainability maintained by the regional and traditional structure of rural life. On the other hand, they argued that villagers were "the people of today" who needed to be modernized. Thus, Abidin Mortaş asserted that village planning should fit the modest and pure living habits of the settlers, but also should be equipped with contemporary components of modern life. Accordingly, general planning should be considered by professionals such as architects; however, the settler should determine the details of the spatial organization himself.[108]

Moreover, architect Zeki Sayar maintained that the tools of modern architecture and planning should be implemented in the countryside to form a culturally and socially improved rural life. To substantiate his ideas, Zeki Sayar referred to Germany's agricultural colonies, established for industrial workers to return to the countryside, and he enthusiastically supported the operation that accomplished the economic agenda and national goals at the same time. According to Zeki Sayar, "nation building with agricultural colonies shows an aim for a new lifestyle in the countryside",[109] and this approach could also be adapted to Turkey's landscape. A systematic practice of "internal colonization" could help the state achieve the economic, national, and socio-cultural transformation of rural Turkey. Zeki Sayar elaborated on the internal colonization model equipped with modern notions in contrast to the tradition and locality to civilize the villagers' lifestyle in the countryside:

> "Although we must consider the habits and lifestyles of peasants when we are constructing the new villages, we should not hesitate to go against these traditions wherever they clash with contemporary social and hygienic standards. The new village plans should also provide the users with the means of civilized living. A revolution in lifestyles is also necessary to teach them to sleep on individual beds rather than together on the earth, to teach them to use chairs and tables rather than sitting and eating on the floor. Kitchens, stoves, and bathrooms should be standardized into a number of different types so as to obtain the most economic and functional results."[110]

According to Sayar, an ideal settlement was organized by three architectural components: standardization, variety in typology, and utilitarian perspective

---

108   Ibid.

109   Zeki Sayar, 'İç Kolonizasyon: Başka Memleketlerde', *Arkitekt*, 68.8 (1936), 231–35 (p. 232).

110   Sayar, 'İç Kolonizasyon: Kolonisation Intérieure', p. 47. Quoted from Bozdoğan, *Modernism and Nation Building*, 101. Author's translation.

in material use. A new lifestyle in the villages would be furnished in the build-ings, which were constructed with the most economic and functional meth-ods. Variation in the housing typology would provide a better living standard for each family. He also suggested involving concrete in the construction of rural houses instead of traditional and regional building techniques and ma-terials.[111] The architect believed the tools of modern architecture to be a spatial translation for the modern construction of Turkish society in the countryside.

By the end of 1930s, it was more apparent that discussions about the village had two sides. One side believed that the new villages should serve as a rational planning mechanism for rural people to adapt their lifestyle to contemporary standards. The other side agreed that ideal rural settlements should concen-trate on the traditional living habits of villagers together with regional build-ing aspects, which could provide a sustainable life in the countryside and avoid alienation in the village community.

Architect Abidin Mortaş, who participated in the architectural competi-tion for the village house in 1935,[112] introduced a project based on combining regional and traditional aspects with contemporary needs. He criticized the new village construction, arguing that the new village houses still needed to be modified to include familiar organizations to the inhabitants. Therefore, the design of the "village house" was a crucial theme of the idea of the settlement and would directly affect peasant life. Besides, rural settlements, which were developed according to urbanized qualities, would cause alienation among vil-lagers.[113] He also proposed a settlement enclosed in a rational geometrical or-ganization: the plan consisted of two areas – housing areas and public space – separated by the main road towards the village. The building program in the public area consisted of a square, a school, the village council, a coffee house, the market, and a mosque. Agricultural activities would be placed in the other quarter, and each house would be located in a garden of equal plots.

As well as the complete settlements for the ideal villages, the dwelling unit emerged as a significant topic among Turkish architects. State-planned set-tlements, which were often a group of houses in organized parcels, practically

---

111   Ibid.

112   In 1935 the RPP and People's House organized an architectural competition for village houses to fulfil the needs for new rural settlements and houses built for mostly Balkan immigrants settled according to the 1934 Settlement Law. The competition and its con-sequences are discussed in the next chapter.

113   Abidin Mortaş, 'Köy Evi Tipleri', Arkitekt, 109–110.1–2 (1940), 8–9 (p. 1940).

made the Village House the *kernel* of the whole implementation so that it was even seen as the beginning of the modernization in the settlement. There were two fundamental viewpoints, the first based on vernacular aspects emphasizing that the traditional and regional customs should determine the design concept of village house. The other proposed a modernized interior adapted to the agrarian livelihood in the countryside.[114]

Abdullah Ziya Kozanoğlu believed that state housing operations in rural areas ignored regional aspects, and this alienated the villagers from their environment. He suggested concentrating on local components to form the village house and teaching the villagers how to build their own houses with vernacular materials and methods to maintain their living conditions. The traditional and accustomed nature of the villager would show the real Turkish culture, and only in this way would the villager feel attached to the Turkish nation and goals of the new republican regime.[115] Accordingly, Kozanoğlu developed two plans for the village house, considering the environmental conditions and local materials in the design.[116] The lowland house consisted of a bedroom with a hall, a dining room, kitchen, and toilet aligned around the semi-open terrace. The stairs led to the second level of the house in which the architect suggested placing another room and a larger terrace. The highland house consisted of four rooms, kitchen and toilet aligned around the semi-open terrace. Likewise, the architect proposed the inclusion of a second level with a room and terrace. The construction materials and techniques would also use local methods, such as timber, stone, or adobe.

On the other hand, architect Arif Hikmet Koyunoğlu designed a village house with a spatial organization evoking a lifestyle between the city and the, a guest room, a bedroom, toilet, cellar, barn, and corral. Although the architect proposed a determined interior with modernized furnishings for the villagers, the construction materials and techniques would be vernacular. In detail, he was suggesting a stone masonry building, with timber separation walls and roof.[117]

---

114 Özge Sezer, 'The Village House: Planning the Rural Life in Early Republican Turkey', in *Spaces / Times / Peoples: Domesticity, Dwelling and Architectural History; Mekanlar / Zamanlar / İnsanlar: Evsellik, Ev, Barınma ve Mimarlik Tarihi*, ed. by Lale Özgenel (Ankara: ODTÜ Basım İşliği, 2016), pp. 51–60.

115 Abdullah Ziya Kozanoğlu, "Köy Evleri Proje ve Yapıları İçin Toplu Rapor," *Arkitekt* 55–56, no. 07–08 (1935): 203.

116 Kozanoğlu, 'Gün Geçiminde Kerpiç Köy Yapısı'.

117 Arif Hikmet, 'Köy Evi', *Arkitekt*, 35.11 (1933), 357.

According to Gülsüm Baydar, Arif Hikmet Koyunoğlu was inspired by the principles of *Existenzminimum*, which was also an influential approach in urban house design in those years. The organization of spaces and furnishing had a minimalist language in this scheme, but unlike the proposal of Abdullah Ziya Kozanoğlu, the idea was not to reference the actual living conditions and traditions of villagers.[118]

Turkish elites (here architects, city planners and politicians) participated in the construction of a rural lifestyle within the framework of modernization and nationalization programs and through scenarios of idealized rural settlements and houses. According to the republican cadre, on one hand, the rural milieu was in great need of economic and socio-cultural development. On the other hand, the rural village was considered the cultural core where the Turkish "nation" hibernated. Despite the different approaches to the village house, based on standardization, vernacular concepts, and the synthesis of modernist and traditional views, the discourse on the Turkish village was meant to establish the "national architecture for rural people" with a nostalgic tone. In theory, housing the rural population in planned settlements emerged as a constructive operation that centered around providing the villagers with a built environment and improved living conditions. However, the discussions and the concepts remained ambiguous, either advocating the *status quo* of accustomed rural life or foregoing traditions in favor of a modernized habitat.

---

118   Gülsüm Baydar (Nalbantoğlu), 'Between Civilization and Culture: Appropriation of Traditional Dwelling Forms in Early Republican Turkey', *Journal of Architectural Education* (1984-), 47.2 (1993), 66–74 (pp. 71–72) <https://doi.org/10.2307/1425168>.

Chapter 4 – Administering the *Rural*: Regulations for the Making of the Modern Turkish Village

Construction of Rural Settlements during the First Years of the Republic

Settlement policy and building typologies in the first years of the republican era were inherited from Ottoman operations which were executed as a result of internal migration and the arrival of refugees from defeated imperial lands into the Anatolian territories. The Ottoman state was confronted with the forced migration of 413,922 people, which required planning, starting from the end of the Balkan Wars between 1913 and 1920.[1] In order to house this group, the Ottoman parliament passed several laws in 1913: initially, a law of 18 March – *Muhacirinin Suret-i İskânı Hakkında Tahrirat-ı Umumiyye ve Talimatnamesi* (General Instructions for Settling the Immigrants) – while on 27 April 1913, within the law *Vilayet İdare-i Sıhhiye Nizamnamesi* (Regulations for Sanitary Matters of the Provinces), the housing of Balkan immigrants came under the administrative purview of the provinces. On 13 May 1913, a new law (*İskan-ı Muhacirin Nizamnamesi* – Regulations for Settling the Immigrants) was enacted to reorganize settlement policies, followed on 29 December by another regulation (*Elli Haneden Aşağı Karye Teşkil Olunmamasına Dair Tahrirat-ı Ummumiye* – Correspondence for Refusal of Village Status of Settlements with Less Than 50 Dwellings), which reorganized the villages along with the new settlements built for the newcomers.

The last legal instructions for settling immigrants were announced by the Ottoman state within the law *Ta'mim ve Talimatname* (Circular Letter and

---

1   Onur Yıldırım, *Diplomacy and Displacement: Reconsidering the Turco-Greek Exchange of Populations, 1922–1934*, Middle East Studies – History, Politics, and Law (New York: London: Routledge, 2006), p. 90.

Instruction) of 22 June 1916.[2] The Ottoman authority passed legislation to construct small houses and cottages for urgent cases, redistributing the abandoned properties of the deported population[3] as building supplies for the Muslim incomers, and planning "exemplar villages" (*Numune Köyler*[4]) in several regions.[5]

Turkey's new parliament was elected, independent of the Ottoman authorities, in 1920 and started Turkey's Independence War after the First World War occupations and the Greco-Turkish War. The parliament continued the Ottoman housing program for 388.146 Muslims immigrating from former Ottoman territories. On the other hand, 1.221.849 Greeks had to leave the country and vacate their houses and agricultural fields.[6] As a result of these relocations, the abandoned properties of the deported Greek Orthodox population served as settlement resources for housing operations conducted during the 1920s.

On 26 April 1922, the 1913 law was reformulated in accordance with the new circumstances of the ongoing war, and within the new regulation it was announced that immigrants who had lived in Anatolian territories for less than six years would be housed by the government. The Ministry of Public Health and Welfare and Ministry of Interior and Economy would determine the location of settlements. In every region, settlement commissions would be established, and each commission would have a civilian authority, a doctor, an

---

2   Cengizkan, *Mübadele konut ve yerleşimleri*, 55–56.; A. Gündüz Ökçün, 'İkinci Meşrutiyet Döneminde Yeni Köylerin Kurulmasına ve Köylerde Çevre Sağlığına İlişkin Tüzel Düzenlemeler', in: *Prof. Fehmi Yavuz'a Armağan*, 528 (Ankara: AÜ Siyasal Bilgiler Fakültesi Yayınları, 1983), pp. 171–200 (p. 171).

3   Referring to the Armenian deportation.

4   The Ottoman authority and, later the republican regime, called the new villages, constructed in accordance with the regulations in planning, "exemplar villages" (*Numune Köyler*) with the idea that the new planned villages would be model settlements for further developments.

5   Fuat Dündar, *İttihat ve Terakki'nin Müslümanları İskân Politikası, 1913–1918*, Araştırma-İnceleme Dizisi, 112, 1. baskı (Cağaloğlu, İstanbul: İletişim, 2001), p. 52.

6   Yıldırım, *Diplomacy and Displacement*, 91.Turkey and Greece signed the *Convention Concerning the Exchange of Greek and Turkish Populations* on 30 January 1923. The agreement contained the population exchange also proclaimed in the Treaty of Lausanne on 24 July 1923. See Article 2 in Part VI of the treaty. *Lausanne Peace Treaty VI. Convention Concerning the Exchange of Greek and Turkish Populations Signed at Lausanne, January 30, 1923*, 24 July 1923 <http://www.mfa.gov.tr/lausanne-peace-treaty-vi_-convention-concerning-the-exchange-of-greek-and-turkish-populations-signed-at-lausanne_.en.mfa>.

engineer, an agriculturist, an accountant, and a secretary. In addition to this, members acquainted with the agricultural and socio-cultural capacities of the regions would participate in the commissions, schools would be built, and dwellers would be assisted and encouraged in agrarian activities with credits and subsidiary payments.[7] On 23 October 1923 the Ministry of Population Exchange and Housing (*Mübadele ve İskan Bakanlığı*) was founded just before the proclamation of the republic on 29 October 1923. These first regulations paved the way for the legal organization of the settlements built in the following years.

The 1924 Village Law and the 1926 Settlement Law

In the first years of the republic, the Village Law (number 442), passed on 18 March 1924, played a crucial role in forming rural settlements for newcomers and the existing population. The law established the village as a legislative body of the republican administration, and the social, cultural, and economic nucleus of the country. It contained ten chapters to define the village in administrative terms: finance (self-sufficient practices and state funding), agricultural and constructive works, organization of elections, and assignments of local authority to bodies such as the council, village guard and imam. The Village Act was basically enacted to construct rural Turkey, and it became a practical guide for how to shape the new rural settlements and reshape the villages demolished in the war up until the first years of 1930s.[8]

The public works and land use plan were detailed within articles in the second chapter, including the architectonic formation of the village. The articles principally determined the border of the village territory, reconstruction methods, infrastructure, housing, hygiene, and administrative and institutional units. Architecture was introduced as a topic for sanitation, together with the construction of water infrastructure and sewage system which were a major part of the village planning. The building program included a square, two main streets crossing each other, a house for the village council, a guesthouse, a school, shops, and ateliers (for a smithy, a grocery, and repairmen), a garbage treatment house outside the village, a cemetery, fountains, and

---

7   30 *Nisan 329 Tarihli İskan-ı Muhacirin Talimatnemesini Değiştiren Nizamnamenin Yürürlüğe Konması*, 1913, TCBCA 030.18.01/04.55.2.; *İskan Tarihçesi* (İstanbul: Hamit Matbaası, 1932), 20–21.; Cengizkan, *Mübadele konut ve yerleşimleri*, 20, 99.

8   *Köy Kanunu*.

a coppice area. On the other hand, the washhouse, public bath, bazaar and shopping area, mill house and irrigation canals around farms were to be built in accordance with the requirements of the villagers and circumstances of the settlement area.[9]

The village building program elaborated in the act was implemented only in a very limited scope. During the first years of the republic, the villages were built to solve the housing problem for immigrants and veterans rather than with the aim of building ideal settlements in the countryside. Although the first implementations of the Village Law consisted of organized dwelling areas with basic infrastructure (housing plots, a school, a mosque, a fountain, and the roads), this act paved the way for the reconstruction of the country beginning with rural areas. It was one of the most significant legal changes the republican regime put on the agenda, even considering later regulations for organization and operation of infrastructure, and dwelling in the rural built environment, such as the Settlement Law of 1926, the Municipal Corporations Law and Public Health Law of 1930, and the Municipal Buildings and Roads Law of 1933.[10]

Following the passage of the Village Law in March 1924, the Ministry of Population Exchange and Housing implemented the building program across 10 regions where the cities and towns had adequate infrastructure, areas for village construction, and properties left by the deported population.[11] First, the settling policy was implemented, utilizing the estates of the leaving population, and renovating houses for newcomers. In a regulation enacted on 6 July

---

9   Ibid, p. 239 (2. Fasıl 13. Madde).

10   Eres, "Türkiye'de Planlı Kırsal Yerleşmelerin Tarihsel Gelişimi ve Erken Cumhuriyet Dönemi Planlı Kırsal Mimarisinin Korunması Sorunu," 101.

11   Kemal Ari states that the first region included the cities of Sinop, Samsun, Ordu, Giresun, Trabzon, Gümüşhane, Amasya, Tokat, Çorum; the second region included the cities of Edirne, Tekfurdağı (Tekirdağ), Gelibolu, Kırkkilise (Kırklareli), Çanakkale; the third region included the city of Balıkesir; the fourth region included the cites of İzmir, Manisa, Aydın, Menteşe, Afyon; the fifth region included the city of Bursa; the sixth region included the cities of İstanbul, Çatalca, Zonguldak; the seventh region included the cities of İzmit, Bolu, Bileceik, Eskişehir, Kütahya; the eighth region included the cities of Antalya, Isparta, Burdur; the ninth region included the cities of Konya, Niğde, Kayseri, Aksaray, Kırşehir; and the tenth region included the cities of Adana, Mersin, Silifke, Kozan, Ayıntab (Gaziantep), Maraş. Kemal Arı, *Büyük Mübadele: Türkiye'ye Zorunlu Göç, 1923–1925*, Türkiye Araştırmaları 17 (İstanbul: Tarih Vakfı Yurt Yayınları, 1995), 52–53.

1924, the ministry declared that the government would distribute the lands after the arrival of the farmer immigrants.[12] In relatively developed provinces like Samsun, Bursa, İzmir, İzmit, Manisa and Adana, new villages were constructed consisting of up to 50 dwellings, a school, and a mosque. In 1933 there were 69 new rural settlements built by the state in accordance with the principles of the Village Law.[13]

Another crucial legislative attempt at solving the rural housing problem was the Settlement Law (number 885) enacted on 31 May 1926. The principles underlying this legislation were housing the exchanged population and seeking low-cost formulas for dwelling and reconstruction works. In other words, the law applied to the organization of existing building reserves as well as to new settlements, considering the economic circumstances and the adaptation of numerous groups into the socio-cultural and economic planning of the country. Within the 1926 Settlement Law, regulations about the new settlements addressed similar concerns as the 1924 Village Law: the building program for each village included a school, mosque, bath, bazaar, police station, cemetery, and pasture for public facilities, along with infrastructure and a dwelling area.[14] Together with the 1924 Village Law, the 1926 Settlement Law shaped the measures for the planning of rural settlements, and hence villages, during the first 10 years of the republic.

---

12   TBMM, *Terkedilmiş Gayrimenkulün İskan Edilme Hakkını Haiz Göçmenler ve Aşiretlere Tevzii Hakkında Yönetmelik*, 1924, TCBCA 030.18.01.01/010.33.20(1+4).; *İskan Tarihçesi*, 22–32.; Cengizkan, *Mübadele konut ve yerleşimleri*, 139–44.

13   Nedim İpek, 'Göçmen Köylerine Dair', *Tarih ve Toplum*, 150.Haziran (1996), 15–21 (p. 19).; Kozanoğlu, "Köy Evleri Proje ve Yapıları İçin Toplu Rapor," 203.: Arı, *Büyük Mübadele*, 66.; Cengizkan, *Mübadele konut ve yerleşimleri*, 28–29. Ali Cengizkan states that in 1924, 14 villages (seven in Samsun, two each in İzmir and Bursa, one each in İzmit, Adana and Antalya) were built; however, Zeynep Eres claimed that there were 32 villages under construction, with some of the settlements not having recorded place names. Eres, "Türkiye'de Planlı Kırsal Yerleşmelerin Tarihsel Gelişimi ve Erken Cumhuriyet Dönemi Planlı Kırsal Mimarisinin Korunması Sorunu," 115–16.

14   *İskan Tarihçesi*, 76–80.

Figure 4.1. *Low-Cost House (Iktisadi Hane), 1925.*[15]

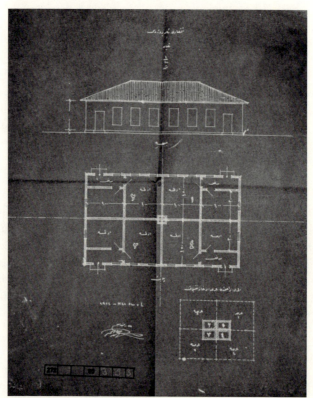

Alongside this legislative framework, ensuring that housing in the settlements met a set standard was one of the most immediate tasks. The state prepared a dwelling typology that could be practically implemented in the given circumstances with low expenses. In 1925, *Iktisadi Hane* (The Low-Cost House) was introduced with the elaboration of proposals for immigrants following the Balkan Wars and during the First World War **(Figure 4.1)**. According to the document dated 10 February 1925, low-cost houses were constructed in several cities in Anatolia in the new rural settlements, differing slightly due to local conditions. But there were building principles that every province abided by:

---

15   *Low-Cost Housing Typology – TCBCA 272.80/3.9.3 (5).*

the wall to separate houses from each other should be made of mud bricks, other walls should be constructed in timber, the chimney should be made of stone, and the roof should be covered with roof tiles. Each unit included four houses, each of which had two rooms without a toilet, kitchen, and bathroom, arrayed under one roof.[16]

Conditions after the wars, particularly from the beginning of the 20th century, designated the program of construction of the new settlements in the first years of the republic. The regulations and instructions, determined during the last years of the Ottoman Empire, also developed a blueprint for the early republican cadre. The previous implementations were adapted to the circumstances of the country; they prepared the legislative framework for the administration of rural Turkey. The 1924 Village Law, the 1926 Settlement Law and the "Low-Cost Dwelling" of 1925 guided the first years of operations in constructing new rural settlements all over the country.

Building the Rural Settlements during the 1920s

One of the first implementations of the Village Law and the low-cost housing typology was constructed in Manisa at the end of 1924. Çobanisa Village was planned by the architect Mesut Özok of the İzmir Population Exchange and Housing Authority and constructed by the engineer Galip Bey.[17]

The plan for a 44.616m^2 area was divided into six streets along the north–south axis, five streets along the west–east axis, and 22 building parcels. Public buildings were located in the middle of the east–west axis, including 12 shops, a mosque, a guesthouse, a gendarmerie station, a school, four fountains, a barn, a bakery, and a bazaar area. The northern part was set aside for agrarian activities, with 12.000m^2 land for each family in the village. The cemetery and coppice were placed in the southern part of the village. The washhouse and the mill were located on the edges of the east–west axis.

The site between the northern and southern part of the village was planned as a dwelling area, with 58 houses according to the plan.[18] The houses, attached

---

16   "Low-Cost Housing Typology – TCBCA 272.80/3.9.3 (5)," TCBCA 272.80/3.9.3 (5) § (1925); Cengizkan, *Mübadele konut ve yerleşimleri*, 182.

17   *Document on Kıyas and Çobanisa*, 1924, TCBCA 30.18.1.1/12.59.12.; Cengizkan, *Mübadele konut ve yerleşimleri*, 39–40, 43, 46, 86., Eres, "Türkiye'de Planlı Kırsal Yerleşmelerin Tarihsel Gelişimi ve Erken Cumhuriyet Dönemi Planlı Kırsal Mimarisinin Korunması Sorunu," 130–32.

18   However, the village was built with 52 houses.

to each other along the east–west axis, were located in a parcel of 200–300m². The units were facing the street with a small garden, and backyards were attached to each other along the north– south axis with larger orchards. Housing units consisted of two dwellings under a single roof. The interior was divided into an entrance hall, two rooms, a kitchen, and a toilet partition.[19] They were designed as one-storey masonry buildings with timber on the room floors and concrete slabs on the toilet partition and kitchen floors. However, the houses were built as two-storey buildings. Each house was situated according to the slope and separated into two layers along the vertical axis: the upper part was the living area and entrance facing the street, while the lower layer was used as a small corral and the backyard entrance, divided into two rooms.

The survey report of 28 April 1924 announced that the Ministry of Population Exchange and Housing planned to construct new villages in several districts in Manisa, such as Soma and Bozköy. The report also focused on the settlement in Bozköy, which was demolished after the deportation of the Greek Orthodox population, but still had 15 houses and a school in the center. Although the town had been destroyed, local people were settled in the abandoned properties in the surrounding villages. But this solution could not fulfil the housing needs of the incoming immigrants. In addition to this, the site was accessible by rail, and the building materials would be easily provided by the quarry in the region. Therefore, the committee of Ministry of Population Exchange and Housing decided to build a settlement in Bozköy, Manisa.[20]

The state sent guidance to the governors in the provinces in March 1924, including İzmir, introducing the village building principles in the city. The Ministry of Population Exchange and Housing communicated to the local authority in İzmir that two rural settlements consisting of 150–200 dwellings would be built in İzmir and Manisa by the end of 1924. To determine the building site, the ministry called the commission to İzmir to propose convenient areas where the transportation network (mostly railways), agricultural potential and resources for building material (mostly quarries) fulfilled the construction plan, and to

---

19   The niche in the wall separating the kitchen and the bigger room was designed as a small part for bathing and a garderobe. The kitchen was located on the wall to which the buildings were attached and here there was a hole left for chimney. This wall was thicker than other separation walls. According to the project, each unit had a 50cm basement wall. The wooden roof had a height of 300cm. The double-sided exterior walls were 240cm high and each window was 125cm X 170cm.

20   *Survey Report on Building Villages in İzmir and Manisa*, 1924, TCBCA 272.80/3.6.8.

prepare the base maps of these areas. Moreover, the ministry instructed the local commission in İzmir to prepare a survey report of demolished rural settlements to improve the living conditions of the local population in these areas.[21]

The document dated 3 December 1924 shows that these two settlements were Çobanisa village in Manisa and Kıyas (or Kayas) village in İzmir. Like Çobanisa Village, Kıyas Village was also planned by architect Mesut Özok,[22] but built by engineer Dervis Bey. It consisted of 50 houses that had been constructed since early 1925 using similar methods and materials to Çobanisa Village in Manisa.[23]

The survey report dated 28 April 1924 introduced the detailed planning and the schemes of other settlements, which would be built in Kuşçular (in Urla district) and Kısıkköy in İzmir. Around Kuşçular village, immigrants had already started to settle into abandoned properties, but the number of buildings did not meet the housing needs of the incoming people. The area was well cultivated, convenient for agrarian activities, and with water access. Also, it was close to the quarries that would be used in construction for building materials. According to the report, houses were planned as stone-masonry buildings with lime-plastered walls and tiled roofs. Likewise, Kısıkköy – a former Greek village demolished during the war – was presented as another suitable place for a new settlement. The area was well connected to the railway between the city harbor and agricultural lands, and close to water sources, while the site was convenient for agrarian activities. Therefore, the committee proposed building another settlement in Kısıkköy consisting of stone-masonry houses for immigrants.[24]

Moreover, a document dated 10 February 1925 announced that the low-cost housing in convenient districts of cities like Samsun, Amasya, and Çorum would efficiently house a large number of newcomers. The construction would also continue in İzmir, the city to which the majority of the population was deported.[25]

Samsun, which was depopulated after the War of Independence and the Greco-Turkish War, was planned to house the newcomers in the abandoned

---

21   Turkish transcription of the letter; Cengizkan, *Mübadele konut ve yerleşimleri*, 172.

22   Ibid, p. 86.

23   Document on Kıyas and Çobanisa.

24   *Survey Report on Building Villages in İzmir and Manisa*, TCBCA 272.80/3.6.8.

25   *Low-Cost Housing Typology*, TCBCA 272.80/3.9.3 (5).

properties in the city and the former villages. However, the condition of the building reserve and the villages did not provide suitable conditions for locals or to settle the immigrants. Therefore in 1924, under the control of Ministry of Population Exchange Housing and Housing, construction of new settlements began with 50 houses in five locations, called Canik, Aksarağaç, Ökse, Çınarağıl, and Çırağman,[26] and continued until 1926.[27]

İsmailzade Osman Bey was employed to construct masonry houses in five villages, using mud bricks as the building material. However, at the end of 1924, the construction method was changed to timber by the ministry in response to climatic conditions.[28] Bey continued building the houses with a timber construction and stone foundation, mud-brick infill walls, and lime plaster.[29]

In addition to the settlements in Canik, Aksarağaç, Ökse, Çınarağıl, and Çırağman, low-cost houses in other villages were built for immigrants and local people who lived in severe circumstances in the city and in the rural areas around Samsun. Also, between 1924 and 1926 cottages were constructed in convenient areas around the city to address urgent housing needs.[30]

A document dated 9 March 1924 describes the government's first attempt at the planning of villages in rural districts of Bursa. As a result of the war conditions, the center and the rural region of the province were demolished. Furthermore, the abandoned properties would not be able to accommodate the

---

26 *Document on Canik, Aksarağaç, Ökse, Çınarağıl, Çırağman,* 18.01.1925, TCBCA 30.18.1.1/ 12.70.1-1. and *Document on Canik, Aksarağaç, Ökse, Çınarağıl, Çırağman,* TCBCA 30.18.1.1/12.70.1-2; *Document on Canik, Aksarağaç, Ökse, Çınarağıl, Çırağman,* 1924, TCBCA 272.11/18.87.7.

27 *Document on Canik, Aksarağaç, Ökse, Çınarağıl, Çırağman,* 1926, TCBCA 030.18.01/ 017.94.2. Cengizkan, *Mübadele konut ve yerleşimleri,* 228.

28 *Document on Canik, Aksarağaç, Ökse, Çınarağıl, Çırağman,* TCBCA 30.18.1.1/12.58.12.

29 *Document on Canik, Aksarağaç, Ökse, Çınarağıl, Çırağman,* 1925, TCBCA 272.80/4.10.9.

30 The implementations of "low-cost houses" in Samsun started in 1925, in accordance with the sources of *Document on Canik, Aksarağaç, Ökse, Çınarağıl, Çırağman,* 1925, TCBCA 272.11/21.103.15. and *Document on Canik, Aksarağaç, Ökse, Çınarağıl, Çırağman,* 1925, 272.80/4.10.15. Ali Cengizkan also pointed out that there were more housing constructions than the five settlements documented in the archives. He referred to the surveys of Nedim İpek about the population exchange in Samsun. Cengizkan, *Mübadele konut ve yerleşimleri,* 42–43. Nedim İpek, *Mübadele ve Samsun,* Türk Tarih Kurumu Yayınları. XVI. Dizi, Sayı 85 (Ankara: Türk Tarih Kurumu Basımevi, 2000), p. 85. For a reading of further documents on construction works and correspondences about the new settlements in Samsun: Eres, "Türkiye'de Planlı Kırsal Yerleşmelerin Tarihsel Gelişimi ve Erken Cumhuriyet Dönemi Planlı Kırsal Mimarisinin Korunması Sorunu," 121–26.

needs of the incoming people and locals. The governor of Bursa declared that in the Kalder, Tepecik and Tahtalı districts in the centre, Armudlu and Kurşunlu in Gemlik district, Emirali, Burgaz and Veledler in Mudanya district, and Baş, Karacaoba, İkizce(oba), Kemerbend and the town center in Karacabey district, the agricultural land was suitable, but the housing areas had been badly destroyed. Therefore, he proposed that these areas be planned by a group of experts – an architect, an engineer, a building contractor, and a technician – from the Ministry of Population Exchange and Housing.[31]

At the beginning of 1925 it was also planned to build low-cost houses in convenient areas, parallel to the construction of new villages.[32] After three months, immigrants were settled in an abandoned Greek village, Filader, in the houses that had been built by the dwellers themselves. But the governor asked the ministry for permission to clear up the demolished houses and to construct an "exemplar village" here.[33]

Moreover, the construction of the new settlements based on the principles of the 1924 Village Law started in the same year in Karacaoba and İkizceoba. Here, the governor of Bursa pointed out convenient locations for the new villages to the commission of the Ministry of Population Exchange and Housing. According to the document dated 3 December 1924, the settlements were built and consisted of 50 timber houses in each village. The completion date of the work was set for 13 November 1924. However, due to the weather conditions, and a delay in the arrival of building elements such as windows and doors provided by the ministry, the construction work was postponed to April 1925.[34] The houses and the organization of dwellings and other buildings were planned by the architect Arif Hikmet Koyunoğlu,[35] who worked in the Ministry of Popula-

---

31 *Document on Village Planning in Bursa*, 1924, TCBCA 272.80/3.5.2. and Cengizkan, *Mübadele konut ve yerleşimleri*, 171.

32 *Document on Building Low-Cost Houses in Bursa*, 1925, TCBCA 272.80/3.8.13.

33 *Document on Filader*, 26.06.1924, TCBCA 272.11/18.87.5. According to Zeynep Eres, the village was being built up until the end of 1920s and was used as an example in a cultural geography book for high school scholars. Eres, "Türkiye'de Planlı Kırsal Yerleşmelerin Tarihsel Gelişimi ve Erken Cumhuriyet Dönemi Planlı Kırsal Mimarisinin Korunması Sorunu," 127.

34 *Document on Karacaoba and Ikizceoba*, 03.12.1924, TCBCA 30.18.1.1/12.59.9.

35 According to a document dated 30 March 1924, Arif Hikmet Koyunoğlu analyzed the work of the ministry and criticized the organization of its housing of immigrants. He criticized the settlements and the bad condition of abandoned houses and construction material in new houses. *Document on Arif Hikmet Koyunoglu*, 1924, TCBCA 30.18.1.1272.11/17.80.11.; Cengizkan, *Mübadele konut ve yerleşimleri*, 229–31. He had a sig-

tion Exchange and Housing and later in the Housing Department within the Ministry of Interior. There, during the first years of the republic, he focused on the planning of villages and village houses, and the reconstruction of abandoned buildings.[36]

During the mid-1920s housing for newcomers in Antalya, Adana, and Mersin – three cities located in southern Anatolia – was built by the government following the same principles of regular village planning practiced in other parts of the country. Documents show that Çirkinoba Village was built in Antalya, and several farms and cultivated areas were transformed into settlements in Adana and Mersin during the second half of 1920s.

According to correspondence dated 12 February 1925, Çirkinoba Village was under construction. However, difficult weather conditions and diseases like influenza and malaria in the district badly affected work in the construction areas. Therefore, the completion of settlement was postponed until April 1925.[37] The building methods and materials were not mentioned in the document, but timber cottages with mud-brick fill were probably used as these were the materials and methods used in the other settlements in Adana and Mersin.

The construction of dwellings for the exchanged population in Adana and Mersin started in April 1924.[38] Mehmet Emin Bey, the director of the Ministry of Population Exchange and Housing in Adana, proposed the Madama farm and surrounding cultivated area to begin the construction, and prepared a scheme for the settlement.[39] In September, the council of ministers agreed to accelerate the operations in Adana and to construct timber cottages in the rural areas for housing the newcomers.[40]

---

nificant impact in forming the early republican conception of rural settlement and the rural house in the 1930s.

36   Nurcan İnci Firat, *Ankara'da Cumhuriyet Dönemi Mimarisinden İki Örnek: Etnografya Müzesi ve Eski Türk Ocağı Merkez Binası; (Devlet Resim ve Heykel Müzesi)*, T. C. Kültür Bakanlığı Yayınları Yayımlar Dairesi Başkanlığı Sanat eserleri dizisi, 2188 203, 1. Baskı (Ankara, 1998), p. 145; Cengizkan, *Mübadele konut ve yerleşimleri*, 84–86.

37   *Document on Çirkinoba*, 1925, TCBCA 30.18.1.1./12.75.13., and Cengizkan, *Mübadele konut ve yerleşimleri*, 42.

38   *Document on Building Houses for Immigrants in Adana*, 1924, TCBCA 272.80/3.6.1. See also Eres, "Türkiye'de Planlı Kırsal Yerleşmelerin Tarihsel Gelişimi ve Erken Cumhuriyet Dönemi Planlı Kırsal Mimarisinin Korunması Sorunu," 116–19.

39   *Document on Madama*, 1924, TCBCA 272.80/3.6.14. Cengizkan, *Mübadele konut ve yerleşimleri*, 174.

40   *Document on Building Cottages in Adana*, 1924, TCBCA 30.18.1.1/10.42.16.

One month later, it was decided to build cottages in Kozan, Adana, and an agreement was concluded between the constructor Hilmi Bey and the director of Population Exchange and Housing commission in Kozan, Halid Bey. The agreement contained the details of eight cottages that were constructed using timber supports, roof and walls filled with mud and sedge, and including four rooms.[41] Furthermore, Bedros farm in Yumurtalik, Adana was organized for a settlement with 50 dwellings. In November 1924, the director of Population Exchange and Housing commission in Yumurtalik, Hüsnü Bey, and the constructor Riza Bey agreed on constructing the cottages with the same technique.[42] Within the same correspondence it was also agreed to start building a settlement for 34 cottages in Yuvanaki farm in Mersin. Another document from 13 July 1925 introduced the base map of the settlement, including 40 dwellings and their conditions.[43]

Housing the newcomers in Izmit province (including Bilecik) was implemented through two government procedures, starting in 1924. For the first, the Ministry of Population Exchange and Housing announced that the immigrants would construct the settlements according to their own ability, and additionally the government would build two settlements in the area. These villages would consist of 150–200 dwellings, 50 of which would be built by the end of 1924. The commissions in the region would decide on the area and prepare the documents (such as base maps). Then a committee of an architect (or civil engineer), engineer and agriculturist would visit the site to develop settlement schemes. For the second procedure, villages that had been demolished in the

---

41   *Document on Building Cottages in Kozan, Adana*, 1924, TCBCA 272.80/3.7.24; Cengizkan, *Mübadele konut ve yerleşimleri*, 175–77. According to the planning details, it was mentioned in the agreement that the each cottage had four rooms. This shows that the cottages were built according to the 'low-cost house' type but using local materials and construction methods. Each cottage had four rooms and each room had a door and window. On the corners, around doors and windows, 45 cm-wide timber pillars should be constructed. The circumference of central pillars should be at least 60 cm between vertical pillars; in every 40–50 cm, horizontal timbers should be located and bays between the grids should be filled with knotgrass. Each side of the wall should be plaster with mud. Interior walls should have a double grid and the roof should be covered with sedge and mud.

42   *Documents on Yuvanaki and Yumurtalık*, 1924, TCBCA 272.80/3.8.2.; Cengizkan, *Mübadele konut ve yerleşimleri*, 178–81.

43   *Document on Yuvanaki*, 1925, TCBCA 272.80/4.10.11.; Cengizkan, *Mübadele konut ve yerleşimleri*, 216.

war would be assessed for the reconstruction of houses and new infrastructure in these areas. The governors would also take into account sanitation and economic circumstances.[44]

A document dated 29 April 1924 shows that the Ministry of Population Exchange and Housing provided site plans and typological plans for houses in the settlements that the immigrants constructed. Engineer Ismail Bey worked on the plan and decided on the final changes during the implementation. The same document also includes correspondence regarding Mihalic village, where construction was completed by the immigrants. Building of the village was accelerated due to the urgency of settling the people, and architect Edhem Bey was sent to the site to reorganize the construction work.[45]

Construction of new villages in Ankara was put on the state's agenda while Ankara was emerging as the capital city of Turkey. A document dated on 9 May 1928 presented the parliament's decision to construct new settlements for immigrants along the railway lines between Eskişehir and Ankara, equipping the area with public facilities and modern infrastructure. The settlements would be built after an agricultural study of the site to provide the agrarian framework for the settlers. It was planned to build Etimesgut (or Ahi-Mes'ud) village along the Yahşihan–Eskişehir line, and Malıköy and Samutlu villages along the Beypazarı–Ayaş-Polatlı line in the west of Ankara.[46]

According to a document of 30 April 1930, Malıköy was constructed with 29 dwellings designed in accordance with the principles of low-cost housing for newcomers from Bulgaria.[47] Other records from 3 September 1930 and 8 October 1930 concerned Samutlu village, which was built for immigrants who had not been settled until that year. The village was organized not only for dwellings, but also for infrastructure to support settlers' agricultural activities.[48]

---

44   Cengizkan, *Mübadele konut ve yerleşimleri*, 172–73; Eres, "Türkiye'de Planlı Kırsal Yerleşmelerin Tarihsel Gelişimi ve Erken Cumhuriyet Dönemi Planlı Kırsal Mimarisinin Korunması Sorunu," 120.

45   Ibid, pp. 172–73, 184; Ibid.

46   *Document on New Villages along the Eskisekir-Ankara Railway Line*, 1928, TCBCA 30.18.1.1/28.29.12.

47   *Document on Malıköy*, 1930, TCBCA 30.18.1.1/02.10.27.11.

48   *Document on Samutlu*, 1930, 30.18.1.1/02.13.5.; *Document on Samutlu*, 1930, TCBCA 30.18.1.1/02.14.64.

Figure 4.2. *Village houses and other public buildings in Etimesgut, 1930s.*[49]

Regulations of the 1924 Village Law and 1926 Settlement Law were implemented in Etimesgut (Ahi Mes'ud). On 16 and 28 May 1928, it was agreed to adapt one of the farms in the Atatürk Forest Farms (*Atatürk Orman Çiftliği*) for model villages,[50] and one month later the first phase of the construction of Etimesgut village started.[51] According to documents of 10 and 21 October 1928, the building program included the dwelling area, train station, village hospital, government house, guesthouse, coffee house, bazaar area, boarding school, and coppice. The land around the settlement was provided for agricultural activities for the dwellers. The northern part of the settlement, separated from the village by the railway line, was planned as a housing area for the agricultural technicians who would assist the villagers in agrarian work. Within two months, 50 houses had already been built. Stone and mud bricks were the construction materials. Each house consisted of two rooms, a penthouse for farming equipments, and a corral for animals **(Figures 4.2)**.[52]

---

49   *Yabancı Gözüyle Cumhuriyet Türkiyesi* (Ankara: Dahiliye Vekaleti, Matbuat Umum Müdürlüğü, 1938).

50   *Document on Etimesgut (Ahi Mes'ud)*, 16.05.1928, TCBCA 30.18.1.1/29.32.1.; *Document on Etimesgut (Ahi Mes'ud)*, 28.05.1928, TCBCA 30.18.1.1/29.35.9.

51   *Document on Etimesgut (Ahi Mes'ud)*, 10.06.1928, TCBCA 30.18.1.1/29.36.18.

52   *Document on Etimesgut (Ahi Mes'ud)*, 10.10.1928, TCBCA 30.18.1.1/30.61.4.; *Document on Etimesgut (Ahi Mes'ud)*, 21.10.1928, TCBCA 30.18.1.1/30.63.9. All agricultural materials

The rural settlements planned during the first years of the republic were mostly constructed as a result of the housing emergency. They were therefore characterized by an agglomeration of dwellings with a simple necessary infrastructure. Nevertheless, Etimesgut was designed in accordance with the modern urbanization building program. Developed simultaneously with the urbanization of Ankara, Etimesgut is key to understanding the patterns and/or distinctness of building actions in the city and countryside during the first years of the republican period.[53]

During the first years of the republican regime, village construction was central in the larger theme of housing the existing population and the exchanged people coming into the country from the former Ottoman terrains. All the correspondence, contracts, and ministry council decisions during the 1920s present a picture of consent about immediately settling the incoming people. They also demonstrate the lack of economic and organizational frameworks for the projects of the early republican state. In other words, until the early 1930s village planning had been undertaken by the republican regime to solve concrete problems of the country, such as reconstructing the building stock and infrastructure in the cities and towns, housing the population consisting of locals and immigrants, and establishing economic welfare in the country. As a result, the first programs had a pragmatic tone in the regime's efforts, rather than forming an idealized land in rural Turkey.

Building the Republican Villages

A general overview of 1930s Turkey leads us to some crucial points. The first is that the Great Depression in the western world had a robust impact on Turkey's economy, and Turkey needed to consolidate its foreign policy due to the approaching war in Europe. The second concerns the domestic programs of the Turkish state: consolidation of the RPP, hence the Kemalist regime, after 1930 had a great impact on the planning the country in its socio-cultural, economic, and political aspects. The newcomers who arrived after the Treaty

---

such as tools, stores, and animals were given to the dwellers by the government. *Document on Etimesgut (Ahi Mes'ud)*, 21.10.1928, TCBCA 30.18.1.1/30.62.14.

53   For the comment, see Cengizkan, "Cumhuriyet Döneminde Kırsal Yerleşim Sorunları: Ahi Mes'ud Numune Köyü," 113–16.

of Lausanne with Bulgaria and the Treaty of Amity with Romania[54] demanded immediate housing. The existing population, of which the majority were living in rural areas, abandoned properties and demolished villages, were also in need of better living conditions. In addition, with the one-party regime, the village as a community – for rural people and the rural administration – emerged as the nucleus of the RPP's nation-building, Turkification, and consolidation of state power. These fundamental facts determined the principles of architectural planning of the villages during the 1930s.

The most significant influence of the political environment appeared in eastern Anatolia. Starting from the first years of the republic, the eastern population forcefully resisted the Kemalist regime due to ethnic and political discrimination and poverty in the region. In response, when the regime gained the tools to consolidate its power in the 1930s, it also developed a radical authority in the country on its way to "building the nation".[55] Relatedly, the or-

---

54 On 18 October 1925 the Treaty of Amity between Turkey and Bulgaria was concluded. From 1930 to 1939, more than 80.000 Turco-Bulgarians immigrated into the country. On 17 October 1933 the Treaty of Amity between Turkey and Romania was concluded. This treaty also paved the way for the immigration of the Turco-Romanian populace up until the early 1950s. See Yüksel Kaştan, "Atatürk Dönemi Türkiye-Bulgaristan İlişkileri," *Atatürk Araştırma Merkezi Dergisi* XXIV, no. 72 (2008), http://www.atam.gov.tr/de rgi/sayi-72/ataturk-donemi-turkiye-bulgaristan-iliskileri.; TBMM, *Türkiye Cumhuriyeti ile Romanya Arasında Dostluk, İyi Komşuluk ve İşbirliği Antlaşmasının Onaylanmasının Uygun Bulunduğuna Dair Kanun Tasarısı ve Dışişleri Komisyonu Raporu (1/323)* (Ankara: TBMM, 13 January 1992), p. 8 <https://www.tbmm.gov.tr/tutanaklar/TUTANAK/TBMM/d19/co 32/tbmm19032080ss0157.pdf>.

55 The first revolt against the new republican government occurred on 13 February 1925 in Diyarbakır, led by Sheikh Mehmet Said on the grounds that the new regime ignored the Kurdish populace and their demands after the legitimation of Turkey in the Lausanne Treaty. Üngör, pp. 124–25. The resistance was forcefully repressed by the state, and the cabinet released a large-scale program to put down resistance in the eastern provinces, hence the Kurdish population, including deportation of the rioters and Kurdish intelligentsia from the region. *Şark Islahat Planı*, the Reformation Plan of the East, was concluded on 25 September 1925 by the cabinet. Before the implementation of the reformation plan, the country separated into general inspectorships the one region that enclosed the Kurdish provinces in the east. The general inspector would work with the experts of the ministries and the military to operate the reformation plan in the east. The regulation included 28 articles in which the Turkification of the region would be discussed and scheduled in various areas, including settling the Turkish people in abandoned properties of Armenians in the Kurdish provinces; assigning the Turkish people in the governmental, administrational and judicial position in the Kur-

ganization of rural Turkey, and hence the construction of villages, reached its second phase, becoming a great instrument of demographic engineering in the country on behalf of the Kemalist government.

Deportation of the Kurdish population from the eastern provinces led to an increase in abandoned property stock, adding abandoned housing from the deportation of Armenians in 1915.[56] The eastern provinces, such as Diyarbakır, Elazığ, Tunceli and Malatya, became emerging areas for the settlement of Turkish-speaking people, especially from Balkan countries. Accordingly, the demographic formation of the country became the fundamental operation in

dish provinces; and inflicting punishment on people who would speak Kurdish. Mehmet Bayrak, "'Şark Islahat Planı' ve TC'nin Kürt Politikası," in *Resmi Tarih Tartışmaları 6: Resmi Tarihte Kürt'ler*, Özgür Üniversite Kıtaplığı 76 (Ankara: Makı, 2009), 389–94. This regulation demonstrated that the state sought to resolve problems with the opposition through ethnic conflicts targeting the Kurdish people. This caused another revolt between 1927 and 1930 in the Ararat province. According to Uğur Ümit Üngör, "the Kurdish-nationalist organization 'Independence' (*Xoybun*) entrenched itself in the Ararat region and forcefully resisted the Kemalist government with demands of autonomy. Again, the Kemalists responded with violence and a local conflagration grew into a guerrilla war quite similar to the Sheikh Said conflict (in 1925)" Ibid, p. 148). After the suppression of the Ararat revolt, the state consolidated political power again, announcing the single-party government of the RPP followed by legislation and regulations for the reorganization of the Kurdish populace on behalf of the Turkish state. Between 1937 and 1938 the state faced another collective resistance from the Kurds in the Dersim Revolt—a more localized opposition in Tunceli Province. This time Kemalist regime used army forces to suppress the rebellion and demolished the area. Faik Bulut, *Dersim Raporları: İnceleme*, 3. Basım, Evrensel Basım Yayın Kürt Tarihi ve Kültürü Dizisi 281–14 (İstanbul: Evrensel, 2005). For another reading of the revolts during the early republican period: Robert Olson, "The Kurdish Rebellions of Sheikh Said (1925), Mt. Ararat (1930), and Dersim (1937–8): Their Impact on the Development of the Turkish Air Force and on Kurdish and Turkish Nationalism," *Die Welt Des Islams* 40, no. 1 (2000): 67–94, h ttp://www.jstor.org/stable/1571104.

56   Notable publications about the Armenian diaspora include the following: *The Armenian Genocide: The Essential Reference Guide*, ed. by Alan Whitehorn (Santa Barbara, California: ABC-CLIO, an imprint of ABC-CLIO, LLC, 2015), pp. 1–11, 17–19.; Taner Akçam, *The Young Turks' Crime Against Humanity: The Armenian Genocide and Ethnic Cleansing in the Ottoman Empire*, Human Rights and Crimes against Humanity (Princeton, N.J.: Princeton University Press, 2012).; Ronald Grigor Suny, Fatma Müge Göçek, and Norman M. Naimark, eds., *A Question of Genocide: Armenians and Turks at the End of the Ottoman Empire* (Oxford; New York: Oxford University Press, 2011).; Tacy Atkinson, '*The German, the Turk and the Devil Made a Triple Alliance': Harpoot Diaries, 1908–1917*, Armenian Genocide Documentation Series (Princeton, NJ: Gomidas Inst, 2000).

domestic politics and dominated building policy in rural Turkey during the 1930s.

Yet, east Anatolia was not the only region where the new population strategy changed the built environment. West Anatolia, east Thrace and some small cities in central Anatolia witnessed the nation-building project through the transfer of people. Establishing new villages, reorganizing existing settlements, and arranging properties for newcomers in towns and cities had been conducted after the population exchange agreements of Lausanne Treaty that brought Muslim people from the Greek hinterlands into the country. Strategies had also been implemented following the 1924 Village Law and the 1926 Settlement Law. However, in the 1930s the state needed new settlement legislation that would emphasize Turkification as a demographic policy. The peace treaties between Bulgaria and Turkey in 1925, and between Romania and Turkey in 1933[57], also paved the way for the new population strategies. This time, the immigrants would play a crucial role in forming a loyal "Turkish" society that merged with the existing population. Furthermore, the newcomers were mostly villagers and peasants in their home countries, making them suitable subjects for the state's socio-cultural and economic policies for rural areas.

Parliamentary discussions also explicitly demonstrated the economic, demographic, and ethnic planning aims of settlement policies. In 1934, Interior Minister Şükrü Kaya announced:

"There are approximately two million pure Turks abroad in our near surroundings. It is almost mandatory for them to come to the homeland little by little [...] It is then our obligation to settle them according to the social and economic principles that the science of settlements necessitates [...] A nation's biggest duty is to annex everybody living within its borders to its own community, to assimilate them. The opposite has been seen with us and has dismembered the homeland."[58]

In another report, Diyarbakır's second General Inspector Ahmet Hilmi Ergeneli detailed the Kurdish deportation and the organization of newcomer settlement. He strongly advised that the living conditions of the new settlements in which the immigrants – "our racial brothers" in his words – would be

---

57   Kaştan, "Atatürk Dönemi Türkiye-Bulgaristan İlişkileri."

58   "TBMM Zabıt Ceridesi, IV. Dönem, 3. Devre (TBMM Journal of Official Report, Period IV, Session 3)" 23 (June 14, 1934): 141, 249. Quoted from: Üngör, p. 149.

settled should be much more developed than their places of origin to comfort them in the country. He suggested building convenient infrastructure and designating economic and social facilities such as "financial rewards and advanced educational opportunities, high-quality housing, children's playgrounds and sport facilities". These groups should be housed near the railways so that "strategic areas would be populated by a 'reliable population'".[59]

Furthermore, from 5 to 22 December 1936, the Interior Minister Şükrü Kaya brought together the General Inspectors – Abidin Özmen, Kazım Dirik, Tahsin Uzer, and Abdullah Alpdoğan – in Ankara to reevaluate, first, the state's control mechanisms in the eastern Anatolian cities, the deportation of Kurds and settlement affairs, and second, the modernization program in rural Anatolia. Discussions during this conference appeared as crucial documents showing a picture of Turkey in the political, socio-cultural, economic, and demographic frameworks from a wider point of view. Yet the consolidation of the regime, and the Turkification of the non-Turkish population in particular, emerged at the center of the debate: the committee agreed that "there is a Kurdishness Cause in the East" that urgently required a response. To ease the obstacles in the eastern provinces, they concluded that the officials who would work in the east would be chosen among Turkish people with encouragement from government through a higher salary, housing, and the possibility of promotion. The new rural settlements would be built on the sides of the railways to house Turkish people. Considering the demographic demand of the state, these settlements could serve the increasing number of Turkish-speaking immigrants. Local commissions and the general inspectors of each region would organize the construction of the new settlements. The government would supply the economic and socio-cultural infrastructure through the People's House, using it as a significant tool to plant Turkishness in "non-Turkish places".[60]

On the other hand, during the conference other groups such as Pomaks, Cherkes and Jews were also discussed in terms of assimilation: Pomaks and Cherkes, who mostly inhabited the Thrace region, were found "adaptable" into Turkish culture because they spoke a dialect close to the Turkish language. Through culture programs they would be practically adapted to "Turkishness".

---

59   Ahmet Hilmi Ergeneli, 'Ergeneli to İnönü', 10 November 1934, BCA, 69.457.24. in: Hüseyin Koca, *Yakın Tarihten Günümüze Hükümetlerin Doğu-Güneydoğu Anadolu Politikaları*, Bilimsel Araştırma Dizisi, 04 (Konya: Mikro, 1998), pp. 416–20. Quated from: Üngör, p. 154.

60   Varlık and Koçak, pp. 16–17.

However, the committee found the Jewish population in the Thrace region a crucial threat because they dominated the local economy in the rural areas, small cities, and towns.[61] The debate on the Jewish people in the Thrace region dated back to the early years of 1930s. When the Thrace region was included in the General Inspectorships, the authority first imposed Turkish dominance by deporting Jews and Bulgarians from provinces in the region such as Kırklareli, Edirne, Çanakkale and Tekirdağ. But the reports mostly concentrated on the Jews, declaring them "unreliable" and condemning their controlling of the trade activities in the cities and towns. In addition to this, nationalist and antisemitic writers[62] paved the way for the increase of hostility among the local Turks against the Jews. In July 1934, the result was another deportation: Jewish people were expelled from the region and forced to Turkify and/or sent to larger cities such as Istanbul and İzmir.[63]

Similar to the tactics in the east, the settlement policy in the western provinces would also center on the legitimation of the state and the domination of "Turkishness". Balkan immigrants would again play a significant role, not only in smoothing out the ethnic characteristics of inhabitants, but also in serving the rural economic program by laboring in agriculture and craftsmanship. The 1934 Settlement Law legislated "building the republican villages" on behalf of population planning and constructing the rural country from top to bottom.

The 1934 Settlement Law

On 14 June 1934, the Kemalist regime implemented a new law that emerged as a critical instrument in the campaign of the RPP to blend the people into one "nation" and to control them in several spheres such as the economy, culture, and social life. As Uğur Ümit Üngör puts it:

"The 1934 Settlement Law read as a typical document of an interwar nation state fortifying its ethnic boundaries through restricting citizenship, expressing a nationalist ideology, and introducing nation formation on an alien

---

61   Ibid, p. 22.

62   Rıfat N. Bali announces here Nihal Atsız (1905–1975) and Cevat Rıfat Atilhan (1892–1967).

63   Rıfat Bali, 'Azınlıkları Türkleştirme Meselesi': Ne İdi? Ne Değildi?, Tarih Dizisi, 93, 1. Baskı (İstanbul: Libra, 2014), pp. 144–45.; Rıfat Bali, 1934 Trakya Olayları, Libra Tarih Dizisi, 54–43, 11. Baskı (İstanbul: Libra, 2014).

population by force. It captures the essence of demographic engineering: The Kemalists sought to increase the relative size and power of the dominant ethnic group, the Turks, at the expense of ethnic minorities. The latter were expected to decrease determinately, and ultimately evaporate into insignificance or disappear sometime in the future."[64]

A detailed look at the law and its annexes discloses that the state's housing agenda, concentrated on rural planning within urbanist concepts, became a nation-building tool and maintained the tone of modernization at the same time. The text of the law, consisting of nine chapters, gradually reveals this objective, describing the settlement regions, registration, and housing of immigrants together with the local people in the settlement regions, the obligations and exemptions of the settlers, and distribution of the agricultural land to the settlers.

The first and second articles introduced the aim of the law. The first article described that revision of the settlement and distribution of the population in Turkey was assigned by the Ministry of the Interior in accordance with the program scheduled by the cabinet, considering the bounds of Turkish culture. The second article detailed the settlement areas that zoned Turkey into three types of territories: territories numbered 1 were places where the concentration of Turkish population was to be located; territories numbered 2 were designated for transporting and housing the population that was intended to "be Turkified"; and territories numbered 3 were areas to be set aside and forbidden from dwelling and settlement due to sanitation, economic, cultural, political, and military circumstances. The Ministry of the Interior suggested the cabinet could amend the zones and territories over time in response to changing needs.[65]

Acceptance of immigrants and refugees became a significant part of the law. The third article of the first chapter presented legal definitions of "immigrants" and "refugees". To settle in Turkey, only people of Turkish origin (and/or who were "culturally Turkish"[66]) immigrating into the country alone

---

64   Üngör, p. 153.

65   "İskan Kanunu," 4003.

66   The text of the 1934 Settlement Law uses the term "culturally Turkish" to refer to people who were traditionally akin to the Turkish language, and easily adopted to the livelihood and customs of Turkey. Here, I interpret the term as a very ambiguous description of Turkishness due to the nature of the concept. As briefly explained in the second chapter, from the beginning of the discourse, the definition of Turkishness retained its

and *en masse*, as well as Turkic nomads, would be accepted according to the instructions of the Ministry of the Interior. Only they were considered "immigrants". The Ministry would determine which people had Turkish origin and/or were culturally Turkish. "Refugees" were defined by the law as groups who sought temporary asylum in the country due to an emergency situation.[67]

The organization of settlement was determined in the seventh article and stated that immigrants and refugees of Turkish origin would be allowed to settle where they chose. However, immigrants and refugees who requested housing assistance from the state had to settle in a location determined by the state. Likewise, non-Turkish groups had to settle and remain where the Ministry of the Interior and the cabinet decided, even though they would not receive housing assistance.[68] In other words, the first chapter centered upon a general ordinance and definitions of the groups who would be organized, instead of a spatial formula to house the population.

The second chapter had the title "Mobilization in the Interior, Circumspections of Culture and Administration". Here, the law detailed the spatial organization according to territorial categorization: the Ministry of the Interior would transport the villagers without arable lands and a source of living as well as people who lived in territories numbered 3 to more suitable areas in terms of the livelihood and sanitation. Additionally, the ministry would decide to relocate the villagers where the settlements were dispersed, and it would organize removing the temporary settlements.[69]

Within the third chapter, the settlement policy was detailed: tribes – *aşirets* – who were not culturally Turkish (referring to the Kurdish groups) would be dispersed and settled in the territories numbered 2; Turkish nomads, who were culturally Turkish, would be transported to favorable areas in terms of the livelihood and sanitation within territories 1 and 3. The Ministry of the Interior would decide to deport non-Turkish nomads. The groups who did not speak Turkish could not establish a community such as a village, neighborhood unit, labor or craft organization. Similarly, the law announced that the

---

conflicting facets in various aspects. Its grounds changed between religion, race, geography, and language under the state's nationalistic legitimations. But it was always questionable to frame "Turkishness", as it is controversial to attempt a description of any nation's characteristics.

67   "İskan Kanunu," 4003.
68   Ibid, pp. 4003–4.
69   Ibid, p. 4004.

tribes and nomads who were not culturally Turkish were certainly not allowed to settle in the territories numbered 1. Here, the non-Turkish locals were separately deported to Turkish villages, towns and city centers and settled with immigrants and refugees of Turkish origin. The territories numbered 2 would be completely designated by the authority under the Turkification aims. The Ministry of the Interior and the cabinet would decide and re-organize the settlements here,[70] having the power to control these groups on behalf of the authorities.

In addition to national resolution and formalization, the settlement policy also focused on work such as the arrangement of houses or housing plots for families, distribution of shops, ateliers and shared lands for the craftsmen and small traders, and distribution of arable lands, livestock, barn and agricultural equipments for the farmers. The land provided for the settlers would be distributed from expropriated areas and the terrains reserved for public use and forestry in and around the villages, towns, and cities. The government organized settlement works, providing building materials, labor[71] and funding. In the newly built and reconstructed villages, public areas such as schools, mosques, village houses, police stations, bazaars, threshing fields, cemeteries, meadows, water resources and marshes would be reserved. Schools, fountains, waterways and channels, and watering facilities would be primarily constructed and/or repaired by the government.[72]

Although the Settlement Law (including provision for housing the locals and newcomers and maintaining the land and workplace) was introduced as if the state conducted the entire operation, people received housing and land support through a debiting plan prepared by the government. Particularly in the territories numbered 2 – places where the state intended to Turkify – people were obligated to pay the prices of the estates within 20 years according to a payment schedule that would start after eight years of occupancy.[73]

During the years after the enactment of the 1934 Settlement Law, the operation was re-arranged with new regulations that consisted of instructions in different scopes of the law. The state sought to fundamentally consolidate the

---

70   Ibid, pp. 4004–5.
71   The government would use public vehicles, experts and officers in order to operate the Settlement Law. If necessary, the settlers would work on the building sites.
72   "İskan Kanunu," 4005.
73   Ibid, pp. 4007–8.

obscure articles that might have caused problems in practice. The first regulations, approved from 7 to 11 August 1934 by the Ministry of Interior, comprised instructions for the implementation of the law within the framework of Turkification of the population, as well as details of the land distribution in accordance with the national categorizations of the population.

The fourth article of regulation, 15035/6599, announced that the government had written a declaration of citizenship (*Tabiiyet Beyannamesi*) for people subjected to the 1934 Settlement Law. Turkish newcomers had to sign this declaration and register as "immigrants". Some groups such as Pomaks, Bosnians, Tatars, and Karapapaks who had already settled in several terrains in East Thrace and Anatolia, and Turkish-speaking Muslim groups such as Lezgis, Chechens, Cherkes, Abkhazians, also had to sign the declaration of citizenship to receive settlement support from the government. Kurds, Arabs, Albanians, non-Turkish Muslims, and non-Turkish Christians and Jews did not sign the declaration of citizenship since they were considered foreigners by the state.[74] The article highlighted that the state sought to resolve the ambiguousness of descriptions of the ethnic groups and their position within the 1934 Settlement Law, and to sort out the population demographically for the purpose of nationalization in particular areas.

Additionally, the regulation introduced general instructions for land and estate distribution. The state mainly referred to the derelicts that remained following the Armenian, Greek and Kurdish deportations. The immigrants who received support from government would be first housed in these abandoned properties and workplaces such as shops and ateliers, and arable lands. If necessary, the government would provide dwellings, land and/or workplaces to the settlers from the expropriated areas in and around villages, towns, and cities.[75]

Another regulation dated 11 August detailed general terms for the settlement operations for the newcomers: "the settlement operation begins with the acceptance and registration of the immigrant at the border. It ends after the meriting properties and lands are resigned with the documents of each title and given to the settlers; the production equipments and food are supplied."[76] Furthermore, the settlement operation of the non-Turkish groups (meaning Kurds) was re-emphasized and elaborated. According to the regulation, these

---

74 T.C. Sıhhat ve İçtimai Muavenat Vekaleti, İskan Umum Müdürlüğü, *İskan Mevzuatı* (Ankara: Köyöğretmeni Basımevi, 1936), 240.

75 Ibid, p. 241.

76 Ibid, p. 247.

groups could not be settled in the villages and neighborhood units where they shared the same language and ethnicity with the locals,[77] and they could not entirely form a new village or neighborhood unit. They could only be settled in Turkish villages and neighborhoods where they constituted a maximum of five percent of the whole populace. They would not abut each other as at least ten Turkish families would live in between. These groups would be obligated to speak Turkish, and they should even be encouraged to engage with Turkish people to Turkify their nations.[78]

The regulations for land organization within the 1934 Settlement Law were basically developed from the 1924 Village Law and 1926 Settlement Law, and this time it was detailed in accordance with the new necessities for the newcomers, the locals, and deported people. In so doing, İskan Toprak Talimatnamesi (the Settlement Land Regulation), which concerned the land distribution and architectural organization of the new and existing settlements, was drafted from 9 to 11 August 1934.[79]

In the second chapter of the regulation, the planning of new villages and the extension of the existing villages were laid out according to the first regulation with which the Ministry of the Interior set out the national organization of the population. In the 15th article of the second chapter, the method of implementing the new villages and extensions was determined. The ministry would sort out the land in the villages or in appropriate rural areas to settle the newcomers with consideration of the interaction between the settlers and locals. However, the village could still be separated into the quarters for newcomers and residents.[80]

The 20th article provided that in each territory a local governor and/or a committee would be established for the village planning operation. They would agree on suitable areas for new rural settlements in cities, towns, and villages by indicating possible housing schemes, and mapping them in scales of 1/20.000, 1/5000 and 1/1000. Thereafter, construction work would begin, and land would be prepared for distribution.[81]

---

77   This article demonstrated that the Ministry of Interior hesitated to name and legitimate the locals, who collaborated with the state within the frame of new settlement program, as Kurds.

78   T.C. Sıhhat ve İçtimai Muavenat Vekaleti, İskan Umum Müdürlüğü, İskan Mevzuatı, 248–49.

79   Ibid, pp. 259–76.

80   Ibid, p. 264.

81   Ibid, p. 266.

Within the following articles of the regulation, the organization of rural settlement construction was defined. The place of the new settlement would be decided by the local governor himself, or by a committee formed by the governor and consisting of a state doctor, engineer, cadaster technician and settlement officer. They would draw up the scheme of the settlements, including the borders, streets, and houses in accordance with the 1924 Village Law. The experts of local government would draw up the settlement plan showing the streets and houses. The local government would also approve the settlement scheme to start the construction.[82]

The law also highlighted that the new settlements would be established in the areas accessible to transportation (close to the railways, highways and harbors, or areas where the extension of the transportation network was planned), suitable for agriculture (in the watery and arable areas) and sanitation (in the areas where the land was reclaimed).[83] In the new rural settlements at least five decares for each person were to be reserved for a forest.[84]

The construction of the new settlements and the reconstruction of the existing villages started with reserving public areas and facilities. For this, the supply of potable water for the inhabitants and the animals emerged as the primary task. According to the regulation, the new settlements would be built with 100 houses. Each house would be divided in 500m² –1000m² parcels, in proportion to the acreage. Each family would have at least 3000m² of arable land around the villages and towns where they were dwelling. In the villages and towns, the farmers and craftsmen would receive a barn and livery stable for at least three animals if they received housing support from the state.[85]

The Settlement Land Regulation dated 9–11 August 1934 gave instructions for land organization. In this regulation, the state detailed not only the distribution of land, which had been decided and elaborated on by the 1934 Settlement Law, but also the architectural program and construction schedules. In this regulation it was declared that the architectural planning of the new settlements and reconstruction of the existing villages would be coordinated and managed by the local governorates, in contrast to operations following the 1924 Village Law and 1926 Settlement Law. With this method, the settlement could

---

82   Ibid, p. 267.
83   Ibid,, p. 267.
84   Ibid, p. 268.
85   Ibid, pp. 269–71.

be individually directed by local authorities in particular areas where the government wished to control the population.

The Land Regulation of the 1934 Settlement Law made the state's intentions clearer, so that the program emerged as much broader than simply housing people as had been the case with the legislation and agenda of the first years of the republic. The most apparent fact was that this time the land organization, and the architectonic, economic, and socio-cultural determination of the housing act, also served nationalization, in contrast to early statutes like the 1924 Village Law and 1926 Settlement Law. It was crystal clear that within the 1934 Settlement Law the regime organized comprehensive population engineering, reflecting the political climate of mid-1930s in Turkey.[86]

Villages of the 1934 Settlement Law

The 1934 Act paved the way for a settlement policy through which locals, Turkish immigrants and Kurds could be blended within the nationalization program. The application of the law and its regulations took place in the rural areas surrounding larger cities, in small Anatolian towns, in villages from which communities were deported, and in the new rural settlements. In particular these villages, which were built as an outcome of the 1934 Settlement Law, became an important tool for the RPP in forming the nation, modernizing and internally colonizing the people through architecture.

Following the passage of the 1934 Settlement Law, it was declared that 50.000 Turco-Romanian immigrants would be welcome and granted Turkish citizenship by the state. The Housing Department of the Ministry of Interior would guide this operation. At the same time the police departments would be responsible for newcomers' security in the arrival cities and would also guard and control immigrants during their transportation to the settlements. The reports announced that immigrants would arrive in Istanbul as the first receiving location. Here they would be registered by the officers registered and prepared for the journey[87] to towns and villages where they would be settled.

---

86   Özge Sezer, 'Modern Köyün İnşası: Erken Cumhuriyet Dönemi Kırsalında İskan Poli-tikaları Üzerine Bir Değerlendirme', *Türkiye Bilimler Akademisi Kültür Envanteri Dergisi*, 0.24 (2021) <https://doi.org/10.22520/tubaked2021.24.007>; Veli Yadirgi, *The Political Economy of the Kurds of Turkey: From the Ottoman Empire to the Turkish Republic*, 2017, p. 180.

87   '50.000 Muhacir Gelecek (50.000 Immigrants Will Come)', *Cumhuriyet* (Istanbul, 7 October 1934), pp. 1, 4.

General Inspectorates in provinces of Thrace conducted the housing program not only in the region but also in eastern Anatolian provinces. However, at the end of 1934 new neighborhoods in the towns and complete settlements in the villages for the immigrants were still under construction.[88]

Immigration continued in the following years and exacerbated the problems of housing organization in rural areas. In May 1935 it was reported that General Inspectors and local governors were forming a commission for the operation. The Thrace region emerged as a target district for the government. Considerable efforts were made to settle the first groups of newcomers, such as arranging building sites for rural houses and land for agriculture,[89] with 90.000 liras spent on the preparations.[90]

Besides, to administer the rehabilitation of villages, the İzmir governor Kazim Dirik established a Village Office in the Local Governorate of İzmir (*İzmir Köy Bürosu*) in 1931. When Kazim Dirik became the General Inspector of Thrace in 1935, he established a similar organization for the whole region, the Village Office of Thrace (*Trakya Köy Bürosu*). This was a forerunner to the state's regulation in 1936 founding "the Province Village Offices" in cities where the 1934 Settlement Law was implemented.[91] Now the village offices became the local authority accommodating the newcomers and people deported from eastern Anatolia. Nevertheless, constructing houses for immigrants emerged as the crucial problem for the government to complete the operation immediately.

On 1 May 1935 the government and the People's House called for an architectural competition for village houses in the new rural settlements, particularly in the Thrace region, and promoted Turkish architects to cooperate. The jury consisted of the director of the People's House, a professor and architect from the Fine Arts Academy, and an architect from the Architect's Chamber. The participants proposed two different housing typologies focusing on local build-

---

88   'Trakya'ya Yerleştirilen Muhacirler (Immigrants Who Are Settled in Thrace)', *Cumhuriyet* (Istanbul, 16 November 1934), p. 2.

89   '50.000 Göçmenin Anayurda Nakli, Bu İşlerle Uğraşacak Bir Komisyon Kuruldu (Transporting 50.000 Immigrants into the Homeland, A Commission Has Been Established for the Operation)', *Cumhuriyet* (Istanbul, 13 May 1935), p. 2.

90   'Göçmenler İçin Malzeme Alındı (Construction Materials Have Been Bought for the Immigrants)', *Cumhuriyet* (Istanbul, 20 May 1935), p. 2.

91   TBMM, *Regulation for 'the Province Village Offices*, 1936. In: Eres, "Türkiye'de Planlı Kırsal Yerleşmelerin Tarihsel Gelişimi ve Erken Cumhuriyet Dönemi Planlı Kırsal Mimarisinin Korunması Sorunu," 148.

ing techniques and materials. (The villagers and settlers could build the houses themselves), as well as considering budget efficiency, sanitation, functionality, the livelihoods of the dwellers, the climate (the first group would be settled in Thrace region and in the villages around Istanbul, and thus the climate and environment of these districts should be considered in the design), and national issues (the houses should architecturally reflect the "Turkish" style).[92]

The Village House Competition was a significant event, demonstrating the state's efforts to develop the housing operation into a standardized project that would be organized by local authorities, and easily carried out by settlers and locals together. Turkish architects also agreed with the concept that the implementation of rural settlements (including constructing brand-new villages and building new quarters around existing villages) should be considered in an architecturally systematic organization. However, they criticized the process in the first years, claiming that the state's early housing solutions were concluded without any research on the village and the village community. The costs of construction were too high for any villager to be able to build a house by his own means. Architect Abdullah Ziya Kozanoğlu pointed out another dimension of this issue: "The son of the villager would expect that the state would build a house for him as well as it built a house for his father. If not, ... he would become an enemy to the regime."[93] And he continued:

"1. Firstly, the existing village houses and the wishes of the villagers who have been already living in the rural settlements should be studied. Accordingly, new planning for villages and the new typology for village houses should be concluded (It could be accomplished by zoning the country and designing 5–6 typologies). 2. A "modern" sanctuary, which would replace the "mosque", should be built to bring the villager under the same roof, to transmit the regime's ideals and the reforms. 3. The new village and village house should be planned in accordance with local techniques and materials [that the villager could easily construct and repair]. 4. They should be as cheap as the villagers could build through their own means. 5. In the party [RPP], a new branch should be established to cope with this assignment. The branch should teach and explain to the villagers [how to build the settlement and the houses]".[94]

---

92   'Köy Evleri Proje Müsabakası', *Arkitekt*, 51.3 (1935), 93.

93   Kozanoğlu, "Köy Evleri Proje ve Yapıları İçin Toplu Rapor," 204.

94   Ibid, p. 204. Author's translation.

The winner was the architect Abdullah Ziya Kozanoğlu. He introduced two typologies for village houses: type one included two rooms, a small interior storage, a porch in the front, and a semi-open barn at the back. The plan was symmetrical, with the entrance in the center. Type two was located on a larger site and included two rooms, a large hall with an opening to the entrance, a kitchen and a storage room, a porch in the front, and a closed barn which was also accessible from the interior. Kozanoğlu also considered the environmental differences, presenting ideas for flat and sloping land. The common concept for both plans was to use local building materials and techniques. In so doing, he suggested timber construction combined with adobe walls. In both interiors he sought to create a "traditional", and/hence "national" life in the houses **(Figure 4.3)**.[95]

Figure 4.3. *Winning project of the Village House Competition for Thrace region, by architect Abdullah Ziya Kozanoğlu.*[96]

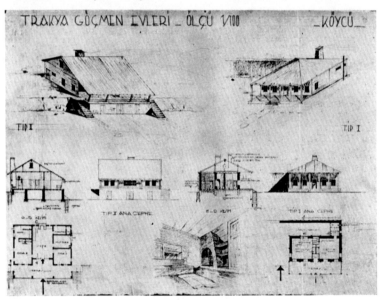

95   Abdullah Ziya Kozanoğlu, 'Halkevi Trakya Göçmen Evleri Proje Müsabakasında Kazanan Eserin Raporu', *Arkitekt*, 55–56.07–08 (1935), pp. 205–6.

96   Kozanoğlu, "Halkevi Trakya Göçmen Evleri Proje Müsabakasında Kazanan Eserin Raporu," 205.

State architect Behçet Ünsal also participated in the competition with two typologies. The house planned for small families consisted of two rooms and a corral, which was not directly connected to the rooms but attached to the house. It was located on approximately 66m² of floor space. The house planned for larger families was designed according to traditional aspects. The rooms were arranged around an atrium, as well as the "traditional Anatolian village house". It consisted of two rooms, a kitchen and cellar, two corrals and a barn. The house was located on approximately 286m² of floor space.[97]

The building expenses associated with these proposed projects, however, were too high for the government's budget. Therefore, the Housing Department of the Ministry of Interior implemented another housing plan, in which the settlers could participate in the construction. The plan was based on a two-room organization, including a small area in the entrance that the settler could use as a cellar, and a corral attached to the house towards the garden. This house cost only 800 liras **(Figure 4.4)**.[98]

The construction of village houses was reported in the newspapers. The Housing Department of Ministry of Interior introduced a prototype for rural houses for the incoming Turco-Romanians and planned to complete the project by the end of the year in several rural areas, especially in Thrace. The operation would continue in other regions by bringing not only more Turkish-speaking immigrants from Romania, but also from other Balkan countries into the country.[99] At the end of the year, within the regulation dated 19 December 1935 (number 3711), the cabinet provided instructions for organizing housing and caring for the immigrants, and sent to the local governorates a procurement list including construction materials (stone, bricks, lime and an assessment of their resources), agricultural equipment and animals, food and animal feed, medicines and medical equipment, and shelters. Another enactment dated 22 June 1936 (number 2/4847) shows that the cabinet budgeted 1,750,000 liras for accommodating Balkan immigrants.[100]

97   Behçet Ünsal, "Bir Köy Evi Tipi," *Arkitekt* 109–110, no. 1–2 (1940): 17.

98   Ünsal, "Bir Köy Evi Tipi."

99   '50.000 Göçmen İçin Trakya'da Hep Bir Tip Evler Yaptırılıyor (For 50.000 Immigrants Prototype Houses Are Being Constructed in Thrace)', *Cumhuriyet* (Istanbul, 29 May 1935), p. 2.

100   T.C. Sıhhat ve İçtimai Muavenet Vekaleti, İskan Umum Müdürlüğü, *İskan Mevzuatı*, 159–60.

Figure 4.4. *A village house constructed by the Housing Department of the Ministry of Interior.*[101]

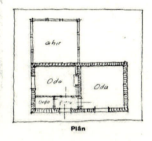

İskân umum müdürlüğü tipine göre inşa edilen bir ev

Plân

In November 1936, Mustafa Kemal Atatürk called attention in parliament to the urgent need to house the Balkan newcomers: "Settling our new-coming citizens who are currently arriving in the homeland, is one of our principal tasks. We are furnishing [the operation] to house the immigrants suitably, and to induce them [in agriculture and other fields of manufacture] readily. The results we have already achieved are reassuring. We will eagerly continue this national matter within the bounds of possibilities."[102] In 1937 in the *Belediyer Dergisi (Journal of Municipalities)* the state announced the intent to complete 18,114 village houses in the rural areas of several cities in Anatolia and Thrace within four years.[103] In addition to the list published in this journal, village houses in the new settlements were constructed in Sincan Village in Ankara and in Harbato and Özmen villages in Diyarbakır.[104]

After the 1934 Settlement Law, the largest number of newcomers and deported people were settled in Tekirdağ province in Thrace. According to the report of the *Journal of Municipalities*, from 1934 to 1937 the government constructed 6.727 village houses for the new dwellers. The new settlement in Muratlı emerged as a crucial example of the project to establish rural life in the

101 Behçet Ünsal, "Sincan Köyü Planı," *Arkitekt* 109–110, no. 1–2 (1940): 16.
102 Mustafa Kemal Atatürk, 1 İkinci Teşrin 1936'da Atatürk'ün Kamutay'daki Nutku, T.C. Trakya Umumi Müfettişliği Köy Bürosu, 40 (İstanbul: Halk Basımevi, 1937), p. 8. Author's translation.
103 'Göçmen Evleri ve Köyleri', *Belediyeler Dergisi*, 29.12 (1937), 53–55.
104 Eres, "Türkiye'de Planlı Kırsal Yerleşmelerin Tarihsel Gelişimi ve Erken Cumhuriyet Dönemi Planlı Kırsal Mimarisinin Korunması Sorunu," 155.

countryside consistent with the new economic, demographic, and cultural ambitions of the Turkish state.

At the beginning of the 20th century, Muratlı was a small rural settlement accessible by rail. Up until the first years of the republic, the population of the town increased, and it became a convenient area to settle the first wave of newcomers. Between 1925 and 1933, 56 dwellings were constructed for 107 immigrants from Bulgaria, Romania, and Yugoslavia. After the 1934 Settlement Law, the area was planned to house the largest "new rural settlement" in the Thrace region, building 700 village houses for the dwellers. Between 1935 and 1939, 656 rural houses were constructed and 23.670 decares of land were provided for the settlers. The site was planned in a grid scheme, but during the implementation of the project some aspects were changed. The houses, constructed of timber and adobe bricks, were placed on 1000 m² plots. Although they followed the same typology as the other implementations of the Housing Department of Ministry of Interior, they had a symmetrical arrangement **(Figure 4.5)**.[105]

Figure 4.5. *Muratlı Village, Tekirdag, Thrace region, 1935.*[106]

---

105   Ibid, pp. 240–44.; Eres, 'Muratlı: Bir Cumhuriyet Köyü'.

106   "L'Immigration En Turquie," *La Turquie Kemaliste* 23, no. Janvier (1938): 15.

Figure 4.6. *Sincan Village, Ankara, by architect Behçet Ünsal in 1937.*[107]

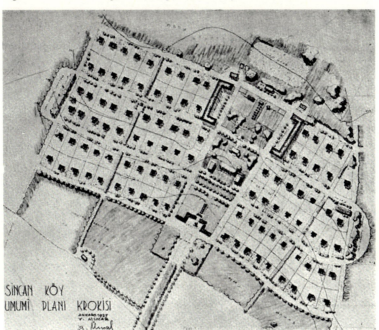

Later, Sincan Village in Ankara was planned by the state architect Behçet Ünsal in 1937 for Turco-Romanian immigrants. This village emerged as another exemplar plan for new rural settlements following the 1934 Settlement Law. Sincan was situated in western Ankara and neighboring Etimesgut village, which had been constructed starting from the late 1920s as one of the first exemplar village projects of the republican state. According to Behçet Ünsal's plan, the new settlement was located on the hillside behind the railway station. A 25-metre-wide road from the railway station was the main access to the village. Agricultural fields and gardens were on the outskirts of the settlement. The main road led to the public core of the village, which included the guesthouse, nursery and its annexes, washhouse, and school. The end of this area was designated for the power plant, village library, coffee house, bazaar and mosque, and the central organization of public facilities was extended by

---

107   Ünsal, "Sincan Köyü Planı," 15.

a public park. The top of the hill was arranged to provide water resources for the dwellers and agricultural activities in the village **(Figure 4.6)**.

The new settlements in Diyarbakır were built to contribute to the demographic transformation of the region. According to the General Inspector of Diyarbakır Abidin Özmen,[108] the province and its surroundings would be developed in accordance with the decisions of a commission consisting of "experts such as artisans, administrators, settlement bureaucrats, judges, doctors, engineers, architects and scientist bureaucrats", aiming to build "three to five Turkish villages of 100 houses every year at a cost of 600 lira". Özmen also declared that "this way our progressive nation can assimilate the backward nation and establish economic dominance in a Turkish center".[109]

The implementation of the 1934 Settlement Law fundamentally had two significant aims for the rural sphere in Turkey. First, settling the incomers would drive the demographic program forward, the objective of which was to conform the whole population to a predominant Turkishness. Thus, either the incomers would be settled in completely restrainable places along the railways and highways, hence in the accessible areas for the state, or they would be settled together with the locals and the deported population to smooth potential conflicts in the countryside. Likewise, the journal *La Turquie Kemaliste* announced that up until 1938, almost 80,000 Turco-Bulgarians and Turco-Romanians, and 10.000 Turco-Yugoslavians, were accommodated by the state, not only in separated settlements but also together with locals. Besides, "350 families from eastern Anatolia" were settled together with Balkan immigrants in the village houses and new rural settlements built in Thrace provinces.[110] The report reveals the demographic ambitions of the settlement operation: Balkan immigrants were instrumentalized in "Turkifying" and easing the strength of the "culturally non-Turkish" population in Turkey.

The second aspiration of the 1934 Settlement Law concerned the economic program of 1930s Turkey. Balkan immigrants were again favored by the economic program grounded in agriculture and agriculture-based industry. A report in the daily newspaper *Cumhuriyet* of 29 May 1935 briefly presented this

---

108   The Inspectorate also included some other provinces in eastern Anatolia such as Elazığ, Urfa, Bitlis, Van, Hakkari, Mardin and Agri.

109   Koca, pp. 495–97; in: Üngör, p. 162.

110   "L'Immigration En Turquie," 16. Ümit Uğur Üngör introduces the statistics report of Turkey Prime Ministry: "According to official sources, the total number of Kurds deported to the west in the 1930s was 25,381 people in 5074 households." Üngör, p. 162.

ideal: 10.000 Turco-Bulgarian immigrants were expected in the county by the end of 1935. The tobacco farmers among these incomers would be settled in places where they could labor in the field and participate in agrarian production.[111] Moreover, around the new settlements and dwellings, the state expropriated agricultural land for farmer and artisan inhabitants. It provided tools and equipment as well as animals and breeds from the state's farms. *La Turquie Kemaliste* announced the goal to establish 85 additional agricultural credit co-operatives by the end of 1939.[112] Once again, the new rural settlements, and the new quarters built as the extensions of existing villages, provided an emerging space that developed into an architectonic language, spoken in the countryside.

111   '50.000 Göçmen İçin Trakya'da Hep Bir Tip Evler Yaptırılıyor (For 50.000 Immigrants Prototype Houses Are Being Constructed in Thrace)'.
112   "L'Immigration En Turquie," 17.

Chapter 5 - Turkification and Planning: New Settlements in Izmir and Elazığ

Building New Rural Settlements in Izmir

An overview of the reconstruction of İzmir during the early republican period shows the intentions behind rural settlement projects in the city. The rehabilitation of İzmir in accordance with republican aims was another focus of the state's agenda, starting from the end of Turco–Greek War in 1922. The first step began after the great fire of İzmir in 1922 that completely destroyed between 20.000 and 25.000 dwellings in the city center. Consequently, from 1924 to 1935 the republican state focused on the restoration of the destroyed area to rebuild dwellings and infrastructure.[1]

During the Lausanne Treaty meetings in 1923, the republican delegates met with architect and planner Henri Prost, on whose advice the municipality of İzmir put urbanist Rene Danger in charge of reconstruction, with a priority focus on ruined areas in the center. Between 1924 and 1925, Danger and Prost first introduced a plan for the economic and residential reorganization of the city. The municipality implemented the plan by expropriating former properties for dwellings, as well as by offering new zones for sale to traders, financial associations, and handicraftsmen.

Together with the Municipalities Law of 3 April 1930 (number 1580), and the urbanist initiatives of the new mayor Behçet Uz, the Danger–Prost plan was revised in 1932 and consulted by Herman Jansen, Ankara's urban planner. In addition to the reconstruction of residential areas, and the organization of

---

1 Cınar Atay, *Osmanlı'dan Cumhuriyet'e İzmir Planları* (İzmir: Yaşar Eğitim ve Kültür Vakfı, 1998), 180–92; Hülya Gedikler Gölgesiz, *1950'li Yıllarda İzmir* (İzmir: Şenocak Yayınları, 2012), 69.

the harbor and industrial districts and the main axis of city center, the revision paved the way for formation of the Culture Park, which emerged as the landmark of the republican state in the city. Between 1934 and 1936 the Culture Park, located on an area of roughly 42 hectares and accessible from the harbor, historical bazaar, and ancient agora, was designed for international fairs representing state planning of İzmir and the capital city Ankara.[2]

The reconstruction of İzmir during the 1930s was also reported on by European scholars such as Lilo Linke, Robert Anhegger and Andreas Tietze. They travelled in the country to observe the Kemalist transformation, not only among the intelligentsia and in the city culture, but also among the people and in the rural landscape. Erik-Jan Zürcher introduces the diaries of travelers that present an important perspective on the circumstances of the country, especially in İzmir:

> "Along the railway line from Eskisehir to Afyonkarahisar and İzmir, she [Linke] sees lots of deserted and ruinous villages and both the diaries and Linke describe how, thirteen to fifteen years after the great fire, the old Greek, and Armenian quarters of İzmir are still in ruins. The debris is still being cleared. Some building activity was going on, but it was still very patchy. By the time the Anhegger/Tietze party arrived, part of the old Greek quarter had been turned into a huge "Culture Park" *(Kültür Parkı)* where the international fair was being held (although the international dimension at this time was very modest indeed)".[3]

The Danger–Prost plan did not account for large-scale urbanization. Therefore, the reconstruction was never implemented completely and systematically. By the end of the 1930s, mayor Behçet Uz attempted to establish an urbanization office within the municipality. This was after he called on Le Corbusier to draw up a master plan for the city center and the surroundings along the gulf, and a development proposal for the hinterland. According to

---

2   Cana Bilsel, 'Ideology and Planning During the Early Republican Period: Two Master Plans for İzmir and Scenarios of Modernization', *METU Journal of Faculty of Architecture*, 16.1–2 (1996), 13–30 (pp. 14–21); Cana Bilsel, 'İzmir'de Cumhuriyet Dönemi Planlaması (1923–1965): 20. Yüzyıl Kentsel Mirası', *Ege Mimarlık*, 71.4 (2009), 12–17 (pp. 12–15); Gedikler Gölgesiz, pp. 69–70.

3   Erik Jan Zürcher, "Two Young Ottomanists Discover Kemalist Turkey, The Travel Dairies of Robert Anhegger and Andreas Tietze," *Journal of Turkish Studies*, Essays in Honour of Barbara Flamming II, 26, no. I (2002): 363.

the agenda, Le Corbusier would prepare the concept and plans, and the urbanization office in the municipality of İzmir would elaborate on and implement the project with his consultancy. Although the parties agreed to the schedule, the project was suspended until 1948 when Le Corbusier visited the city for the first time as up until then he had not presented any plans to the urbanization office of the municipality of İzmir. In early 1949 the architect submitted a master plan including 22 drafts and diagrams. He proposed a larger port capable of importing and exporting goods all over the country and to which the industrial areas would be well connected. Le Corbusier also introduced the "Green Industrial Settlement", extending the existing industrial area, railway line and harbor towards the north of the gulf. According to the project report, the principal "Green Industrial Settlement" concept was based on an organization that embraced the industrial production bases and workers' habitat in a wide green zone. Here the workers would benefit from a clean and healthy environment without needing to leave the domain.[4]

The reconstruction of the city was never completely concluded by the early republican cadre until mid-1950s.[5] The center was partially built and developed in accordance with the most urgent necessities such as regenerating the harbor area, the bazaar and small production ateliers, and constructing dwellings for locals and newcomers. In other words, the urbanization of İzmir during the early republican period concentrated on the coastal strip, with an emphasis on the city center and its transportation connections to the hinterland. The Culture Park, planned by the office of civil works in the municipality of İzmir, gradually became the most significant component of the reconstruction operation in the city. The project not only followed the European public park model, but also transformed the area into a green plaza and fairground and provided an affordable solution for the ruined district instead of rebuilding the demol-

---

4   Bilsel, 'Ideology and Planning During the Early Republican Period: Two Master Plans for İzmir and Scenarios of Modernization', pp. 21–26; Cana Bilsel, 'Le Corbusier'nin İzmir Nazım Planı ve "Yeşil Endüstri Sitesi" Önerisi', *Ege Mimarlık*, 31.3 (1999), 13–17; Özlem Genel Altınkaya, 'İzmir Nazım Planı: Le Corbusier'nin Mimarlığı'nda Mekânsal Bir Strateji Olarak Lineerlik', *Ege Mimarlık*, 96.2 (2017), 40–43.

5   In 1951 the municipality of İzmir organized an international competition for urban planning of the city, establishing a jury including the mayor, civil servants, a Turkish architect, German architect Paul Bonatz, and British architect Sir Patrick Aber`bie. Architect Kemal Ahmet Aru won the competition. However, the implementation was postponed until 1955. Gedikler Gölgesiz, *1950'li Yıllarda İzmir*, 71–72.

ished houses. It also emerged as a memorial space for the new republic in the city center – rather than representing inhabitants of the former state.

Neither plan – Rene Danger and Henri Prost's plan or Le Corbusier's master plan –addressed agricultural geography and its potential. Both plans lacked a defined strategy for the rural edges of İzmir, despite the fact that the city had a tradition of industrial production based on agrarian goods. This approach reflects the bifurcation of the state's urbanization and countryside rehabilitation agendas. Namely, the reconstruction of the city was not paired with the planning of new settlements in rural İzmir in the demographic, socio-cultural and economic programs of the republican state.

Despite the urbanization politics applying only to a small territory of the city, İzmir was crucially important for agriculture and trade in the early republican economic program. The city was home to an expanding harbor, and at the same time the infrastructure of its hinterland was convenient not only for advancing agrarian activities, but also for the production and transportation of goods.[6] Furthermore, the rural population was still the majority in broader İzmir.[7] Along with the state's focus on the economic capacity of the city and its region, Turkish scholars during the mid-1930s studied İzmir and its domain through an academic lens. This work assisted the republican cadre in first forming an economic plan, and later a demographic plan, for western Anatolia.[8]

---

6   The city and its hinterland started to develop with the Levantine groups in the Ottoman State from the 19th century. British traders in particular concentrated on the agricultural and industrial activities in the region and built the first railway line between the harbor and Aydın – a city in İzmir's hinterland with a remarkable agricultural potential. The line provided for the transportation of industrial raw material and agricultural goods. A second line was constructed between the harbor and Turgutlu – a small town in the hinterland towards the east of the city. Philip Mansel, 'Cities of the Levant – The Past for the Future?', *Asian Affairs*, 45.2 (2014), 220–42 <https://doi.org/10.1080/030683 74.2014.907006>; Abdullah Martal, *Belgelerle Osmanlı Döneminde İzmir* (İzmir: Ankara: Yazıt Yayıncılık, 2007), pp. 38–61.

7   According to the population census in 1935, 310,063 of a total population of 596,078 were living in the rural towns and villages. *1935 20 İlkteşrin Genel Nüfus Sayımı; Türkiye Nüfusu, Vilayet, Kaza, Şehir ve Köyler İtibarile Muvakkat Rakamlar – Population de La Turquie 20 Octobre-1935 Recensement General de La Population Par Provinces, Districts, Villes et Villages, Chiffes Provisoires*, Başvekalet Devlet İstatistik Genel Müdürlüğü, 74 (Ankara: Ulus Basımevi, 1935), p. 1.

8   Danyal Bediz, 'İzmir (Smyrna); Und Sein Wirtschaftsgeographisches Einzugsgebiet' (unpublished Dissertation, Ludwig-Maximilians-Universität München, 1935); A. Naim

In addition to this, the administrative structure of the city was also developed in the rural regions. The government plans were uncomplicatedly installed in smaller towns and villages. Thus, the People's House and its Village Affairs Branch actively participated in the rehabilitation of rural İzmir from the foundation of the institution in 1932. The local governor Kazim Dirik, who held this post until 1935, established a committee, including a veterinarian, an agriculturalist, a teacher and a doctor, which started to work in nearby villages.[9] The Village Affairs Branch worked together with the Village Office in the city governorate established by Kazim Dirik in 1931.

In the same year, the governor and the committee held a conference series in Bornova Agriculture School to instruct 40 village teachers. This group visited the villages in the region to survey the condition of the countryside. During excursions in the following years, doctors and veterinarians worked on public health in the villages, agriculturalists assisted and instructed the villagers, and officials observed the priorities of the rural community. The branch encouraged villagers to trade their agricultural products in the urban markets. Also, governor Kazim Dirik started a series of lectures in 1935 for the village headmen about "Village Affairs in the Turkish Revolution", focusing on administrative and legislative subjects in the village community. Nevertheless, from 1934 the branch engaged in state propaganda in the countryside by requesting the participation of villagers in national celebrations in İzmir and the town centers of the city. The visiting groups also concentrated on republican reforms and programs in the village community.[10]

The agenda of Village Affairs Branch of İzmir People's House was to assist the rehabilitation of the rural city at the beginning of 1930s. The focus of the organization shifted from fulfilling the urgent needs of villages to including them in the state's programs. In rural İzmir and its hinterland, the People's House sought to modernize the villages with instruction in sanitation and public health, to develop the economy through guidance in agricultural methods, to consolidate the state's administrative structure with the 1924 Village Law and 1934 Settlement Law, and finally to use education to effect social reforms in the village community.

(Hakim) Öktem, 'Die Stellung (İzmir) Smyrna Im Weltverkehr Und Welthandel' (unpublished Dissertation, Friedrich-Wilhelms Universität zu Berlin, 1935).

9   Yaşar Akyol, *İzmir Halkevi (1932–1951)*, Kent Kitaplığı Dizisi 60 (İzmir: İzmir Büyükşehir Belediyesi, 2008), 66.

10   Ibid, pp. 120–23.

Together with the surveys, studies and practices of the People's House and the Village Affairs' Branch, the state also intensely focused on the *village* as a crucial social unit, along with the regions and provinces. On 31 July 1936, the Interior Ministry announced five-years plans for villages in every province of the country to implement the 1934 Settlement Law and the 1924 Village Law, and to boost social and economic rural life. The local governors would establish a committee to prepare plans and report to the parliament.[11]

Early in 1937, the preparation for the Five Years Plan of the Villages in İzmir continued to focus on village schools and education. With the permission of the Culture Ministry a new educational institute for village teachers, which focused on instruction for the villagers in agriculture and socio-cultural topics, began to accept scholars in İzmir.[12] In accordance with the development plan, the governorate provided farm animals and working animals for peasants to improve agricultural conditions in the rural areas. Moreover, the Agriculture Ministry proposed building a modern dairy farm in rural İzmir within the five-year plan. The governorate began to expropriate land in favorable areas, especially in the town of Torbalı.[13]

On 25 March 1937 the Turkish parliament promulgated the "Five-Year Cultural Development Plan for Villages in İzmir Province". To fulfil the cultural agenda of the Kemalist regime in the villages of İzmir, a committee gathered under the cultural directorship of A. Rıza Özkut in the Village Affairs' Branch of People Houses and introduced a program in ten articles addressing the socio-cultural situation of rural İzmir. This program was also designed to also improve the economic circumstances of the city. Thus the development plan included assessments of İzmir's villages as compared to other villages in the

---

11   'Köyler İçin Beşer Yıllık Plan', *Anadolu* (İzmir, 31 July 1936), p. 5.

12   According to a news item dated 21 March 1937, the Institute for the Village Teachers was scheduled to begin operations in the following academic semester. The institute was one of the first village institutes, which started to open in 1938 and were legitimated by law in 1940.

13   'Mektepsiz Köy Kalmayacak, Beş Yıllık Program Tamamlanmak Üzere', *Anadolu* (İzmir, 16 January 1937), p. 2; 'Beş Yıllık Köy Kalkınma Programımızda Köy Mekteplerinin Tamamlanması İşi Başta Gelmektedir', *Anadolu* (İzmir, 17 January 1937), pp. 1, 7; 'Köy Öğretmeni Enstitüsü Önümüzdeki Ders Yılında Açılacaktır.', *Anadolu* (İzmir, 21 March 1937), p. 2; 'Köy Kalkınma Planına Göre Hazırlanan Program, Elli Aygır, Yetmiş Eşek Aygırı ve Dörtyüzelli Boğa Satın Alınacaktır', *Anadolu* (İzmir, 21 February 1937), p. 4; 'Modern İnekhane, Yerin İstimlakına Derhal Başlanıyor', *Anadolu* (İzmir, 13 March 1937), p. 2.

country, demographic estimations to plan socio-cultural programs in the villages, evaluation of the culture and demography of the villages, organization
of schools in underpopulated villages in İzmir and keeping village instructors
for İzmir's villages, cultural politics in İzmir's villages, programs for the assimilation of non-Turkish groups and consolidation of Turkish culture among the
immigrants, periodical inspections of village schools in İzmir, development of
new maneuvers to connect the village teachers to villages in İzmir, and finally
development of new methods for village teachers to assist the government in
village affairs.[14]

The report noted that in 1937 only 263 villages out of 629 in İzmir had
schools that provided primary and secondary education. It therefore suggested the need to construct more educational buildings in the villages, to
organize school associations among smaller villages, to supply more teaching
and training equipment for the children, and to regulate the village community via a systematized education program with the better assistance of village
teachers in rural İzmir.[15]

One of the crucial tenets of the program was to integrate the rural population into the nationalization project. The report pointed out that a cultural
program for İzmir's villages should emphasize the assimilation and consolidation of Turkish culture. In particular, non-Turkish people and immigrants
would be the initial target group. The culture director A. Rıza Özkut advocated
the desire "to remove and cause to forget the national classifications of Alba-
nian, Bosnian, Pomak, Cretan, Romanian and Bulgarian", and it was necessary
to begin Turkification tactics especially for children. He therefore campaigned
primarily for schools and libraries in the new settlements to acquaint rural people with Turkish culture.[16]

On the other hand, the demographic character of the city changed during
the Greco-Turkish War in 1922. After the Lausanne Treaty and the proclamation of the republic in 1923, it was declared that İzmir should be legitimated as
a Turkish city, even though it had never been referred to as Turkish for at least
the last two hundred years.[17] However, there were still Turkish villages on the

14   *Umumi Meclisce 937 Yılı Toplantısında Kabul Edilen İzmir İli Köylerinin Kültür Bakımından
      Beş Yıllık Kalkınma Programı*, vol. 7 (İzmir: Cumhuriyet Basımevi, 1937), 1–2.

15   Ibid, pp. 6–10, 12–15.

16   Ibid, p. 11.

17   Sibel Zandi-Sayek, *Ottoman İzmir: The Rise of a Cosmopolitan Port, 1840–1880* (Minneapo-
      lis; London: University of Minnesota Press, 2012); Bilsel, 'Ideology and Planning During

outskirts of the city. And the abandoned Greek villages – including properties and lands – were the resource for accommodating incoming Turkish people in and around the city. Therefore, the housing programs played a crucial role in the demographic formation of İzmir, starting in the first years of the republic and continuing with the 1934 Settlement Law. Accordingly, at the beginning of 1936 the local newspaper of İzmir, *Anadolu*, announced housing programs for Balkan immigrants in the Thrace region. This article was consistent with the government line that the settling of newcomers was a national duty and a crucial part of the social and economic program in the country. More than 10.000 new houses would be constructed in the following year to "enliven the villages" and "enrich the prosperity of the country".[18]

According to an official document of 1938, Balkan immigrants started to be housed in the city from the end of the Balkan Wars in 1912 to the beginning of the First World War in 1914. The municipality of İzmir under the Ottoman state sought to settle the incomers within the limitations imposed by the war climate and without a well-organized settlement policy. The first Balkan immigrants were housed with the assistance of locals in the city and in the rural expansion of the city. On 8 September 1932, the republican state enacted a new law (number 2664) regarding the former and new Balkan immigrants to record the incoming population and provide them with abandoned properties in the cities and their rural areas. In İzmir particularly, the republican state implemented regulations to house the locals, Balkan incomers immigrating in the city since 1912, and the populace coming into the country from Greece after the population exchange agreement in the Lausanne Treaty.[19]

After the enactment of the law (number 2664) in 1932, 5049 households, including 22.207 family members, were registered as Balkan immigrants in İzmir. The local government of İzmir also provided 4629 houses, two stores, six coffee shops, one bakery, 66 small shops, 92 gazebos and stables, 38.919 decares of agricultural fields, 16,353 decares of vineyards, 736 decares of orchards, 3248 decares of fig orchards, and 79.923 olive trees. A total of 14.387 households, including 61.763 family members, were registered as the Turco–Greek populace arriving via population exchange. The local government of İzmir supported this population with 13.150 houses, 79 stores, 23 gristmills, 60 coffee shops,

the Early Republican Period: Two Master Plans for İzmir and Scenarios of Modernization'.

18   'Her Göçmenin Evi Olacak', *Anadolu* (İzmir, 2 February 1936), p. 5.

19   *İzmir Cumhuriyetin 15. Yılında* (İzmir Cumhuriyet Basımevi, 1938), pp. 133–34.

16 hostelries and hotels, four hammams, 59 bakeries, 1240 shops, 11 rendering plants, 209 gazebos and stables, nine factories, three tileries, nine tanneries, six soaperies, 43 warehouses, three music halls, one club, three cinemas, four pharmacies, 18.330 decares of agricultural fields, 34.275 decares of vineyards, 4920 decares of vegetable gardens, 326.314 olive trees, 42.818 decares of fig orchards, and 1328 orchards. In addition, the government provided 833 houses to 932 people whose dwellings were destroyed in the great fire of İzmir in 1922.[20]

Within the scope of the 1934 Settlement Law, 7383 Turco–Romanians from Constanza and Turco–Bulgarians from Varna immigrated to İzmir in 1936 and 1937, as well as to the other cities in the region such as Manisa and Aydın. Starting from early 1937, the governorate of İzmir received these immigrants in the city and accommodated them in available properties in the city, rural towns, and villages. The governor Fazli Gülec and the Housing Director of İzmir Tahsin Akgün led the general operation with the assistance of governmental organizations such as The Red Crescent of Turkey, which provided food and the first health control of immigrants in Urla, in İzmir's rural harbor. The state provided the settlers with 1.358.452 kilos of common wheat and 706.365 kilos of wheat seed for the first year.[21]

Officials registered the immigrants and prepared them for transportation to the places where they were temporarily settled. Up until summer 1937, 815 families in rural İzmir were housed in several towns in existing properties: 20 households in Seydiköy, 20 households in Değirmendere, 65 households in Foça, 25 households in Menemen, 180 households in Seferhisar, 60 households in Kemalpaşa, 110 households in Urla, 85 households in Bergama, 200 households in Torbalı, and 50 households in Dikili.[22]

Particularly after the arrival of the first groups, new rural settlements, and new dwellings to extend villages were needed due to the conditions of the places where the immigrants were settled. Within the governorate of İzmir, a commission was established consisting of the directors of public health (Cevdet Saraçoğlu), public works (Galip Bey) and agriculture (Nadir Uysal) to determine appropriate areas for new village construction and land provision for the incomers. First, the commission visited Torbalı and confirmed the

---

20   Ibid, p. 136.

21   Ibid, p. 136; 'Göçmenler Geliyor, Bu Yıl Vilayetimize 5296 Göçmen Gelecek', *Anadolu* (İzmir, 30 June 1937), p. 2.

22   'Vilayetimizde 5260 Göçmen İskan Edilecek', *Anadolu* (İzmir, 6 February 1937), p. 5.

existence of sufficient land for the construction of new villages and agricultural activities. Later, the commission visited and surveyed several towns – in the south Kuşadası and Selçuk, in the north Menemen, Foça, Bergama and Dikili, in the east Kemalpaşa, and in the west Urla and Çeşme – to survey new settlement possibilities and abandoned village houses.[23]

At the beginning of March 1937, the local governorate began to expropriate the land in Torbalı and its rural surroundings. Almost 1000 decares were provided for the settlements and 25.000 decares of the Beleric farm in the region were provided for agricultural land. In other towns the governorate decided to construct dwellings as extensions of the settlements, but in Kayas in Torbalı, where the land reclamation had continued since 1936, it agreed to build three new settlements.[24]

On 13 July 1937 the governorate of İzmir announced a tender offer for the construction of village houses. According to the statement published in the local newspaper, the construction work would include:

"A. In Maltepe Village in Menemen 91 single village houses; the estimated cost is 17.328,22 Liras.

B. In Bergama 20 single village houses; the estimated cost is 3.808,40 Liras.

C. In Dikili 31 single houses, in Çandarlı 158 single village houses and 31 semi-detached village houses; the estimated cost is 46.939,14 Liras.

D. In Foça 17 single village houses and 10 semi-detached village houses; the estimated cost is 6557,64 Liras.

E. In Kızılca and Parsa villages in Kemalpaşa 21 single village houses; the estimated cost is 3998,82 Liras.

F. In Torbalı in Kayas 32 single village houses, in Ahmetli village 156 single village houses and 32 semi-detached village houses, in Havuzbaşı village 54 single village houses, in Taşkesik village 145 single village houses and 16 semi-detached village houses; the estimated cost is 89.631,42 Liras.

G. In Kalambaki Farm in Kuşadası 29 single village houses; the estimated cost is 5522,18 Liras".[25]

---

23   "Göçmen Köyleri, Komisyon Kazalara Tetkikata Gidiyor," Anadolu, January 19, 1937; "Göçmen Köyleri, İnşaata Haziran İçinde Başlanacak," Anadolu, May 28, 1937.

24   'Göçmenlere Verilecek Arazi İstimlak Ediliyor', Anadolu (İzmir, 3 May 1937), p. 2; 'Göçmen Evleri, Yakında İnşa Edilmeye Başlanacak', Anadolu (İzmir, 3 June 1937), p. 1; 'İskan İşleri, Kayas Çiftliğinde Yeni Köyler Kurulacak', Anadolu (İzmir, 26 May 1937), p. 2; 'Yeni Göçmenler İçin Yer Hazırlandı', Anadolu (İzmir, 14 July 1937), p. 2.

25   "İzmir İskan Müdürlüğünden," Anadolu, July 17, 1937. Author's translation.

The tender offer was also announced in the towns and villages where the dwellings and settlements would be built. The Housing Department of İzmir Governorate requested stone masonry techniques and timber roofs in the houses, with building materials, such as stone and timber, to be provided to the building contractors. Also, the government would bring the necessary amount of timber from the national forest in Denizli province.[26]

Since local building contractors did not respond to the first announcement, the tender was postponed until the end of August and the estimated costs increased by 100 Liras. However, still no one applied for the construction work and the Interior Ministry sent a committee from the Housing Department to oversee the operation. After a survey of the committee, the Ministry of Public Health and Welfare prepared draft plans to send to the governorate of İzmir to start the operation.[27]

By 1938 in İzmir, the state completed 521 rural dwellings out of a planned 931 houses, including the new rural settlements. In all, 74.020 decares land (44.943 decares in 1936 and 29.077 decares in 1937), 1346 ploughs and 1312 working animals were provided to the settlers coming into the province.[28]

Three New Rural Settlements in the Torbalı District of Izmir

Following the early immigrant housing announcement after the 1934 Settlement Law, Torbalı district in İzmir became the focus of the governorate housing commission's agenda.[29] The commission addressed this region because British companies had started to implement infrastructure for agricultural settlements under Ottoman rule in the late 19th century. The area had already been cultivated in the early 19th century and the tradition of agrarian production continued from that time. The first railway line in the region was constructed between 1856 and 1860 with the goal of bridging the agricultural land from Aydın to İzmir and to the harbor. The İzmir–Torbalı line was completed in 1860, making Torbalı an important stop between Aydın and İzmir for the transport of agrarian goods and people, connecting the local rural bazaar to the city. Up until the end of the 19th century, construction of the railway

---

26   "İzmir İskan Müdürlüğünden"; "Göçmen Evleri," *Anadolu*, May 9, 1937.

27   'Göçmen Evleri Emaneten İnşa Ettirilecek', *Anadolu* (İzmir, 29 July 1937), p. 2; 'Göçmen Evleri, Bir Hafta Sonra İnşaata Başlanacak', *Anadolu* (İzmir, 17 August 1937), p. 2.

28   *İzmir Cumhuriyetin 15. Yılında*, pp. 136–37.

29   "Göçmen Köyleri, Komisyon Kazalara Tetkikata Gidiyor."

network in the region continued, connecting the cultivated area between the lowlands of the Maeander River.[30]

In 1881 Sultan Abdul Hamid II bought almost 30.000 decares of farmland, including 20 villages and agriculture areas in Torbalı reaching to Tire – another town to the southeast of Torbalı. After this step, the sultan practically owned the land around the railway line passing through Torbalı district, and during the 1890s the Ottoman state built new agricultural farms and villages to serve his interests. When the sultan was dethroned in 1908, the imperial farms in Torbalı district contained an administration office, a guild, a granary and two warehouses (for cotton), two slaughterhouses, two gristmills, seven orchards, 89 shops, 23 gazebos in vineyards, three bakeries, two hostelries, a hippodrome, an aviary, and a garden.[31]

At the end of the 19th century, Turkish Muslims, non-Turkish Muslims, and Turkic nomads represented the majority of the population in rural Torbalı, and Orthodox Greeks were the minority.[32] The dominance of Muslims and Turkic nomads also continued during early republican years. This fact probably made the district even more attractive for immigrants who came into the country within the scope of the 1934 Settlement Law. After an earthquake hit the district in 1928 and caused damage in the settlements, the state paid much more attention to reconstruction works in rural Torbalı in the following years,[33] resulting

---

30　A. Nedim Atilla, *İzmir Demiryolları*, Kent Kitaplığı Dizisi, 36, 1. Basım (İzmir: İzmir Büyükşehir Belediyesi Kültür Yayını, 2002), pp. 63–65, 89–91, 145.; Atay, *Osmanlı'dan Cumhuriyet'e İzmir Planları*, 83–86.

31　"Aydın Vilayeti Salnamesi," 1894, 214; "Aydın Vilayeti Salnamesi," 1896, 184; "Aydın Vilayeti Salnamesi," 1908, 263; Yasin Kayış, *Aydın Vilâyeti Salnâmelerinde Torbalı ve Sultan II. Abdülhamid'in Hayır Eserleri*, Kültür Yayınları, I (İzmir: Torbalı Belediyesi, 2012), 36. For further reading on the extension of the İzmir–Aydın railway line in İzmir's city centre, and the role of British and French entrepreneurs in construction work, see Sibel Zandi-Sayek, *Ottoman İzmir: The Rise of a Cosmopolitan Port, 1840–1880* (Minneapolis, London: University of Minnesota Press, 2012), pp. 115–49.

32　"Aydın Vilayeti Salnamesi," 1889, 187; Kayış, *Aydın Vilâyeti Salnâmelerinde Torbalı ve Sultan II. Abdülhamid'in Hayır Eserleri*, 63. And, according to official document on population census in 1935, in 1927 the population of the town was 1771, which increased to 1935 in 8 years. *1935 20 İlkteşrin Genel Nüfus Sayımı; Türkiye Nüfusu, Vilayet, Kaza, Şehir ve Köyler İtibarile Muvakkat Rakamlar – Population de La Turquie 20 Octobre-1935 Recensement General de La Population Par Provinces, Districts, Villes et Villages, Chiffes Provisoires*, 18.

33　İbrahim Hakkı and Hamit Nafiz, *30–31 Mart 1928 Tarihindeki Tepeköy-Torbalı Zelzelesi*, Darülfünun Jeoloji Enstitüsü Neşriyatından, 1 (İstanbul: Kader Matbaası, 1929).

in the decision to construct three new rural settlements – Yeniköy, Havuzbaşı and Taşkesik villages – in the area. **(Figure 5.1.)**

Figure 5.1. *Location of Yeniköy, Taşkesik and Havuzbaşı villages.*[34]

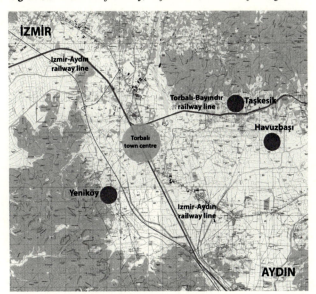

According to the report from 1891 in the Ottoman annual, Yeniköy village in Torbalı district had already been established at that time with 26 dwellings and a population of 116. Between 1892 and 1894 a mosque, a fountain with an ornamental pool, and a primary school were built in the public space in the village center.[35] Traditionally the mosque referred to the imperial power as well as to the Islamic community in rural Anatolia. It also represented an important social space uniting the people in the village. In Yeniköy, as in other settlements built in the region by the Ottoman authority at the end of 19th century, the school and the fountain with its annexes also emerged as spaces referring to the imperial state, religious community, and social life in the village.

---

34   Drawn after *Akdeniz Harita* (Office for Carthography and Land Survey).

35   'Aydın Vilayeti Salnamesi', 1891, p. 461; 'Aydın Vilayet Salnamesi', 1893, p. 409; 'Aydın Vilayeti Salnamesi', pp. 501–2; Kayış, pp. 65, 113 – 115, 142 – 144, 153 – 154.

The building program included new components that differed from traditional Anatolian villages.

In 1937 construction started on the republican settlement of Yeniköy from the eastern edge of the former Ottoman village. It emerged as a larger settlement in terms of inhabitants and dwellings, but the objective of this republican settlement was to implement a much more comprehensive building program to be finished in the following years by the government and settlers together.[36]

The new settlement consisted of four main streets, each 10 meters wide, on the north– south axis that crossed five main streets of the same width on the west–east axis. The intersections created building blocks of land spread over nearly 10 decares. Each building block included 10 dwellings located on a 1000 m² site. Two blocks between the second and third streets on the north–south axis, and the first and third streets on the west–east axis, were left for the public area that included shops, coffee house, village office, gendarmerie, and the school that was built in the 1940s with the financial help of villagers.[37]

The earliest cadastral plan of the settlement was dated back to 1969. This plan consisted of ten complete blocks and two incomplete blocks extended with new dwellings in the north-south direction. The area built in 1937 included 111 dwellings, mostly single houses in a large garden, except for some of the parcels that were divided in two for private use.[38]

In summer 1937, the Housing Director of İzmir Tahsin Akgün transferred his role to Ziya Fuad, the former Housing Director of Elazığ, who then led the building operation in Yeniköy.[39] According to an official document, the arrangement of building plots and construction of the houses were completed in 1938. The houses were 50,5m² (9.1m x 5.5m) one-storey single buildings situated in a 1000 m² garden. They consisted of two rooms, a niche for storage in the entrance, and a porch on the back front. The construction material was mainly stone, and the timber roof was extended towards the porch on the back of the house. Each garden had a bathing cubicle that was also used as a toilet **(Figure 5.2)**.

---

36   Interview with the settler.
37   Interview with the settler.
38   The earliest cadastral plan of republican settlement in Yeniköy Village, dated 1969, has been found in the archives of the General Directorate of Land Registry and Cadastre of Torbalı.
39   'İzmir İskan Müdürlüğü', *Anadolu* (İzmir, 20 August 1937), p. 2.

Figure 5.2. *Yeniköy Village in 1938, after construction.*[40]

The housing programs in the Havuzbaşı and Taşkesik villages were different from the Yeniköy operation. In 1937 it was announced that 54 single houses were to be constructed in Havuzbaşı, and 145 single houses and 16 semi-detached houses were planned for Taşkesik.[41] However, by 1938 only 24 houses in Taşkesik and 28 houses in Havuzbaşı were completed. In both settlements, the dwellings were located along the side of a 10-metre-wide main street. Each house was situated on a 600 m² building plot. The housing typology that was implemented in Havuzbaşı and Taşkesik villages was identical to that of Yeniköy village, though the houses were placed on smaller plots **(Figure 5.3, Figure 5.4).**[42]

Figure 5.3. *Havuzbaşı Village in 1938, after construction.*[43]

40   *İzmir Cumhuriyetin 15. Yılında*, p. 136.
41   "İzmir İskan Müdürlüğünden."
42   See in Appendix: "House Typology in Yeniköy, Havuzbaşı and Taşkesik Villages, İzmir".
43   *İzmir Cumhuriyetin 15. Yılında*, p. 137.

Figure 5.4. *Taşkesik Village in 1938, after construction.*[44]

Building the New Rural Settlements in Elazığ

Zeynep Kezer discusses Elazığ as a "spatial border" in the middle of eastern Turkey, referring to the Turkification and modernization policies of the state in the region, starting in the early years of the republic:

> "Elazığ provides a particularly illustrative case in point. During the 1930s and 1940s, the province's mountains and valleys, streets and squares, homes and school classrooms, as well as the myriad activities these places engendered, revealed how components of physical environment served as social sorters. Spatial practices ranging from innocuous daily encounters between schoolchildren to solemn collective ceremonies or military raids, which accentuated the uneven power relations between the state, its agents, and the local population, generated and reified differences among people, depending on their ethno-religious tribal affiliations and relationship with the central authorities.
>
> ... Their [republican cadre's] interventions profoundly altered this region's built environment and its broader geography, affecting how local populations and agents of the state engaged with and moved through it, ultimately changing how this landscape was imaged by all".[45]

Construction began on the "imaged landscape" of Elazığ by the late 19th century when the Ottoman state proclaimed the first constitutional monarchy in 1876.

---

44   *İzmir Cumhuriyetin 15. Yılında*, p. 137.

45   Zeynep Kezer, 'Spatializing Difference: The Making of an Internal Border in Early Republican Elazığ, Turkey', *Journal of the Society of Architectural Historians*, 73.4 (2014), 507–27 (p. 509).

Together with the new legislative form of the state, the administrative framework had to be reorganized in a hierarchical system of provinces (*Vilayet*), departments (*Sancak*), and districts (*Kaza*). In 1879, Mamuret-ül Aziz (later Elaziz and then Elazığ), comprising the Elazığ, Dersim (Tunceli) and Malatya departments, became one of the 29 provinces in the Ottoman Empire.[46]

The ethnic composition of Elazığ had been heterogeneous: the religious, social, and economic structures were abundant and manifold, based on various traditional aspects among the locals who were predominantly Kurds and Armenians. From 1915 to 1916, Armenians and other Christians had been forced into exile and deported under Ottoman rule.[47] Starting from 1916, Kurds had been forced to leave their homes and deported out of the eastern region in the country, especially after the revolts in 1925 in Diyarbakır, in 1930 in Ararat, and in 1937 in Dersim (Tunceli).[48] Elazığ, on the other hand, remained loyal to the Turkish state and developed into "a secure" island of the republican regime in eastern Anatolia. The consolidation ambitions of the republican regime shaped Elazığ and its rural terrain during the 1930s.

The position of Elazığ in the state's interior policy started to become clearer with the Dersim Reports, which were prepared by the Interior Minister Şükrü Kaya after his survey of the region, along with the General Inspector of Elazığ and other military officials. On 18 November 1931, Kaya reported on the conflicts between Kurdish tribes and locals, briefly addressing the Kurds as perils for the state and arguing that an urgent repossession was needed in the area. He pointed out that the Aghas – tribal leaders –should be distracted from the city, and the rural people should be deported and resettled in rural Elazığ.[49]

---

46   Donald Quataert, *The Ottoman Empire, 1700–1922* (Cambridge, UK; New York: Cambridge University Press, 2005), pp. 63–64; Metin Heper, 'Center and Periphery in the Ottoman Empire: With Special Reference to the Nineteenth Century', *International Political Science Review*, 1.1 (1980), 81–104.

47   Majeed R. Jafar, *Under-Underdevelopment: A Regional Case Study of the Kurdish Area in Turkey*, Studies of the Social Policy Association in Finland; No 24 (Helsinki: Social Policy Association in Finland, 1976); Suny, Göçek, and Naimark.

48   Üngör, *The Making of Modern Turkey*, 124–25; Bayrak, "'Şark Islahat Planı' ve TC'nin Kürt Politikası"; Bulut, *Dersim raporları*; Olson, "The Kurdish Rebellions of Sheikh Said (1925), Mt. Ararat (1930), and Dersim (1937–8): Their Impact on the Development of the Turkish Air Force and on Kurdish and Turkish Nationalism."

49   Bulut, *Dersim raporları*, 265–70.

Nevertheless, the maneuvers first resulted in an administration law for Dersim (Tunceli) enacted at the end of 1935.[50] Then, in 1937, the state performed a military operation against the rebellions and deported civilians, not only to Elazığ but also to other cities in the region such as Malatya, Sivas, Erzincan, Erzurum, Gümüşhane and Bingöl.[51]

From this point of view, the General Inspectorates Conference in 1936 in Ankara was, again, a significant attempt to form the region on the macro scale, and Elazığ on the micro scale. In the meeting with the general inspector of the Fourth Region (which comprised Elazığ, Dersim, Erzincan, Bingöl, and later Muş), Abdullah Alpdogan presented the works which had been completed on behalf of "public order", meaning the consolidation of state power in the region. One of the main attempts was to connect Dersim to the surrounding provinces. Therefore, transport to and from Elazığ, which had been already built in the west and south terrains, was important to ease the mobility problem in the tough topography of Dersim. Abdullah Alpdoğan announced that the construction of a bridge in Pertek would be a critical solution to the transport problem, hence ensuring the state's military access to the region.[52]

Railway construction had played a key role in the modernization program during the early republican period across the country. The plans for the eastern provinces however, had a central place in the state's agenda. The intent was not only to develop the region via public works, especially with the "innovated" component of transportation, but also to control the area by equipping the region with agents of modernization. Therefore, the general inspectors and officials of the interior ministry agreed that the priority should be railway construction in the region. But the military capabilities should be also increased by creating seven-kilometer-wide buffer zones on each side of railways to protect the infrastructure from any kind of treason.[53]

These policies resulted in large-scale infrastructure projects in East Anatolia, focusing on Elazığ. In other words, from the early 1930s the railway, highway and bridge projects started to be implemented in and around Elazığ, with the city as a nucleus. In 1931 the railway was extended to Malatya, while in 1934 the line between Malatya and Elazığ was completed, followed in 1935 by the line between Elazığ and Diyarbakır. In 1932 the Kömürhan–İsmet Paşa Bridge was

---

50   TBMM, *Tunceli Vilayetinin İdaresi Hakkında Kanun*, 1935, pp. 112–16. (number 2884).
51   Bulut, *Dersim raporları*, 369–80.
52   Varlık and Koçak, pp. 136–37.
53   Kezer, 'Spatializing Difference', pp. 516–17.

constructed, followed in 1935 by the Keban Bridge on the Malatya–Elazığ highway, and in 1939 the Pertek Bridge on the Elazığ–Dersim (Tunceli) highway.[54]

To keep the centralized position of the city in the east, the government developed a plan for Elazığ–Van railways in the direction of the Iran border. The project started in 1935, together with the Diyarbakır –Kurtalan line. The law numbered 3,813 arranged the financing of the construction of these two lines. However, the construction of Elazığ–Iran railway was postponed until 1941 and not finished until 1947. According to the plan, the railway headed east, passed through the Elazığ and Muş lowlands, and reached Tuğ village next to Lake Van. The conditions of the highways in the area were difficult, and therefore the railroads became the primary solution for transportation.[55]

In addition to the operation connecting Elazığ with its periphery, institutional agents of the state transformed the cityscape during the 1930s. From 1933 to 1937 local governor Tevfik Sırrı Gür and general inspector Abdullah Alpdoğan led the public projects. First, in 1934 the train station was built, and from the train station to the center a 20-metre-wide boulevard – Station Boulevard – was developed and ornamented with a statue of Atatürk. The municipality and theatre buildings, Elazığ People's House, Atatürk Primary School, and Elazığ Girls' Institute were other rising "modern" buildings around the city center. A public park – Culture Park (sharing the name with İzmir's Fairground) – and a stadium were built. In the city center, streets were reorganized to include landscaping on the pedestrian walkways.[56] In 1936 general inspector Abdullah Alpdoğan also announced that seven schools were under construction in the towns, and a state hospital with larger capacity was built in the intersection of the south-north and east-west roadways.[57]

In eastern Anatolia the state invested in a development program based on agrarian and mining enterprises. From the early 1930s In Elazığ, cotton agri-

---

54   Sezer, "Railways and Bridges as Expression of Rural in Early Republican Period, 1930–1945 (Erken Cumhuriyet Döneminde Kırsalın İfadesi Bağlamında Demiryolları ve Köprüler)," 178–84; Varlık and Koçak, *Umumî müfettişler*, 146–48; *Elazığ-Genç Demiryolu Hattının İşletmeye Açılışı* (Ankara: TCDD, 1945); *Nafia Sergisi Kataloğu*, vol. 13, T.C. Nafia Vekaleti Neşriyatı 5 (Ankara: T.C. Nafia Bakanlığı, 1944); "İsmetpaşa (Kömürhan) Köprüsü," *Demiryollar Mecmuası*, 1931.

55   *Elazığ-Genç Demiryolu Hattının İşletmeye Açılışı.*

56   "Elaziz Vilayetinin Bayındırlık İşleri," *Altan*, ubat 1937, 6; "Valimizin Mühim Bir Eseri Daha," *Turan Gazetesi*, June 25, 1934.

57   Varlık and Koçak, *Umumî müfettişler*, 149–53; Hurşit Nazlı, *Elazığ İlinin Coğrafi, Zirai, Ticari, Tarih, Nüfus ve Jeolojik Durumu* (Ankara: Zerbamat Basımevi, 1939), 41–64.

culture (and in some areas silk farming), supported by the government, dominated the rural economy. To process agrarian goods, several foundries were established in the region, and the manufactured goods were transported to other local markets in the neighboring provinces. In 1933 the cotton harvested in the lowlands of Elazığ was processed in Gaziantep's weaving ateliers.[58] According to state's schedule, in 1937, 40.000 kilograms of cottonseeds would be planted in the cultivated areas of rural Elazığ.[59] In 1936 the state financial institution Etibank established the Chrome Mining Processing Plant in Keban district,[60] where the construction of a hydroelectric dam was planned in the same year but postponed until 1966.[61]

In other words, the target was to boost economic activities in the region by supporting agricultural production, selling processed agricultural goods within local markets and trade organizations and generating new industrial fields to engage the labor of the population not working in agriculture. Relatedly, the local governor of Elazığ, Tevfik Sırrı Gür, established the "Commerce Club", which was associated with the Chamber of Commerce and Industry and founded agriculture cooperatives in rural towns. The club was not only a meeting place for local traders, small manufacturers, and peasants, but also became an educational center offering courses on manufacturing and agricultural production processes and a market for the people.[62]

---

58   *Büyük Türk Cumhuriyetimizin On Yılında Elaziz'de İktisadi Umran ve Refah Adımları* (Elaziz: Sinan Matbaası, 1933), 30.

59   Varlık and Koçak, p. 157.

60   Koca, pp. 493–94.

61   The Keban Dam Project was completed in 1974. It was not a part of Southeast Anatolia Development Project (GAP) – the largest energy development project of the Turkish state in eastern Anatolia – but became an inseparable part of it. The construction of the Keban Dam Lake dramatically altered the geography of the city and its districts. John Kolars, 'Problems of International River Management: The Case of the Euphrates', in *International Waters of the Middle East: From Euphrates-Tigris to Nile*, ed. by Asit K Biswas (Oxford: Oxford University Press, 1994), pp. 44–94 (p. 59); John F. Kolars and William A. Mitchell, *The Euphrates River and the Southeast Anatolia Development Project*, Water, the Middle East Imperative (Carbondale: Southern Illinois University Press, 1991), pp. 18–30.

62   *Büyük Türk Cumhuriyetimizin On Yılında Elaziz'de İktisadi Umran ve Refah Adımları*, 10.

Executing the Turkification Agenda and Four New Rural Settlements in Elazığ

According to the 1936 survey of the general inspectorate, the total population of the Elazığ area, including Erzincan, Bingöl and Dersim (Tunceli), was 350.826, of which 198.508 were Kurds and 107.965 were Turks.[63] Despite these numbers, authorities insisted on establishing the Turkishness of the region, including the rural territories where people were much more attached to tradition and religion. Early republican officials referred to the Kurdish tribes as "the natural born rebellions and bandits who aimed to transform a Turkish region into Kurdish one".[64] This view informed cultural operations in the city, and the extension of these operations strongly affected the rural areas and altered the spatial form of the countryside.

In this respect, Elazığ People's House played a critical role and deliberately furthered the establishment of Turkishness in the region. Under the directorship of the local governor Tevfik Sırrı Gür, a committee in the People's House set the organization's agenda based on the demonstration of the Turkish nation with lectures and conferences on Turkish history, culture, and language. Indeed, this committee worked to Turkify the names of almost 3000 villages in the Elazığ terrain.[65]

Additionally, the symbolism of the People's House had an important role in Elazığ, as well as in other eastern provinces. Starting from the early years, the institution became influential in disseminating state propaganda, and was intended to be a place bridging the people and the regime. The organization concentrated on the transmission of republican reforms, and at the same time on the building of the Turkish nation in the eastern provinces. The People's House offered a completely new program for cultural life in the city and in rural areas different from the typical instruments of the state. Particularly in Elazığ, it was meant to transform the cultural panorama, along with the physical panorama, by adding a new institution for modernization and nationalization to the city.

---

63   Varlık and Koçak, p. 30.

64   Ibid, pp. 130–32.

65   Between 1963 and 1964 the Ministry of Village Affairs prepared an inventory report for the villages in Elazığ province. This report gave wide publicity to the altered place names of the villages (from Armenian and Kurdish placenames to Turkish placenames). *Köy Envanter Raporlarına Göre Elazığ*, Köy İşleri Bakanlığı Yayınları 44 (Konya: Yıldız Basımevi, 1966), 126–52.

Moreover, the implementation of the 1934 Settlement Law became another key nationalization instrument, especially in the rural areas of the region. Within the scope of the law, the deportation of Kurds and the settling of Balkan immigrants paved the way for the transformation of the rural landscape in Elazığ. By 1936 a total of 6428 immigrants had arrived in Elazığ, including 3,875 people from Romania, 1,963 from Yugoslavia, 176 from Bulgaria, 59 from Greece, and 355 from Russia. Out of 1653 families, 1234 had been housed, with the remaining 419 families still waiting to be settled by the state. By 1935, 29.033 decares of agricultural land had been provided to the incomers, followed in 1936 by a further 28.019 decares. In addition to this, the state supplied equipment for agrarian activities such as ploughs, farm animals, and seeds.[66] For the state it was crucial to provide equipment for the settlers in the region since Balkan immigrants fulfilled the profile of the "loyal" and "hardworking" citizens that the state idealized.

The immigrant population was meant to plant a "Turkish" population in the eastern provinces, especially in Elazığ and Diyarbakır. Therefore, state officials agreed on a crucial consensus to establish "strong and collective Turkish settlements" along the railways and highways, and every year a set number of Balkan immigrants would be housed in these villages. A local commission affiliated with the general inspectorates would organize the construction.[67] Relatedly, the housing operation in Elazığ was led by local governor Tevfik Sırrı Gür and general inspector Abdullah Alpdoğan.

According to a report dated June 1935, Etminik village in the center, and Kapuaçmaz, Nirhi and Hoşmat villages in Palu, which were abandoned after the Armenian deportation, were reconstructed for Turco–Romanian incomers starting from 1934. When the settlers arrived in the city, officials registered them as "Turkish citizens" and transported them to the settlements. The immigrants also worked in the construction of village houses.[68] According to another report from July 1935, 41 immigrants arrived in the city. Nine of these (from three families) were housed in Hölvenk (or Hulvenk), which was also an abandoned village following the Armenian deportation, and 32 immigrants waited to be settled. But in the northern part of the city, while the construction of village houses for immigrants was still to be completed, some of the villages

---

66   Varlık and Koçak, Umumî müfettişler, 148–49; Nazlı, Elazığ İlinin Coğrafi, Zirai, Ticari, Tarih, Nüfus ve Jeolojik Durumu, 51.

67   Varlık and Koçak, pp. 72–73.

68   "Şarımızda Olup Bitenler: İskanda," Altan, Haziran 1935.

were reconstructed for the incomers.[69] In August 1935 it was announced that the director of Land Registry Office of Elazığ, Celal Tuna, was to lead the land provision operation for the incomers and for the locals who were covered by the 1934 Settlement Law and housed by the government in the province.[70]

The intention to build "Turkish" rural settlements around the railways to strengthen the political authority in the region was apparent with these housing operations. After 1935, almost ten new settlements that had been abandoned after the Armenian and Kurdish deportations were constructed for Balkan immigrants along the railways in the province **(Figure 5.5.)**[71]

Figure 5.5. *Villages in which new rural settlements were built from 1934 to 1936 along the railway lines in Elazığ.*[72]

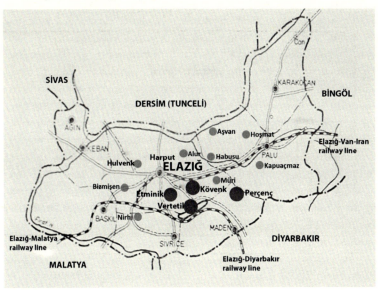

---

69   'Şarımızda Olup Bitenler: İskan İşleri', *Altan*, Temmuz 1935, 10.

70   'Şarımızda Olup Bitenler: Tapuda', *Altan*, Aralık 1935, 9, 12 (p. 9).

71   *Cumhurluk Devrinde Elaziz, İl ve İlçelerde Bayındırlık İşleri* (Ankara: Resimli Ay Basımevi, 1935).

72   Drawn after *Köy Envanter Raporlarına Göre Elazığ*, 13.

Rural settlements, including "Hölvenk (or Hulvenk) with 80 houses, Bizmişen (or Pazmaşen) with 80 houses, Etminik with 89 houses, Vertetil with 18 houses, Habusu (or Habusi) with 26 houses, Kövenk (or Hövenk) with 21 houses, Alur with 21 houses, Şerusi with 11 houses, Müri with 18 houses, Kuyuk with 20 houses",[73] were built for the incomers. According to an official document from 1935, another settlement with 26 houses was built in Perçenç for the immigrants.[74] In Etminik a village school with two classrooms, in Bizmişen a village school with one classroom, in Habusu a village school with one classroom, and in Vertetil a village school with two classrooms, were constructed together with the village houses.[75] This program of building schools demonstrated that educating the settlers was as crucial as housing them in the planned settlements.

The rural settlements constructed in Elazığ after the 1934 Settlement Law were mostly incomplete housing areas in abandoned villages that were first reconstructed for the Balkan incomers and deported population in 1934. However, the 1924 Village Law, which essentially determined the spatial organization and administration of the rural settlements, was not applied in all of the villages in Elazığ.[76] The rural settlements were constructed without a large-scale plan. On the other hand, the housing typologies varied and differed from the examples of other housing programs in the western part of the country.

In Kövenk (Güntaşı), 26 houses were constructed. The houses were 28m² (7mx4m) one-storey semi-detached buildings in a 300m² garden, and they consisted of two rooms and an interior barn with a small porch at the entrance. The construction material was adobe and the houses were covered by flat mud roofs. Although the building material and techniques were local and traditional, the rectangular form of the houses and white-washed walls evoked a modernized landscape.

The houses in Vertetil (Yazıkonak), Etminik (Altınçevre) and Perçenç (Akçakiraz) differed from other rural dwelling programs in the country. In Vertetil, the state built 18 two-storey masonry single houses,[77] which had

73   "Elaziz Vilayetinin Bayındırlık İşleri," 6.

74   Cumhurluk Devrinde Elaziz, İl ve İlçelerde Bayındırlık İşleri.

75   "Elaziz Vilayetinin Bayındırlık İşleri," 6.

76   According to the General Inspectorares Conference reports, in 1936 there were 1,050 villages associated with the cities of Elazığ, Bingol and Tunceli, which were under the control of 4. General Inspectorate. In 314 villages the 1924 Village Law was still not applied. Varlık and Koçak, p. 357.

77   "Elaziz Vilayetinin Bayındırlık İşleri," 6.

48m² (8.7mx5.5m) floor space in a 500m² garden. Between each housing plot was a 10-metre space where a garden wall was built. The houses were located facing each other and framing a 10-metre-wide street. Although there were fewer houses in Vertetil than in other settlements, the organization of houses clearly represented a modernist perspective in the rural environment **(Figure 5.6)**.[78]

Figure 5.6. *Settlement in Vertetil (Yazikonak), 1935, under construction.*[79]

The houses consisted of two separate rooms and two halls. On the ground floor, there was one room and a large entrance hall where the timber stairs were located. On the first floor, there was another hall and one room. It was also intended to add a balcony facing the street that could be reached from the hall in the first floor. However, the balcony was not put in place and later this area was filled in. The construction material was brick and timber, which was also used on the floor and roof. In the garden there was a cubicle for bathing and a toilet.

The Etminik settlement, the construction of which started in the early 1930s, was one of the largest operations in Elazığ.[80] Eighty-nine two-storey masonry single houses were built in Etminik, following the same typology as the dwellings in Vertetil. Likewise, the houses were located on a 40.5m² (9mx4.5m) floor space, with one room and an entrance hall on the ground floor and one room and a living area on the first floor connected by the timber stairs. Brick and timber were used in the construction **(Figure 5.7)**.[81]

---

78   Naşit Hakkı Uluğ, *Tunceli Medeniyete Açılıyor* (İstanbul: Cumhuriyet Matbaası, 1939), 168.

79   *Cumhurluk Devrinde Elaziz, İl ve İlçelerde Bayındırlık İşleri.*

80   "Şarımızda Olup Bitenler: İskanda," 10; "Elaziz Vilayetinin Bayındırlık İşleri," 6.

81   *Cumhurluk Devrinde Elaziz, İl ve İlçelerde Bayındırlık İşleri.*

Figure 5.7. *Settlement in Etminik (Altınçevre), 1935.* [82]

Figure 5.8. *Settlement in Perçenç (Akçakiraz), built in 1935.* [83]

On the other hand, in Perçenç (Akçakiraz) the housing was slightly different from the dwellings in Etminik and Vertetil. The houses were constructed as two-storey semi-detached masonry buildings. Each house had 35m² (7.8mx4.5m) of floor space. The interior organization was the same as

---

82   Ibid.
83   Ibid.

the dwellings in Vertetil and Etminik villages; the entrance hall and one room were on the ground floor, and on the first floor was a living space consisting of a hall and a room. The timber stairs ensured circulation between the floors. The construction material was brick and timber. According to the photographs taken at the construction site, the housing plots were clearly designated. However, information about the measurements was not included in the official documents.[84] **(Figure 5.8)**

The Clash of Turkification and Planning: An Interpretation of the Rural Settlements of the Early Republic

The state authorities' intentions for the village community and the rural population, starting from the early years of the republican regime, were varied. The projects aimed to develop the country by fostering rural life in its sociocultural, economic, and national aspects. Nevertheless, the spatial programs, which were physical extensions of these motives, *de facto* formed the rural landscape of Anatolia. In other words, these operations developed an architectural culture in the countryside, with a powerful impact on the Turkish village, for which there had been no precedent.

Before 1930 these projects were a response to critical post-war conditions: the incomers from former Ottoman terrains in the Balkans urgently needed to be housed, and the reconstruction of the built environment for the locals arose as another obligation for the state. On the other hand, the population of the villages and small towns were the majority of the country. The new settlers were also small farmers and peasants who were associated with the rural community in their lands of origin. Indeed, during the first years of the republic, the village evolved into the nucleus of the country.

Although the insufficiency of infrastructure in the cities and in the rural areas was a tremendous obstacle for the new programs, legislation for the village community became the major concern. Therefore, the 1924 Village Law was enacted by the government even earlier than other critical laws such as the first Settlement Law in 1926 and the Municipalities Law in 1930. The Village Law

---

84   In Perçenç, today's Akçakiraz, from the republican settlement only one house has remained to enable a historic architectonic analysis. However, the plot, comprising the house and the garden, has mostly been altered by the settlers. Therefore, information about the measurements of housing site is missing.

identified the village as the communal and spatial midpoint of Turkey and as an administrative unit of the new secular state. It was one of the first modernizing attempts that resulted in planning, and hence reconstruction, of the existing villages and the formation of new settlements. The 1924 Village Law introduced the fundamental idea for the building program required for Turkey's new villages. The government produced settlement plans and housing typologies, and constructed "exemplar villages", based on this law, paving the way for a significant phase in the transformation of the appearance of rural Turkey as well as the questioning of village architectural planning during the early republican period.

In 1930 the single-party government of the RPP reinforced the political power of the Kemalist regime. In addition to administrative and regulatory operations, the republican state had an important impact in the economic and socio-cultural fields. These two facts changed the development of rural settlements, especially from the early 1930s: starting from mid-1920s the Kurdish conflict prompted the state to use force against any social and political resistance in the country. In the 1930s the strength of state's authority and its self-confidence developed into the formula with which the theme of nationalization (read as Turkification) was materialized and systematically introduced. Involving all agents of the government, the regime bridged the modernization program to the demographic program, which also included Turkish-speaking people from eastern Europe.

The second settlement law, enacted in 1934, briefly and clearly addressed instructions for the legal and spatial organization of the demographic engineering that the regime decisively engaged in during the 1930s and 1940s. The implementation of the 1934 Settlement Law shaped the population in the countryside as well as the rural built environment by producing the new form of the Turkish village. The law was primarily directed at housing settlers within a state-determined framework in accordance with national characteristics – simply defined as Turkish folks and non-Turkish folks. Secondly, the settlement law assisted the application of the 1924 Village Law on a broader scale in rural areas. And finally, the 1934 law guided the building of new rural settlements and the housing of people in these new habitations.[85]

During the implementation of the 1934 Settlement Law, Balkan immigrants played a critical role in population planning. Since the 19th century Turkey had

---

85   According to the documents introduced above, until the early 1940s new settlements and rural dwellings were under construction in several provinces of Turkey.

been confronted with movements of people as refugees and exchanged populations. After the Balkan Wars, the First World War, and the Greco-Turkish War,
and up until early 1920s, the migration of masses occurred within the circumstances of war. However, during the 1930s the state undoubtedly encouraged
Turkish-speaking people from Bulgaria, Yugoslavia, and Romania to come to
the country, particularly within the scope of 1934 Settlement Law.

As emphasized in the 1934 Settlement Law, the Turkish language was the
most important instrument for identifying the Turkish nation and melting
all ethnicities into the same pot. Therefore, the state considered Balkan immigrants, who had spoken Turkish in their origin countries, as key to the
demographic program to unite rural folks under Turkishness. Beside the national codes, Turco–Yugoslavians, Turco–Romanians and Turco–Bulgarians
were principally accustomed to rural tradition as peasants and farmers in
their homelands. In fact, they were better oriented in agricultural production
and small manufacturing than the locals.

For these reasons, the Kemalist regime acknowledged Balkan immigrants
as "loyal" and "hardworking" people who assisted in modernizing and nationalizing the country. This viewpoint – that the state regarded them as model citizens for a developing Turkey – prompted large-scale efforts in the planning of
new rural settlements and dwellings, providing agrarian land and equipment,
preparing them for agricultural production, and consolidating Turkishness in
the countryside via a majority of Turkish-speaking settlers.

Moreover, the 1934 Settlement Law legitimated and regulated the deportation of Kurds in the eastern provinces to western Anatolia. Erik Jan Zürcher
introduces the diaries of German travelers Lilo Linke, Robert Anhegger and
Andreas Tietze, who witnessed the deportation of people from Dersim to Afyonkarahisar and Aydın in 1937 after the revolt. They had been told to where they
were to be deported by state officials in the train station. The party came across
another group when they arrived in Aydın. The travelers depicted the scene:
"They are simply removed from there and distributed over the country. They are
then dumped anywhere, without a roof over their head or employment. They
do not know a single word of Turkish".[86] In accordance with the law they would
be settled together with Turkish-speaking folks and finally Turkified. Supporting these narratives, in 1938 *La Turquie Kemaliste* – a state-promoted journal –

---

86   Zürcher, 'Two Young Ottomanists Discover Kemalist Turkey: The Travel Dairies of
      Robert Anhegger and Andreas Tietze', pp. 368–69.

announced that in the new rural settlements people from the eastern provinces were settled together with Balkan immigrants.[87] **(Figure 5.9)**

Figure 5.9. *The photograph, on the left, was seen in the journal La Turquie Kemaliste with the title "Young immigrants preparing to milk their cows".[88] The photograph, on the right, was published in the book Tunceli Medeniyete Açılıyor (Tunceli is developing towards civilization) with the title of "An immigrant from Rumelia Turks, settled in Elazığ's lowlands".[89]*

The settlement policies, which evolved into not only the case for building new village communities but also for relocating people according to a demographic scheme, gives the topic a geographical focus. Thus, the introduction of new rural settlements in İzmir and Elazığ become critical to understanding the discussion, especially in a political climate in which the Interior Minister Şükrü Kaya argued the need to "separate the country into west and east" to accomplish the national, socio-cultural and economic program of the state.[90]

The methods the state adopted in the housing operations were compatible to each other in the whole country: the settlements were organized by the local governors and the settlers labored at the construction site. They were equipped

---

87   "L'Immigration En Turquie."
88   'Ibid, p. 16.
89   Uluğ, *Tunceli Medeniyete Açılıyor*, 168.
90   "TBMM Zabıt Ceridesi, IV. Dönem, 3. Devre (TBMM Journal of Official Report, Period IV, Session 3)," 139. Quoted from Üngör, p. 149.

by the government with agricultural instruments, land, farming animals, and seed to plant. However, major differences occurred in the various settlements that reflected differences in on-site plans, housing typologies, and organization of the construction.

From this point of view, the programs in İzmir were influential for the circumstances of the larger region. The city had been urbanized since the late Ottoman period. The trade tradition and infrastructure had been ruled city life for a long time, and the agricultural facilities in the rural areas were much more developed than in the eastern part of Anatolia. Thus, starting from the early years of the republic, İzmir promised a strong potential for the development plan of the country. The deportation of the Greek and Armenian populations and the Great Fire of İzmir in 1922 demolished city life, and the Greco-Turkish war also overwhelmed the rural towns and villages at the beginning of 1920s. There was therefore a need for city development as well as rehabilitation of the rural areas.[91]

During the first years, population exchange largely influenced the settlement operations, and the state mostly used abandoned villages and houses to accommodate the incoming people. However, the practices associated with the 1934 Settlement Law included the rural districts in the demographic plan as well as the housing of Turkish-speaking immigrants in the region. The most significant characteristic of the programs in İzmir was the use of infrastructure in rural areas that had been constructed by foreign allies since the late 19th century. This enabled a settlement planning in which modernist features like wide regular streets, determined building plots, water infrastructure, and an extended building program were achieved in the new villages.

Nevertheless, Elazığ – a city in eastern Anatolia, which witnessed the deportation of the Armenians and Kurds during the First World War – started to develop in a "republican" manner from the 1920s. Especially in the 1930s, the state definitively implemented its spatial agents and formed a rigid administration in the province. The city was overseen by the general inspector and governor during the 1930s. In Elazığ the state put a great effort into economic and social improvement projects and continued to develop transportation, particularly to facilitate the mobility of the military in this region. Railroads, highways, and bridges were prominent on the government's agenda, with the city

---

91   Orhan Özcan, 'İngiliz Basınında İzmir Yangını ve Mülteci Sorunu (Eylül 1922)', *Çağdaş Türkiye Tarihi Araştırmaları Dergisi*, 15.31 (2015), 177–200.

emerging as the symbolic, administrative, bureaucratic, and military basis of the state in the east.[92]

The city and the countryside did not have determined spatial borders in Elazığ. First, the center was furnished with features of the republican urban program, such as a public square and park, large boulevards, running water infrastructure, Girls' Institute, People's House, new municipality and theatre, hospital, and so on. Urbanization was attempted on the micro-scale, but an urban planning project for the whole city and its hinterland was not completed during the 1930s and 1940s. Similar to the republican program that transformed the city center, rural Elazığ changed with the application of the 1934 Settlement Law that resulted in the deportation of Kurds from the region and the transportation of Balkan immigrant into the villages and new settlements. Thus, both the city architecture and rural development evolved into powerful tools for the regime's propaganda in the region.

The images of new settlements in Elazığ dramatically illustrate the contrasting panorama between the landscape, which was still untouched, tough, and wild, and the "extremely" modern village houses, which were more improved and articulated than those in the western provinces. In other words, the village houses, and their arrangements as new rural settlements in Elazığ were not only architectonic components of the built environment, but also the greatest agents of the state in transforming the country to consolidate and maintain political stability, and to concentrate on one "harmonic" nation by shaping it within the framework of Kemalist ideology.

The "republican villages", which were created during the 1930s and elaborated during the 1940s, evolved into a micro-cosmos of the Kemalist regime negotiating with rural Anatolia. They were specifically formed and planned, and were important to the economic, socio-cultural, and national agenda of state. They became significant components of an idealized land to demonstrate a particular rural built environment, to nurture devoted citizens, and finally to

---

92   Zeynep Kezer emphasizes that Turkey's first military airport was built in Elazığ in 1940, making the province the nucleus of the state in the east. Kezer, 'Spatializing Difference', p. 517. For further reading on how Elazığ was transformed into a state's secure-space and its reflection on the entanglements of rural hertitage, see also Özge Sezer, "Contectualization, Realization, and Contestation of the Village: Inheriting from Early Republican Elazığ, Turkey" pp.183-196, in Praktiken des Erbes. Metaphern, Materialisierungen, Machtkonstellationen, Schriftenreihe des DFG-Graduiertenkollegs "Identität und Erbe", Band III, ed. Simone Bogner et.al (Weimar: Bauhaus Universitätsverlag, 2022).

serve a "harmonic" nation adapted to the political authority. Analyzing these forms through a historiography of the Early Republican Period uncovers another layer of this complex narrative and presents clear motivations for an instrumentalized architecture in the countryside of Turkey.

Conclusion

Yaşar Kemal starts his masterpiece Memed, My Hawk with a sharp description of the rural landscape of Anatolia. He romantically describes the landscape through the Taurus Mountains rising from the Mediterranean coast "covered with a tangle of brushwood, reeds, blackberry brambles, wild vines, and rushes, its deep green expanse seems boundless, wilder and darker than a forest."[1] Yet, when the story continues, he dramatically portrays a picture of the Turkish village and villagers still grappling with poverty and social underdevelopment after more than 30 years of republican rule. Kemal's novel, based on an insider's observation of a village community, shows the impact of the early republican deal, which often emphasized modernizing and nationalizing the country rather than the actual needs and problems of the rural community. Moreover, this book intends to unfold different layers of nation-building and modernization endeavors in Turkey during the early republic by addressing this disconnection between the government and the governed society via village planning. Therefore, the research concentrated on clarifying relevant facts through the historiography of early republican village planning, highlighting the argument in a spatial context, and considering the theme in different geographical, cultural, social, and economic circumstances. At the beginning of the studies for this book, other rural settlement implementations were trialed in various locations for possible consideration. Many of these rural settlements have disappeared due to uncontrolled urbanization approaching rural areas, the underdevelopment of the settlements, and/or the state's larger projects.

The cases of İzmir and Elazığ presented here have been chosen among because they allowed an architectural investigation followed by an architectural documentation. Yeniköy Village especially retains the original form of the republican settlement in its site organization and houses. This settlement gen-

---

1   Yaşar Kemal, Memed, My Hawk, 3.

erated a sample of the "modern Turkish village" after the construction of other buildings such as a school, gendarmerie, public park, nursery, and shops. On the other hand, in Havuzbaşı and Taşkesik villages the settlements have been reformed due to the contemporary needs of the village community, and the houses have been modified by the residents themselves.

According to official documents, ten new settlements were built in Elazığ during the 1930s. However, today only four of these survive in the neighborhoods of (Kövenk) Güntaşı, (Vertetil) Yazıkonak, (Etminik) Altınçevre, (Perçenç) Akçakiraz, along with the houses built in the former republican settlements. Most of the rural settlements were demolished following uncontrolled growth after the population flow from neighbouring provinces in the 1950s. Some of them were submerged due to construction of the Water Reservoir of Keban Dam, starting in 1966. Today, the best-preserved settlement is located in Yazıkonak district – the former Vertetil Village – where it still displays the characteristics of the original settlement.

Residents of the planned rural settlements built in the 1930s in İzmir and Elazığ express a common feeling of nostalgia for the history of the adaptation period to their new "homeland". In İzmir, Yeniköy, Havuzbaşı and Taşkesik, the whole immigration story – from leaving the land of origin to landing and settling into Turkey – has been told to residents by preceding generations in the form of significant personal memoirs. Most of them referred to the settlements as "Atatürk's Villages", even promoting the "heroic-character" of the founder and the first president of Turkey. Current residents show a great respect and nostalgia towards the early republican programs as they gave them "a house to sleep in, bread to eat, animal and land to survive" in this particular brand new place. In other words, they carry the immigration story with them and add the bond with the new home as their "national" origin place.

In Elazığ today's residents acquaint themselves with the early republican implementations in their villages. However, many settlers who were housed in these settlements in 1930s moved to the western provinces, starting in the 1950s. The people who remained there narrate how their ancestors struggled to survive in the harsh land, which was much less fertile than that of their countries of origin. And they state that their ancestors, most of the time, taught them how to cultivate the land and animals with the new techniques of the locals. Those who left reunited with their relatives in the western provinces where the soil and climate were more similar to their home countries.

The rural settlements, constructed in the early republican period of Turkey, had a great impact on the rural landscape by changing the physical environment and relocating people. From the 1930s they became models of Kemalist interventions, of which the consequences and traces are still observable in the countryside. They were elaborated as particular forms to generate the modern Turkish village in accordance with the socio-cultural, economic, and demographic programs in which the regime often sought a formula through regulations, legislative instructions, specific associations, and actors, and building practices aiming to re-shape rural Turkey.

Starting from the early republican period, methods to reform the countryside have been altered by different governments under different ideologies in Turkey's political milieu, while the rural population – still the largest group in the country – has remained underprivileged. Up until the 1980s the focus of the state remained on the rural population, despite the urbanization of Turkey that gradually started in the 1950s. In other words, Turkey witnessed the instrumentalization of rural people for political purposes for a long time in its history. In this regard, villages built during the early republic have maintained a critical position in the maneuvers that regimes have usually negotiated between the consolidation of political power and the community in rural Turkey.

These specific settlements have emerged as representative sites to comprehend the profound strategies of the state legitimation practices that still affect the lives in the social, economic, and cultural spheres. Their values in architecture and planning correspond with the modernist aesthetic and technique while becoming examples of places to build a controlled environment that appears to be prevalent among authoritarian regimes even today. Consequently, the documentation of *Forming the Modern Turkish Village* discloses another vein of the architectural history of early republican Turkey and contributes to an interdisciplinary observation field by suggesting a critical reading for idealized rural Turkey, its history, and its people.

Literature

30 Nisan 329 tarihli iskan-ı muhacirin talimatnemesini değiştiren nizamnamenin yürürlüğe konması, TCBCA 030.18.01/04.55.2 § (1913).

Cumhuriyet. "50.000 Göçmen Için Trakya'da Hep Bir Tip Evler Yaptırılıyor (For 50.000 Immigrants Prototype Houses Are Being Constructed in Trace)." May 29, 1935.

Cumhuriyet. "50.000 Göçmenin Anayurda Nakli, Bu İşlerle Uğraşacak Bir Komisyon Kuruldu (Transporting 50.000 Immigrants into the Homeland, A Commission Has Been Established for the Operation)." May 13, 1935.

Cumhuriyet. "50.000 Muhacir Gelecek (50.000 Immigrants Will Come)." July 10, 1934.

1935 20 İlkteşrin Genel Nüfus Sayımı; Türkiye Nüfusu, Vilayet, Kaza, Şehir ve Köyler İtibarile Muvakkat Rakamlar – Population de La Turquie 20 Octobre-1935 Recensement General de La Population Par Provinces, Districts, Villes et Villages, Chiffes Provisoires. Başvekalet Devlet İstatistik Genel Müdürlüğü 74. Ankara: Ulus Basımevi, 1935.

Adiv, M. Uriel. "Richard Kauffmann (1887–1958): Das Architektonische Gesamtwerk." Dissertation, Technische Universität Berlin: Fachbereich 8 Architektur, 1985.

Afetinan, A. Medeni bilgiler ve M. Kemal Atatürk'ün el yazıları. Ankara: Türk Tarih Kurumu Basimevi, 1998.

Ağaoğlu, Ahmet. Serbest Fırka Hatıraları. 3. bs. İletişim Yayınları Anı Dizisi, 253 15. İstanbul: İletişim, 1994.

Ahmad, Feroz. From Empire to Republic: Essays on the Late Ottoman Empire and Modern Turkey. 1st ed. İstanbul Bilgi University Press; History 218–219. 25–26. İstanbul: İstanbul Bilgi University Press, 2008.

Akçam, Taner. The Young Turks' Crime Against Humanity: The Armenian Genocide and Ethnic Cleansing in the Ottoman Empire. Human Rights and Crimes against Humanity. Princeton, N.J.: Princeton University Press, 2012.

Akçura, Yusuf. "Halka." *Halka Doğru* I (1930).

———. *Yeni Türk Devletinin Öncüleri: 1928 Yılı Yazıları*. Ankara: Kültür Bakanlığı, 1981.

Akkaya, Serpil. *Sumerer, Hethiter und Trojaner – Urahnen der anatolischen Türken? Eine rezeptionsgeschichtliche Betrachtung der Rolle antiker Kulturen in den Identitätskonzeptionen der Atatürk'schen Reformpolitik*. 1. Aufl. Thesis series. Innsbruck: Innsbruck Univ. Press, 2012.

Aksakal, Mustafa. *The Ottoman Road to War in 1914: The Ottoman Empire and the First World War*. Cambridge Military Histories. Cambridge, UK; New York: Cambridge University Press, 2008.

Akşin, Sina. *Jön Türkler ve İttihat ve Terrakki*. 5. Baskı. İstanbul: İmge Kitabevi, 2014.

Akyol, Yaşar. *İzmir Halkevi (1932–1951)*. Kent Kitaplığı Dizisi 60. İzmir: İzmir Büyükşehir Belediyesi, 2008.

Ankara Halkevi. "Birkaç Söz." In *Küçükyozgat Köyü: Köy Tetkiki*, 3–4. Ankara Halkevi Neşriyatı Köycüler Şubesi 17/2. Ankara: Ankara Halkevi, 1936.

Arı, Kemal. *Büyük Mübadele: Türkiye'ye Zorunlu Göç, 1923–1925*. Türkiye Araştırmaları 17. İstanbul: Tarih Vakfı Yurt Yayınları, 1995.

Atatürk. *Atatürk'ün söylev ve demeçleri: açıklamalı dizin ile*. Ankara: Atatürk Araştırma Merkezi, 2006.

Atatürk, Mustafa Kemal. *1 İkinci Teşrin 1936'da Atatürk'ün Kamutay'daki Nutku*. T.C. Trakya Umumi Müfettişliği Köy Bürosu 40. İstanbul: Halk Basımevi, 1937.

———. *Atatürk'ün Söylev ve Demeçleri: I-III*. Ankara: Atatürk Araştırma Merkezi, 2006.

———. *Nutuk, 1919–1927: Tam Metin*. Edited by Mustafa Bayram Mısır. Ankara: Palme Yayınları;, 2010.

———. *Hâkimiyeti Milliye*. ubat 1931.

Atay, Cınar. *Osmanlı'dan Cumhuriyet'e İzmir Planları*. İzmir: Yaşar Eğitim ve Kültür Vakfı, 1998.

Atilla, A. Nedim. *İzmir Demiryolları*. 1. Basım. Kent Kitaplığı Dizisi 36. İzmir: İzmir Büyükşehir Belediyesi Kültür Yayını, 2002.

Atkinson, Tacy. *"The German, the Turk and the Devil Made a Triple Alliance": Harpoot Diaries, 1908 – 1917*. Armenian Genocide Documentation Series. Princeton, NJ: Gomidas Inst, 2000.

(Aydemir), Şevket Süreyya. *İnkılâp ve Kadro: İnkılâbın Ideolojisi*. Ankara: Muallim Ahmet Halit Kitaphanesi, 1932.

"Aydın Vilayet Salnamesi," 1893.

"Aydın Vilayeti Salnamesi," 1889.

"Aydın Vilayeti Salnamesi," 1891.

"Aydın Vilayeti Salnamesi," 1894.

"Aydın Vilayeti Salnamesi," 1896.

"Aydın Vilayeti Salnamesi," 1908.

Bali, Rıfat. *1934 Trakya Olayları*. 11. Baskı. Libra Tarih Dizisi 54–43. İstanbul: Libra, 2014.

———. *"Azınlıkları Türkleştirme Meselesi": Ne Idi? Ne Değildi?* 1. Baskı. Tarih Dizisi 93. İstanbul: Libra, 2014.

Baltacıoğlu, İsmail Hakkı. *Edebiyatta Türk'e Doğru, Türk'e Doğru*. Ankara: Atatürk Kültür, Dil, Tarih Yüksek Kurumu, 1994.

———. *Millet Nedir?, Türk'e Doğru*. Ankara: Atatürk Kültür, Dil, Tarih Yüksek Kurumu, 1994.

———. *Milleti Anla!, Türk'e Doğru*. Ankara: Atatürk Kültür, Dil, Tarih Yüksek Kurumu, 1994.

———. *Problemler, Türk'e Doğru*. Ankara: Atatürk Kültür, Dil, Tarih Yüksek Kurumu, 1994.

Bartal, Israel. "Farming the Land on Three Continents: Bilu, Am Oylom, and Yefe-Nahar." *Jewish History* 21, no. 3/4 (2007): 249–61.

Bartók, Béla. *Küçük asya'dan türk halk musıkisi*. Translated by Bülent Aksoy. Pan Yayıncılık 16. İstanbul: Pan Yayıncılık, 1991.

Başgöz, Ilhan. *Türkiye'nin eğitim çıkmazı ve Atatürk*. Istanbul: Pan, 2005.

Bayar, Yeşim. *Formation of the Turkish Nation-State, 1920–1938*. New York, NY: Palgrave Macmillan, 2014.

Bayrak, Mehmet. "'Şark Islahat Planı' ve TC'nin Kürt Politikası." In *Resmi Tarih Tartışmaları 6: Resmi Tarihte Kürt'ler*, 389–94. Özgür Üniversite Kıtaplığı 76. Ankara: Makı, 2009.

Bediz, Danyal. "Izmir (Smyrna); Und Sein Wirtschaftsgeographisches Einzugsgebiet." Dissertation, Ludwig-Maximilians-Universität München, 1935.

Beer, M. "Introduction." In *The Pioneers of Land Reform*. London, UK: G. Bell & Sons, 1920.

Berkes, Niyazi. "Translator's Introduction." In *Turkish Nationalism and Western Civilization: Selected Essays of Ziya Gökalp*, by Zıya Gökalp. New York: Columbia University Press, 1959.

———. *Türkiye'de çağdaşlaşma*. Edited by Ahmet Kuyaş. 7. baskı. Yapı Kredi yayınları Cogito, 1713 117. İstanbul: Yapı Kredi Yayınları, 2005.

Berman, Marshall. *All That Is Solid Melts into Air, The Experience of Modernity*. London, UK: Penguin Books, 1988.

Anadolu. "Beş Yıllık Köy Kalkınma Programımızda Köy Mekteplerinin Tamamlanması İşi Başta Gelmektedir." January 17, 1937.

Bilsel, Cana. "Ideology and Planning During the Early Republican Period: Two Master Plans for Izmir and Scenarios of Modernization." *METU Journal of Faculty of Architecture* 16, no. 1–2 (1996): 13–30.

———. "İzmir'de Cumhuriyet Dönemi Planlaması (1923–1965): 20. Yüzyıl Kentsel Mirası." *Ege Mimarlık* 71, no. 4 (2009): 12–17.

———. "Le Corbusier'nin İzmir Nazım Planı ve 'Yeşil Endüstri Sitesi' Önerisi." *Ege Mimarlık* 31, no. 3 (1999): 13–17.

"Birinci Köy Kalkınma Kongresi Komisyonlar Mazbatası." Ankara: TBMM, 1938. 75–920. TBMM Kütüphanesi.

Birinci Köy ve Ziraat Kalkınma Kongresi: Belgeler. Ankara: T.C. Ziraat Vekaleti, 1938.

Birinci Köy ve Ziraat Kalkınma Kongresi Yayını: Türk Ziraat Tarihine Bir Bakış. İstanbul: Devlet Basımevi, 1938.

Bozdoğan, Sibel. *Modernism and Nation Building: Turkish Architectural Culture in the Early Republic*. Studies in Modernity and National Identity. Seattle: University of Washington Press, 2001.

Breuilly, John. *Nationalism and the State*. 2nd ed. Manchester: Manchester University Press, 1993.

Bulut, Engin, Çağdaş. "Devletin Taşradaki Eli: Umumi Müfettişlikler." *Cumhuriyet Tarihi Araştırmaları Dergisi* 11, no. 21 (Bahar 2015) (2015): 83–110.

Bulut, Faik. *Dersim Raporları: İnceleme*. 3. Basım. Evrensel Basım Yayın Kürt Tarihi ve Kültürü Dizisi 281–14. İstanbul: Evrensel, 2005.

Burchardt, Jeremy. "Agricultural History, Rural History, or Countryside History?" *Cambridge University Press* 50, no. 2 (Jun., 2007) (2007): 465–81. http://www.jstor.org/stable/4140139 .

———. "Editorial: Rurality, Modernity and National Identity between Wars." *Cambridge University Press*, Rural History, 21, no. 2 (2010): 143–50.

Burnett, John. "Introduction." In *Change in the Village*. Dover, N.H: Caliban Books, 1984.

Büyük Türk Cumhuriyetimizin On Yılında Elaziz'de İktisadi Umran ve Refah Adımları. Elaziz: Sinan Matbaası, 1933.

Caferoğlu, Ahmet. *Anadolu Dialektolojisi Üzerine Malzeme I: Balıkesir, Manisa, Afyonkarahisar, Isparta, Aydın, İzmir, Burdur, Antalya, Muğla, Denizli, Kütahya Vi-*

layetleri Ağızları. Edebiyat Fakültesi Dil Seminerleri 105. İstanbul: İstanbul Üniversitesi Yayınları, 1940.

Çağlar, Kerim, Ömer. *Yüksek Ziraat Enstitüsü: Kanunlar, Kararnameler, Bütçe ve Talimatnameler*. T.C. Yüksek Ziraat Enstitüsü Neşriyatı 101. Ankara: Yüksek Ziraat Enstitüsü Basımevi, 1940.

Can Bilsel, S. M. "'Our Anatolia': Organicism And The Making Of Humanist Culture In Turkey." In *Muqarnas, Volume 24 Muqarnas, Volume 24 History and Ideology: Architectural Heritage of the "Lands of Rum,"* edited by Gülru Necipoglu Bozdoğan, 223–42. Brill Academic Publishers, 2007. https://doi.org/10.116 3/ej.9789004163201.i-310.39.

Çeçen, Anıl. *Atatürk'ün Kültür Kurumu Halkevleri*. Cağaloğlu, İstanbul: Cumhuriyet Kitapları, 2000.

Cengizkan, Ali. "Cumhuriyet Döneminde Kırsal Yerleşim Sorunları: Ahi Mes'ud Numune Köyü." *Arredomento Mimarlık*, no. 06 (2004): 110–19.

———. *Mübadele Konut ve Yerleşimleri*. 1. baskı. Ankara: Orta Doğu Teknik Üniversitesi, Mimarlık Fakültesi, 2004.

Çetin, Sıdıka. "Erken Cumhuriyet Döneminde Köyün Modernizasyonu, Örnek Köyler Üzerinden Okuma." *Arredomento Mimarlık*, no. 6 (2003): 99–105.

Çetin, Türkan. "1929 Dünya Ekonomik Bunalimi Sonrası Türkiye'nin Tarım Politikasında Arayışlar: Birinci Türkiye Ziraat Kongresi." *DEÜ Atatürk İlkeleri ve İnkılap Tarihi Enstitüsü Çağdaş Türkiye Tarihi Araştırmaları Dergisi 2*, no. 6–7 (1996): 213–26.

———. "Cumhuriyet Döneminde Köycülük Politikaları: Köye Doğru Hareketi." In *75 Yılda Köylerden Şehirlere*, 213–30. Bilanço' 98 Yayın Dizisi. Istanbul: Türkiye Ekonomik ve Toplumsal Tarih Vakfı, 1999.

Christensen, Peter H. *Germany and the Ottoman Railways: Art, Empire, and Infrastructure*. New Haven: Yale University Press, 2017.

Çiftçiyi Topraklandırma Kanunu, Pub. L. No. 4753 (1945). http://www.resmiga zete.gov.tr/arsiv/6032.pdf.

Cumhuriyet Halk Partisi Onbeşinci Yıl Kıtabı. Ankara: TBMM, 1938.

Cumhurluk Devrinde Elaziz, İl ve İlçelerde Bayındırlık İşleri. Ankara: Resimli Ay Basımevi, 1935.

Dewey, John. *Türkiye Maarifi Hakkında Rapor*. Edited by Hasan Ali Yücel. T.C. Maarif Vekilliği, Ana Programa Hazırlıklar, B.1. Istanbul: Devlet Basımevi, 1939. http://hdl.handle.net/11543/928.

Altan. "Dil, Edebiyat, Tarih Komitesi," ubat 1936.

Dirik, Kazım. İdeal Cumhuriyet Köyü, TCBCA, 30.1.0.0/111.705.8 § (n.d.).

Document on Arif Hikmet Koyunoglu, TCBCA 30.18.1.1272.11/17.80.11 § (1924).

Document on Building Cottages in Adana, TCBCA 30.18.1.1/10.42.16 § (1924).

Document on Building Cottages in Kozan, Adana, TCBCA 272.80/3.7.24 § (1924).

Document on Building Houses for Immigrants in Adana, TCBCA 272.80/3.6.1. § (1924).

Document on Building Low-cost Houses in Bursa, TCBCA 272.80/3.8.13 § (1925).

Document on Building Villages in Izmit, TCBCA 272.80/3.6.9. § (1924).

Document on Canik, Aksarağaç, Ökse, Çınarağıl, Çırağman, TCBCA 272.11/18.87.7 § (1924).

Document on Canik, Aksarağaç, Ökse, Çınarağıl, Çırağman, 272.80/4.10.15 § (1925).

Document on Canik, Aksarağaç, Ökse, Çınarağıl, Çırağman, TCBCA 30.18.1.1/12.70.1-1 § (1925).

Document on Canik, Aksarağaç, Ökse, Çınarağıl, Çırağman, TCBCA 272.11/21.103.15 § (1925).

Document on Canik, Aksarağaç, Ökse, Çınarağıl, Çırağman, TCBCA 272.80/4.10.9 § (1925).

Document on Canik, Aksarağaç, Ökse, Çınarağıl, Çırağman, TCBCA 030.18.01/017.94.2 § (1926).

Document on Canik, Aksarağaç, Ökse, Çınarağıl, Çırağman, Pub. L. No. 18.01.1925, TCBCA 30.18.1.1/12.70.1-2 (n.d.).

Document on Canik, Aksarağaç, Ökse, Çınarağıl, Çırağman, Pub. L. No. 03.12.1924, TCBCA 30.18.1.1/12.58.12 (n.d.).

Document on Çirkinoba, TCBCA 30.18.1.1./12.75.13 § (1925).

Document on Etimesgut (Ahi Mes'ud), TCBCA 30.18.1.1/29.32.1 § (1928).

Document on Etimesgut (Ahi Mes'ud), TCBCA 30.18.1.1/29.35.9 § (1928).

Document on Etimesgut (Ahi Mes'ud), TCBCA 30.18.1.1/29.36.18 § (1928).

Document on Etimesgut (Ahi Mes'ud), TCBCA 30.18.1.1/30.63.9 § (1928).

Document on Etimesgut (Ahi Mes'ud), TCBCA 30.18.1.1/30.62.14. § (1928).

Document on Etımesgut (Ahi Mes'ud), TCBCA 30.18.1.1/30.61.4 § (1928).

Document on Filader, TCBCA 272.11/18.87.5 § (1924).

Document on Karacaoba and Ikizceoba, TCBCA 30.18.1.1/12.59.9 § (1924).

Document on Kıyas and Çobanisa, TCBCA 30.18.1.1/12.59.12 § (1924).

Document on Madama, TCBCA 272.80/3.6.14 § (1924).

Document on Malıköy, TCBCA 30.18.1.1/02.10.27.11 § (1930).

Document on New Villages along the Eskisekir-Ankara Railway line, TCBCA 30.18.1.1/28.29.12 § (1928).

Document on Samutlu, 30.18.1.1/02.13.5 § (1930).

Document on Samutlu, TCBCA 30.18.1.1/02.14.64 § (1930).

Document on Village Planning in Bursa, TCBCA 272.80/3.5.2 § (1924).

Document on Yuvanaki, TCBCA 272.80/4.10.11 § (1925).

Documents on Yuvanaki and Yumurtalık, TCBCA 272.80/3.8.2. § (1924).

Dündar, Fuat. *İttihat ve Terakki'nin Müslümanları İskân Politikası, 1913–1918*. 1. baskı. Araştırma-İnceleme Dizisi 112. Cağaloğlu, İstanbul: İletişim, 2001.

Efroymson, C.W. "Collective Agriculture in Israel." *Journal of Political Economy* 58, no. 1 (1950): 30–46.

Altan. "Elaziz Vilayetinin Bayındırlık İşleri," ubat 1937.

Elazığ-Genç Demiryolu Hattının İşletmeye Açılışı. Ankara: TCDD, 1945.

Eley, Geoff, and Ronald Grigor Suny, eds. *Becoming National: A Reader*. New York: Oxford University Press, 1996.

———. "Introduction: From the Moment of Social History to the Work of Cultural Representation." In *Becoming National: A Reader*, edited by Geoff Eley and Ronald Grigor Suny. New York: Oxford University Press, 1996.

Epikman, Refik. "Türk Ressamlarının Yurt Gezisi." *Ülkü* 21, no. Temmuz (1939): 461–62.

Erbay, Fethiye, and Mutlu Erbay. *Cumhuriyet Dönemi (1923–1938), Atatürk'ün Sanat Politikası*. 1. basım. İstanbul: Boğaziçi Üniversitesi, 2006.

Eres, Zeynep. "Erken Cumhuriyet Döneminde Çağdaş Kırsal Kimliğin Örneklenmesi: Planlı Göçmen Köyleri." *Mimarlık*, Cumhuriyet Dönemi Mimarlığı, 375, no. Ocak-Şubat (2014). http://www.mimarlikdergisi.com/index.c fm?sayfa=mimarlik&DergiSayi=389&RecID=3306.

———. "Muratlı: Bir Cumhuriyet Köyü." *Mimarlık*, Kırdan / Kentten, 386, no. Kasım-Aralık (2015). http://www.mimarlikdergisi.com/index.cfm?sayfa= mimarlik&DergiSayi=400&RecID=3798.

———. "Türkiye'de Kırsal Alanda Çağdaşlaşma ve Mübadil Köyleri." In *90. Yılında Türk-Yunan Zorunlu Nüfus Mübadelesi Sempozyumu: Yeni Yaklaşımlar, Yeni Bulgular Sempozyum Bildiri Metinleri, 16–17 Kasım 2013*, edited by Bilge Gönül, Hakan Uzbek, Sefer Güvenç, Süleyman Mazlum, and Tutku Vardağlı, 174–201. İstanbul: Lozan Mübadilleri Vakfı Yayınları, 2016.

———. "Türkiye'de Planlı Kırsal Yerleşmelerin Tarihsel Gelişimi ve Erken Cumhuriyet Dönemi Planlı Kırsal Mimarisinin Korunması Sorunu." Dissertation, Istanbul Technical University, 2008.

Ergeneli, Ahmet Hilmi. "Ergeneli to İnönü," November 10, 1934. 69.457.24. BCA.

Ersanlı, Büşra. *İktidar ve Tarih*. İletişim Yayınları 880, Araştırma İnceleme Dizisi 139. İstanbul, Turkey: İletişim Yayınları, 2003.

Etzioni, Amitai. "Agrarianism in Israel's Party System." *The Canadian Journal of Economics and Political Science / Revue Canadienne d'Economique et de Science Politique*, 23, no. 3 (1957): 363–75.

Evrenol, Malik. *Revolutionary Turkey*. Ankara: Istanbul: Librairie Hachette, 1936.

Falke, Friedrich. "Die Landwirtschaftliche Hochschule Ankara Am Schluss Ihres Zweiten Studienjahres." *La Turquie Kemaliste* 9, no. Octobre (1935): 2–9.

Fehl, Gerhard. "The Nazi Garden City." In *The Garden City: Past, Present and Future*, 88–106. London: E & FN Spon, 1992.

Figes, Orlando. "The Russian Revolution of 1917 and Its Language in the Village." *The Russian Review* 56, no. July (1997): 323–45.

Firat, Nurcan İnci. *Ankara'da Cumhuriyet Dönemi Mimarisinden İki Örnek: Etnografya Müzesi ve Eski Türk Ocağı Merkez Binası; (Devlet Resim ve Heykel Müzesi)*. 1. Baskı. T. C. Kültür Bakanlığı Yayınları Yayımlar Dairesi Başkanlığı Sanat eserleri dizisi, 2188 203. Ankara, 1998.

Frost, Ruth Sterling. "The Reclamation of the Pontine Marshes." *American Geographical Society* 24 (1934): 584–95.

"Geçen 4 Yılda Yapılan İşler." *Belediyeler Dergisi* 1, no. 6 (1936): 30–36.

Gedikler Gölgesiz, Hülya. *1950'li Yıllarda İzmir*. İzmir: Şenocak Yayınları, 2012.

Gellner, Ernest. *Thought and Change: The Nature of Human Society*. London, UK: Wiedenfeld and Nicholson, 1964.

Genel Altınkaya, Özlem. "İzmir Nazım Planı: Le Corbuiser'nin Mimarlığı'nda Mekânsal Bir Strateji Olarak Lineerlik." *Ege Mimarlık* 96, no. 2 (2017): 40–43.

Georgeon, François. *Osmanlı-Türk Modernleşmesi 1900–1930*. Translated by Ali Berktay. 2. Tarih 26. İstanbul: Yapı Kredi Yayınları, 2009.

———. *Türk milliyetçiliğinin kökenleri Yusuf Akçura: (1876–1935)*. 2. baskı. Tarih Vakfı Yurt yayınları 40. Beşiktaş, İstanbul: Tarih Vakfı Yurt Yayınları, 1996.

Gerngross, Otto. *Şarap Kurulması: Bağbozumundan İçkiyi Elde Edinceye Kadar Şarap İçin Yapılacak İşler Hakkında Çiftçiye Öğütler – Weinbereitung: Ratgeber Für Den Praktischen Landwirt Zur Richtigen Behandlung Des Weines von Der Traubenlese Bis Zum Fertigen Getränk*. Translated by Turgut Küşat. Çiftçiye Öğütler 1. Ankara: Yüksek Ziraat Enstitüsü Basımevi, 1934.

Gessner, Dieter. "Agrarian Protectionism in the Weimar Republic." *Sage Publications* 12, no. 4 (1977): 759–78.

Ghirardo, Diane Yvonne. *Building New Communities: New Deal America and Fascist Italy*. Princeton: Princeton University Press, 1989.

Giddens, Anthony. *The Consequences of Modernity*. Reprint. Cambridge: Polity Press, 2008.

Giray, Kıymet. "Örneklerle Cumhuriyet Dönemi Türk Resim Sanatı." In *Cumhuriyet Dönemi Türk Resim Sanatından Örnekler: 22 Ekim – 03 Aralık 2003 Ankara Devlet Resim ve Heykel Müzesi Sergi Kataloğu*. Ankara: TC Merkez Bankası – Kültür Bakanlığı, 2003.

———. "Yurdu Gezen Türk Ressamları-1: 1939–1944 Yurt Gezileri." *Türkiye'de Sanat* 18, no. Mart-Nisan (1995): 34–38.

Anadolu. "Göçmen Evleri." May 9, 1937.

Anadolu. "Göçmen Evleri, Bir Hafta Sonra İnşaata Başlanacak." August 17, 1937.

Anadolu. "Göçmen Evleri Emaneten İnşa Ettirilecek." July 29, 1937.

"Göçmen Evleri ve Köyleri." *Belediyeler Dergisi* 29, no. 12 (1937): 53–55.

Anadolu. "Göçmen Evleri, Yakında İnşa Edilmeye Başlanacak." March 6, 1937.

Anadolu. "Göçmen Köyleri, İnşaata Haziran İçinde Başlanacak." May 28, 1937.

Anadolu. "Göçmen Köyleri, Komisyon Kazalara Tetkikata Gidiyor." January 19, 1937.

Anadolu. "Göçmenler Geliyor, Bu Yıl Vilayetimize 5296 Göçmen Gelecek." June 30, 1937.

Cumhuriyet. "Göçmenler İçin Malzeme Alındı (Construction Materials Have Been Bought for the Immigrants)." May 20, 1935.

Anadolu. "Göçmenlere Verilecek Arazi İstimlak Ediliyor." March 5, 1937.

Gökalp, Zıya. *Turkish Nationalism and Western Civilization: Selected Essays of Ziya Gökalp*. Translated by Niyazi Berkes. New York: Columbia University Press, 1959.

Greverus, Ina-Maria. *Der Territoriale Mensch: Ein Literaturanthropologischer Versuch Zum Heimatphänomen*. Frankfurt Am Mein, Germany: Athenäum Verlag, 1972.

Grift, Liesbeth van de. "Cultivating Land and People: Internal Colonization in Interwar Europe." In *Governing the Rural in Interwar Europe*, edited by Liesbeth van de Grift and Amalia Ribi Forclaz, 68–92. New York: Routledge/Taylor & Francis Group, 2018.

———. "Introduction: Theories and Practices of Internal Colonization, the Cultivation of Lands and People in the Age of Modern Territoraliality," *International Journal of History*, 3, no. 2 (2015).

Grift, Liesbeth van de, and Amalia Ribi Forclaz, eds. *Governing the Rural in Interwar Europe*. London; New York: Routledge, Taylor & Francis Group, 2018.

Grill, Johnpeter Horst. "The Nazi Party's Rural Propaganda before 1928." *Central European History* 15, no. 2 (1982): 149–85. http://www.jstor.org/stable/45459 55.

Guha, Amalendu. "Lenin on the Agrarian Question." *Social Scientist* 5, no. 9 (April 1977): 61–80. https://doi.org/10.2307/3516720.

Güleç, Alaettin. *Küçükyozgat Köyü: Köy Tetkiki*. Ankara Halkevi Neşriyatı Köycüler Şubesi 17/2. Ankara: Ankara Halkevi, 1936.

Gürcan, Metin, and Robert Johnson, eds. *The Gallipoli Campaign: The Turkish Perspective*. Routledge Studies in First World War History. London: Routledge/ Taylor & Francis Group, 2016.

Hamit Bey. *Devlet İnhisarlarına Müteallik Mevzuat*. İnhisarlar Umum Müdürlüğü Hukuk Müşavirliği, I, II. İstanbul: İnhisarlar Matbaası, 1932.

Hamit Sadi. *İktisadi Türkiye: Tabii, Beşeri ve Mevzii Coğrafya Tetkikleri*. Yüksek İktisat ve Ticaret Mektebi 14. İstanbul: Ahmet Sait Matbaası, 1932.

Harf İnkılabı, 1928–1938: Tarih, Tahlil, Tasvir. C.H.P. Beşiktaş Halkevi Yayınları, Sayı 1. İstanbul: İstanbul: Kader Basımevi, 1938.

Hechter, Michael. *Internal Colonialism: The Celtic Fringe in British National Development, 1536–1966*. International Library of Sociology. London: Routledge and Kegan Paul, 1975.

Henderson, Susan R. "Ernst May and the Campaign to Resettle the Countryside: Rural Housing in Silesia, 1919–1925." *Journal of the Society of Architectural Historians* 61, no. 2 (2002): 188–211. https://doi.org/10.2307/991839.

Heper, Metin. "Center and Periphery in the Ottoman Empire: With Special Reference to the Nineteenth Century." *International Political Science Review* 1, no. 1 (1980): 81–104.

Anadolu. "Her Göçmenin Evi Olacak." February 2, 1936.

Heyd, Uriel. *Foundations of Turkish Nationalism: The Life and Teachings of Ziya Gökalp*. Westport, Conn: Hyperion Press, 1979.

Horváth, Béla. *Anadolu 1913*. Translated by Tarık Demirkan. Tarih Vakfı Yurt Yayınları 36. İstanbul: Tarih Vakfı, 1996.

Howard, Douglas A. *The History of Turkey*. The Greenwood Histories of the Modern Nations. Westport, Conn: Greenwood Press, 2001.

Howard, Ebenezer. *Garden Cities of To-Morrow*. Edited by F. J. Osborn. London, UK: Faber, 1965.

Hutchinson, John, and Anthony D. Smith, eds. *Nationalism*. Oxford Readers. Oxford; New York: Oxford University Press, 1994.

İbrahim Hakkı, and Hamit Nafız. *30–31 Mart 1928 Tarihindeki Tepeköy-Torbalı Zelzelesi.* Darülfünun Jeoloji Enstitüsü Neşriyatından 1. İstanbul: Kader Matbaası, 1929.

İhtisas Raporları: 1931 Birinci Türkiye Ziraat Kongresi. Vol. 1. Ankara: Milli İktisat ve Tasarruf Cemiyeti, 1931.

İmset, İsmet Hulusi. "Köye Gidelim." *Köy Postası* 52, no. 09 (1948): 13.

Inan, Afet (Ayşe). "Afet İnan: Prolegomena to an Outline of Turkish History." In *Discourses of Collective Identity in Central and Southeast Europe (1770–1945): Texts and Commentaries*, edited by Ahmet Ersoy, Maciej Górny, and Vangelis Kechriotis, translated by Ahmet Ersoy, 54–61. Budapest; New York: Central European University Press, 2010.

Inan, Afet Ayşe. *Cumhuriyet'in Ellinci Yılı Için: Köylerimiz.* Vol. XVI. 36. Ankara: Türk Tarih Kurumu Basımevi, 1978.

———, ed. "İktisat Esaslarımız: 17 Şubat 339 – 4 Mart 339 Tarihine Kadar İzmir'de Toplanan İlk Türk İktisat Kongresinde KAbul Olunan Esaslar ve İrat Olunan Nutuklar." In *İzmir İktisat Kongresi, 17 Şubat – 4 Mart 1923*, 17–90. Türk Tarih Kurumu Yayınları XVI. Dizi 46. Ankara: Türk Tarih Kurumu Basımevi, 1982.

İpek, Nedim. "Göçmen Köylerine Dair." *Tarih ve Toplum* 150, no. Haziran (1996): 15–21.

———. *Mübadele ve Samsun.* Türk Tarih Kurumu Yayınları. XVI. Dizi, Sayı 85. Ankara: Türk Tarih Kurumu Basımevi, 2000.

Anadolu. "İskan İşleri, Kayas Çiftliğinde Yeni Köyler Kurulacak." May 26, 1937.

Resmi Gazete. "İskan Kanunu." 04 1934, sec. 2733. http://www.resmigazete.go v.tr/arsiv/2733.pdf.

İskan Tarihçesi. İstanbul: Hamit Matbaası, 1932.

Demiryollar Mecmuası. "İsmetpaşa (Kömürhan) Köprüsü," 1931.

İstatistik Göstergeler– Statistical Indicators, 1923–1992. 1682. Ankara: T.C. Başbakanlık Devlet İstatistik Enstitüsü, 1994.

Izmir Cumhuriyetin 15. Yılında. Izmir Cumhuriyet Basımevi, 1938.

Anadolu. "İzmir İskan Müdürlüğü." August 20, 1937.

Anadolu. "İzmir İskan Müdürlüğünden." July 17, 1937.

Jafar, Majeed R. *Under-Underdevelopment: A Regional Case Study of the Kurdish Area in Turkey.* Studies of the Social Policy Association in Finland; No 24. Helsinki: Social Policy Association in Finland, 1976.

Jongerden, Joost. *The Settlement Issue in Turkey and the Kurds: An Analysis of Spatical Policies, Modernity and War.* BRILL, 2007.

Kaplan, Ramazan. *Cumhuriyet Dönemi Türk Romanında Köy*. 3. baskı. Kaynak Eserler 32. Kızılay, Ankara: Akçağ, 1997.

Karaömerlioğlu, Asım. *Orada Bir Köy Var Uzakta: Erken Cumhuriyet Döneminde Köycü Söylem*. 1. baskı. Araştırma-İnceleme Dizisi 200. Cağaloğlu, İstanbul: İletişim, 2006.

Karaömerlioğlu, M. Asim. "The People's Houses and the Cult of the Peasant in Turkey." *Middle Eastern Studies* 34, no. 4 (1998): 67–91. http://www.jstor.org/stable/4283970.

Karaömerlioğlu, M. Asim. "The Village Institutes Experience in Turkey." *British Journal of Middle Eastern Studies* 25, no. 1 (May 1998): 47–73. http://www.jstor.org/stable/195847.

Karaosmanoğlu, Yakup Kadri. *Yaban*. 34. baskı. Y. Kadri Karaosmanoğlu Bütün Eserleri Dizisi 1. İstanbul: İletişim, 1999.

Kaştan, Yüksel. "Atatürk Dönemi Türkiye-Bulgaristan İlişkileri." *Atatürk Araştırma Merkezi Dergisi* XXIV, no. 72 (2008). http://www.atam.gov.tr/dergi/sayi-72/ataturk-donemi-turkiye-bulgaristan-iliskileri.

Katz, Elihu, and S. N. Eisenstadt. "Some Sociological Observations on the Response of Israeli Organizations to New Immigrants." *Administrative Science Quarterly* 5, no. 1 (1960): 113–33.

Kayış, Yasin. *Aydın Vilâyeti Salnâmelerinde Torbalı ve Sultan II. Abdülhamid'in Hayır Eserleri*. Kültür Yayınları, I. İzmir: Torbalı Belediyesi, 2012.

Keyder, Caglar. "Genesis of Petty Commodity Production in Agriculture: The Case of Turkey." In *Culture and Economy: Changes in Turkish Villages*, edited by Paul Stirling, 171–86. Huntingdon: Eothen, 1993.

Keyder, Çağlar. *The Definition of a Peripheral Economy: Turkey, 1923–1929*. Studies in Modern Capitalism = Etudes Sur Le Capitalisme Moderne. Cambridge [Cambridgeshire]; New York: Paris: Cambridge University Press; Editions de la Maison des sciences de l'homme, 1981.

Kezer, Zeynep. *Building Modern Turkey: State, Space, and Ideology in the Early Republic*. Culture Politics and the Built Environment. Pittsburgh, Pa: University of Pittsburgh Press, 2015.

———. "Spatializing Difference: The Making of an Internal Border in Early Republican Elazığ, Turkey." *Journal of the Society of Architectural Historians* 73, no. 4 (December 2014): 507–27. https://doi.org/10.1525/jsah.2014.73.4.507.

Kirby, Fay. *Türkiye'de Köy Enstitüleri*. Translated by Niyazi Berkes. 3. Baskı. İstanbul: Tarihçi Kitabevi, 2010.

Koca, Hüseyin. *Yakın Tarihten Günümüze Hükümetlerin Doğu-Güneydoğu Anadolu Politikaları*. Bilimsel Araştırma Dizisi 04. Konya: Mikro, 1998.

Kocabaş Yıldırır, Özlem. *Türkiye'de Tarımsal Kooperatifçilik Düşüncesinin Gelişimi.* 1. baskı. Libra Kitap 35. Osmanbey, İstanbul: Libra Kitap, 2010.

Kocak, Seval, and Gulsun Atanur Baskan. "Village Institutes and Life-Long Learning." *Procedia – Social and Behavioral Sciences* 46 (2012): 5937–40. http s://doi.org/10.1016/j.sbspro.2012.08.009.

Kohn, Hans. *Nationalism: Its Meaning and History.* Toronto, Canada: Princeton, N.J.: Van Nostrand, 1955.

Kolars, John. "Problems of International River Management: The Case of the Euphrates." In *International Waters of the Middle East: From Euphrates-Tigris to Nile*, edited by Asit K Biswas, 44–94. Oxford: Oxford University Press, 1994.

Kolars, John F., and William A. Mitchell. *The Euphrates River and the Southeast Anatolia Development Project.* Water, the Middle East Imperative. Carbondale: Southern Illinois University Press, 1991.

Kop, Kadri, Kemal, Murad Sertoğlu, and Necaettin Atasagon. "Köy Dergisi'nin Prensip ve Gayesi." *Köy Dergisi* 1, no. 1 (1939): 2.

Köy Envanter Raporlarına Göre Elazığ. Köy İşleri Bakanlığı Yayınları 44. Konya: Yıldız Basımevi, 1966.

"Köy Evleri Proje Müsabakası." *Arkitekt* 51, no. 3 (1935): 93.

Anadolu. "Köy Kalkınma Planına Göre Hazırlanan Program, Elli Aygır, Yetmiş Eşek Aygırı ve Dörtyüzelli Boğa Satın Alınacaktır." February 21, 1937.

Köy Kanunu, Pub. L. No. 442, 237 (1924). http://www.mevzuat.gov.tr/Mevzuat Metin/1.3.442.pdf.

Anadolu. "Köy Öğretmeni Enstitüsü Önümüzdeki Ders Yılında Açılacaktır." March 21, 1937.

Anadolu. "Köyler İçin Beşer Yıllık Plan." July 31, 1936.

Köymen, Nusret Kemal. "Forward to the Progressive Village." *La Turquie Kemaliste* 32, no. Avril (1939): 15–18.

(Köymen), Nusret Kemal. *Halkçılık ve Köycülük.* Ankara: Tarık Edip Kütüphanesi, 1934.

———. *Köycülük Esasları.* Ankara: Tarık Edip Kütüphanesi, 1934.

———. *Meksika'da Köycülük.* Ankara: Tarık Edip Kütüphanesi, 1934.

Köymen, Nusret Kemal. *Türk Köyünü Yükseltme Çareleri.* Ankara: Çankaya Matbaası, 1939.

Köymen, Oya. "Cumhuriyet Döneminde Tarımsal Yapı ve Tarım Politikaları." In *75 Yılda Köylerden Şehirlere*, 1–30. Bilanço' 98 Yayın Dizisi. Istanbul: Türkiye Ekonomik ve Toplumsal Tarih Vakfı, 1999.

(Koyunoğlu), Arif Hikmet. "Köy Evi." *Arkitekt* 35, no. 11 (1933): 357.

Kozanoğlu, Abdullah Ziya. "Gün Geçiminde Kerpiç Köy Yapısı." *Ülkü* 13, no. 2 (1934): 66–70.

———. "Halkevi Trakya Göçmen Evleri Proje Müsabakasında Kazanan Eserin Raporu." *Arkitekt* 55–56, no. 07–08 (1935): 205–6.

———. "Köy Evleri Proje ve Yapıları İçin Toplu Rapor." *Arkitekt* 55–56, no. 07–08 (1935): 203–4.

(Kozanoğlu), Abdullah Ziya. "Köy Mimarisi." *Ülkü* 7, no. Ağustos (1933): 37–41.

———. "Köy Mimarisi." *Ülkü* 5, no. Haziran (1933): 370–74.

Kushner, David. *The Rise of Turkish Nationalism, 1876–1908.* London; Totowa, N.J: Cass, 1977.

Kutlu, Sacit. *Didâr-ı Hürriyet: Kartpostallarla İkinci Meşrutiyet 1908–1913.* 1. baskı. İstanbul Bilgi Üniversitesi Yayınları 57. İstanbul: İstanbul Bilgi Üniversitesi, 2004.

"Lausanne Peace Treaty VI. Convention Concerning the Exchange of Greek and Turkish Populations Signed at Lausanne, January 30, 1923.," July 24, 1923. http://www.mfa.gov.tr/lausanne-peace-treaty-vi_-convention-conc erning-the-exchange-of-greek-and-turkish-populations-signed-at-lausa nne_.en.mfa.

Lewis, Bernard. *The Emergence of Modern Turkey.* Oxford University Press, 1961.

"L'Immigration En Turquie." *La Turquie Kemaliste* 23, no. Janvier (1938): 15–18.

Low-Cost Housing Typology – TCBCA 272.80/3.9.3 (5), TCBCA 272.80/3.9.3 (5) $ (1925).

Makal, Mahmut. *A Village in Anatolia.* Edited by Paul Stirling. Translated by Sir Wyndham Deedes. 1. Edition. London: Vallentine, Mitchell & Co. Ltd., 1954.

Maksudyan, Nazan. *Türklüğü Ölçmek: Bilimkurgusal Antropoloji ve Türk Milliyetçiliğinin Irkçı Çehresi, 1925–1939.* İlk basım. Beyoğlu, İstanbul: Metis, 2005.

Mango, Andrew. *From the Sultan to Atatürk: Turkey.* Haus Histories. London: Haus Publishing, 2009.

Mansel, Philip. "CITIES OF THE LEVANT – THE PAST FOR THE FUTURE?" *Asian Affairs* 45, no. 2 (May 4, 2014): 220–42. https://doi.org/10.1080/03068 374.2014.907006.

Mardin, Şerif. *Bütün eserleri dizisi. 1: Jön Türklerin syasî fikirleri: 1895–1908.* 5. baskı. İletişim yayınları 13. Cağaloğlu, İstanbul: İletişim Yayınları, 1994.

———. *Bütün eserleri dizisi. 3: İdeoloji.* 3. baskı. İletişim yayınları 191. Cağaloğlu, İstanbul: İletişim Yayınları, 1995.

———. *Türk Modernleşmesi.* 1. baskı. Makaleler 4. Cağaloğlu, İstanbul: İletişim Yayınları, 1991.

Martal, Abdullah. *Belgelerle Osmanlı Döneminde İzmir*. İzmir: Ankara: Yazıt Yayıncılık, 2007.

Anadolu. "Mektepsiz Köy Kalmayacak, Beş Yıllık Program Tamamlanmak Üzere." January 16, 1937.

Anadolu. "Modern İnekhane, Yerin İstimlakına Derhal Başlanıyor." March 13, 1937.

Mortaş, Abidin. "Köy Evi Tipleri." *Arkitekt* 109–110, no. 1–2 (1940): 8–9.

———. "Köy Projesi: Mimar Burhan Arif." *Arkitekt* 59–60, no. 11–12 (1935): 320.

Muşat, Raluca. "Lessons for Modern Living: Planned Rural Communities in Interwar Romania, Turkey and Italy." *Journal of Modern European History* 13, no. 4 (2015): 534–48.

———. "The 'Social Museum' of Village Life." In *Governing the Rural in Interwar Europe*, edited by Amalia Ribi Forclaz and Liesbeth van de Grift, 117–41. New York: Routledge, 2018.

———. "'To Cure, Uplift and Ennoble the Village': Militant Sociology in the Romanian Countryside, 1934–1938." *East European Politics and Societies* 27, no. 3 (2012): 353–75.

Nafia Sergisi Kataloğu. Vol. 13. T.C. Nafia Vekaleti Neşriyatı 5. Ankara: T.C. Nafia Bakanlığı, 1944.

Nalbantoğlu Baydar, Gülsüm. "Silent Interruptions: Urban Encounters with Rural Turkey." In *Rethinking Modernity and National Identity in Turkey*, edited by Sibel Bozdoğan and Reşat Kasaba, 192–210. Publications on the Near East 3. Seattle: London: University of Washington Press, 1997.

Nalbantoglu, Gulsum Baydar. "Between Civilization and Culture: Appropriation of Traditional Dwelling Forms in Early Republican Turkey." *Journal of Architectural Education (1984-)* 47, no. 2 (November 1993): 66–74. https://doi.org/10.2307/1425168.

Nazlı, Hurşit. *Elazığ İlinin Coğrafi, Zirai, Ticari, Tarih, Nüfus ve Jeolojik Durumu*. Ankara: Zerbamat Basımevi, 1939.

Ökçün, A. Gündüz. "İkinci Meşrutiyet Döneminde Yeni Köylerin Kurulmasına ve Köylerde Çevre Sağlığına İlişkin Tüzel Düzenlemeler." In *Prof. Fehmi Yavuz'a Armağan*, 171–200. 528. Ankara: AÜ Siyasal Bilgiler Fakültesi Yayınları, 1983.

Oktay, Ahmet. *Cumhuriyet Dönemi Edebiyatı*. Kültür Bakanlığı Yayınları; Sanat-Edebiyat Dizisi / Yayımlar Dairesi Başkanlığı, 1562. 69–6. Ankara: Kültür Bakanlığı, 1993.

Öktem, A. Naim (Hakim). "Die Stellung (Izmir) Smyrna Im Weltverkehr Und Welthandel." Dissertation, Friedrich Wilhelms Universität zu Berlin, 1935.

Okyar, Osman, and Mehmet Seyitdanlıoğlu. *Fethi Okyar'ın Anıları: Atatürk-Okyar ve Çok Partili Türkiye*. İstanbul: Türkiye İş Bankası Kültür yayınları, 1999.

Olson, Robert. "The Kurdish Rebellions of Sheikh Said (1925), Mt. Ararat (1930), and Dersim (1937–8): Their Impact on the Development of the Turkish Air Force and on Kurdish and Turkish Nationalism." *Die Welt Des Islams* 40, no. 1 (2000): 67–94. http://www.jstor.org/stable/1571104.

Oral, Haluk. *Gallipoli 1915: Through Turkish Eyes*. 1st ed. Beyoğlu, İstanbul: Türkiye İş Bankası Kültür Yayınları, 2007.

Özcan, Orhan. "İngiliz Basınında İzmir Yangını ve Mülteci Sorunu (Eylül 1922)." *Çağdaş Türkiye Tarihi Araştırmaları Dergisi* 15, no. 31 (2015): 177–200.

Özen, Hulusi. *Köy Tetkikleri: Genezin ve Göynük*. Kırşehir Halkevi Neşriyatından 7–8. Kırşehir: Köy Basımevi, 1941.

Özsezgin, Kaya. *Cumhuriyetin 75 Yılında Türk Resmi*. Türkiye İş Bankası, Kültür Yayınları; Cumhuriyet Dizisi, Genel yayın no. 436. 20. İstanbul: Türkiye İş Bankası Kültür Yayınları, 1999.

———. *Cumhuriyetin Elli Yılında Plastik Sanatlar*. Tunca Sanat, 2010.

Öztan, Ramazan Hakkı. "Settlement Law of 1934: Turkish Nationalism in the Age of Revisionism." *Journal of Migration History* 6, no. 1 (February 17, 2020): 82–103. https://doi.org/10.1163/23519924-00601006.

Pappenheim, Fritz. *The Alienation of Modern Man: An Interpretation Based on Marx and Tönnies/ Fritz Pappenheim*. New York: Modern Reader Paperbacks, 1968.

Parker, John, and Charles Smith, trans. "Appendix: Programme of Republican People's Party." In *Modern Turkey*, 1. Ed., 235–51. London: George Routledge & Sons, Ltd., 1940.

Parla, Taha, Füsun Üstel, and Sabir Yücesoy. *Ziya Gökalp, Kemalizm ve Türkiye'de korporatizm*. 3. baskı. İletişim Yayınları Araştırma İnceleme Dizisi, 76 9. İstanbul: İletişim Yayınları, 1999.

Parssinen, T. M. "Thomas Spence and the Origin of English Land Nationalization," Journal of the History of Ideas, 34, no. 1 (1973).

Popkins, Gareth. "Peasant Experiences of the Late Tsarist State: District Congresses of Land Captains, Provincial Boards and the Legal Appeals Process, 1891–1917." *The Slavonic and East European Review* 78, no. 1 (2000): 90–114. http://www.jstor.org/stable/4213009.

Quataert, Donald. *The Ottoman Empire, 1700–1922*. Cambridge, UK; New York: Cambridge University Press, 2005. http://dx.doi.org/10.1017/CBO9780511 818868.

Rathbun, Carole Leslie. "The Village in the Turkish Novel and Short Story 1920 to 1955." Thesis (Ph. D.), Princeton University, 1968.

Rayman, Paula. *The Kibbutz Community and Nation Building.* Princeton, N.J: Princeton University Press, 1981.

Reşit Galip. "Tarih, Arkeologya ve Etnografya Dergisi Niçin Çıkıyor?" *Türk Tarih, Arkeologya ve Etnografya Dergisi* Temmuz, no. 1 (1933).

Rogger, Hans. *Russia in the Age of Modernisation and Revolution, 1881–1917.* Longman History of Russia. London; New York: Longman, 1983.

Sadoğlu, Hüseyin. *Türkiye'de Ulusçuluk ve Dil Politikaları.* 1. baskı. İstanbul Bilgi Üniversitesi Yayınları 44. İstanbul: İstanbul Bilgi Üniversitesi Yayınları, 2003.

Altan. "Şarımızda Olup Bitenler: İskan İşleri," Temmuz 1935.

Altan. "Şarımızda Olup Bitenler: İskanda," Haziran 1935.

Altan. "Şarımızda Olup Bitenler: Tapuda," Aralık 1935.

Savran, Cevdet Nasuhi. "Yurdun Bucaklarından: Kantrancı Köyü." *Karınca: Türk Kooperatifçilik Cemiyetinin Aylık Mecmuası* 14, no. Haziran (1935): 5–6.

Sayar, Zeki. "İç Kolonizasyon: Başka Memleketlerde." *Arkitekt* 68, no. 8 (1936): 231–35.

———. "İç Kolonizasyon: Kolonisation Intérieure." *Arkitekt* 62, no. 2 (1936): 46–51.

Schmidt, Carl. "Land Reclamation in Fascist Italy." *The Academy of Political Science* 52 (1937): 340–63.

Schmidt, K. Rudolf. "Zur Heimatideologie," Das Heft, Zeitschrift für Literatur und Kunst, 6 (1965).

Schnaidt, Claude. *Hannes Meyer: Bauten, Projekte Und Schriften; Buildings, Projects and Writings.* Stuttgart: Verlag Gerd Hatje, 1965.

Seeher, Jürgen and Deutsches Archäologisches Institut, eds. *"Hattuşa'da 106 Yıl": Hitit Kazılarının Fotoğraflarla Öyküsü = "106 Years in Hattusha": Photographs Tell the Story of the Excavations in the Hittite Capital.* 1. baskı. Yapı Kredi yayınları 3712. Beyoğlu, İstanbul: Yapı Kredi Yayınları: DAI, 2012.

Semerci, Bekir. "Yeni Arayışlar." In *Köy Enstitüleri: Amaçlar İlkeler Uygulamalar,* edited by Mustafa Aydoğan, 18–27. Tanıtım Dizisi 1. İstanbul: Köy Enstitüleri ve Çağdaş Eğitim Vakfı Yayınları, 1997.

Sezer, Özge. "Contectualization, Realization, and Contestation of the Village: Inheriting from Early Republican Elazığ, Turkey" pp.183-196, in Praktiken des Erbes. Metaphern, Materialisierungen, Machtkonstellationen, Schriftenreihe des DFG-Graduiertenkollegs "Identität und Erbe", Band III, ed. Simone Bogner et.al (Weimar: Bauhaus Universitätsverlag, 2022).

———. "Idealization of the Land: Forming the New Rural Settlements in the Early Republican Period of Turkey, 1923–1950." Dissertation, Berlin Technical University, 2020. http://dx.doi.org/10.14279/depositonce-9811.

———. "Imagining the Fascist City: A Comparison between Rome and New Towns in the Pontine Marshes during the Fascist Era." In *History Takes Place: Rome: Dynamics of Urban Change*, edited by Anna Hofmann and Martin Zimmermann, 96–107. Berlin: Jovis Berlin, 2016.

———. "Modern Köyün İnşası: Erken Cumhuriyet Dönemi Kırsalında İskan Politikaları Üzerine Bir Değerlendirme." *Türkiye Bilimler Akademisi Kültür Envanteri Dergisi* 0, no. 24 (December 31, 2021). https://doi.org/10.22520/t ubaked2021.24.007.

———. "Modernizasyon Düşleri; Erken Cumhuriyet Dönemi Türkiyesi'nde Anadolu Kırsalında İstasyon Yapıları ve Köprüler." In *International Symposium on Theories of Art / Design and Aesthetics, 19–21 October 2011 Faculty of Fine Arts Antalya University Turkey, Papers*, 278–85. Antalya: Akdeniz Üniversitesi Güzel Sanatlar Fakültesi Dekanlığı, 2012.

———. "Railways and Bridges as Expression of Rural in Early Republican Period, 1930–1945 (Erken Cumhuriyet Döneminde Kırsalın İfadesi Bağlamında Demiryolları ve Köprüler)." Master Thesis, Istanbul Technical University, 2010.

———. "The Village House: Planning the Rural Life in Early Republican Turkey." In *Spaces / Times / Peoples: Domesticity, Dwelling and Architectural History; Mekanlar / Zamanlar / Insanlar: Evsellik, Ev, Barinma ve Mimarlik Tarihi*, edited by Lale Özgenel, 51–60. Ankara: ODTÜ Basım İşliği, 2016.

Shaw, Stanford Jay, and Ezel Kural Shaw. *Reform, Revolution, and Republic: The Rise of Modern Turkey, 1808 – 1975*. 1. publ. History of the Ottoman Empire and Modern Turkey, Stanford Shaw ; Vol. 2. Cambridge: Cambridge Univ. Press, 1978.

Simons, Tal, and Paul Ingram. "Organization and Ideology: Kibbutzim and Hired Labor, 1951–1965." *Administrative Science Quarterly* 42, no. 4 (1997): 784–813.

Smith, Anthony D. *National Identity*. Ethnonationalism in Comparative Perspective. Reno: University of Nevada Press, 1991.

———. *The Ethnic Origins of Nations*. 17. [reprint]. Malden, Mass.: Blackwell, 2008.

Snowden, Frank. "Latina Province, 1944–1950." *Sage Publications* 43, no. Relief in the Aftermath of War (2008): 509–26.

Soer, Josh van, and Michael Marek. *Kibbuzhandbuch: Leben und Arbeiten in Kibbuz und Moshav; Hinweise für Volunteers*. 5. Aufl. Stuttgart: Zündhölzchen Verl, 1985.

Soylu, Gafur. *Köy Nedir ve Nasıl İdare Edilir*. 2. Basılış. İstanbul: Marifet Basımevi, 1940.

Spence, Thomas. *Das Gemeineigentum Am Boden*. Translated by F. Eichmann. Leibzig, Germany: Hirschfeld, 1904.

Spiegel, Daniela. *Die Città Nuove Des Agro Pontino Im Rahmen Der Faschistischen Staatsarchitektur*. Berliner Beiträge Zur Bauforschung Und Denkmalpflege 7. Petersberg: M. Imhof, 2010.

Sturt, George. *Change in the Village*. Dover, N.H: Caliban Books, 1984.

Suny, Ronald Grigor, Fatma Müge Göçek, and Norman M. Naimark, eds. *A Question of Genocide: Armenians and Turks at the End of the Ottoman Empire*. Oxford; New York: Oxford University Press, 2011.

Survey Report on Building Villages in Izmir and Manisa, TCBCA 272.80/3.6.8 § (1924).

Taglia, Stefano. *Intellectuals and Reform in the Ottoman Empire: The Young Turks on the Challenges of Modernity*. SOAS/Routledge Studies on the Middle East 23. London: Routledge/Taylor & Francis Group, 2015.

Tansuğ, Sezer. *Çağdaş Türk sanatı*. 3. basım. İstanbul: Remzi Kitabevi, 1993.

Tanyeri-Erdemir, Tuğba. "Archaeology as a Source of National Pride in the Early Years of the Turkish Republic." *Journal of Field Archaeology* 31, no. 4 (2006): 381–93. http://www.jstor.org/stable/40025296.

Tapu Kadastro Umum Müdürlüğü. "Mübadil ve Yerli Ahaliye Tevzi Edilen Arazi Kayıtları Hakkında Tamim." *Resmi Gazete*. March 13, 1930, sec. 1444. http://www.resmigazete.gov.tr/main.aspx?home=http://www.resmigaze te.gov.tr/arsiv/1444.pdf&main=http://www.resmigazete.gov.tr/arsiv/144 4.pdf.

TBMM. İskan Kanunu, Pub. L. No. 2510 (1934). http://www.resmigazete.gov.t r/arsiv/2733.pdf.

―――. İtibarı Zirai Birliği Kanunu, Pub. L. No. 498, 396 (1924). https://www.t bmm.gov.tr/tutanaklar/KANUNLAR_KARARLAR/kanuntbmmc002/kanu ntbmmc002/kanuntbmmc00200498.pdf.

―――. Köy Eğitmenleri Kanunu, Pub. L. No. 3238 (1937). https://www.tbmm .gov.tr/tutanaklar/KANUNLAR_KARARLAR/kanuntbmmc017/kanuntbm mc017/kanuntbmmc01703238.pdf.

———. Köy Enstitüleri Kanunu, Pub. L. No. 3803, 233 (1940). https://www.tb mm.gov.tr/tutanaklar/KANUNLAR_KARARLAR/kanuntbmmc021/kanun tbmmc021/kanuntbmmc02103803.pdf.

———. Maarif Teşkilâtına Dair Kanun, Pub. L. No. 789 (1926). https://www.tb mm.gov.tr/tutanaklar/KANUNLAR_KARARLAR/kanuntbmmc004/kanun tbmmc004/kanuntbmmc00400789.pdf.

———. Regulation for "the Province Village Offices," Pub. L. No. 45/175 (1936).

———. Tarım Kredi Kooperatifleri Kanunu, Pub. L. No. 2836, 764 (1935). https ://www.tbmm.gov.tr/tutanaklar/KANUNLAR_KARARLAR/kanuntbmmc 015/kanuntbmmc015/kanuntbmmc01502836.pdf.

———. Terkedilmiş gayrimenkulün iskan edilme hakkını haiz göçmenler ve aşiretlere tevzii hakkında yönetmelik, Pub. L. No. 683, TCBCA 030.18.01.01/010.33.20(1+4) (1924).

———. Tunceli Vilayetinin İdaresi Hakkında Kanun, Pub. L. No. 2884, 112 (1935).

———. "Türkiye Cumhuriyeti Ile Romanya Arasında Dostluk, İyi Komşuluk ve İşbirliği Antlaşmasının Onaylanmasının Uygun Bulunduğuna Dair Kanun Tasarısı ve Dışişleri Komisyonu Raporu (1/323)." Ankara: TBMM, January 13, 1992. https://www.tbmm.gov.tr/tutanaklar/TUTANAK/TBMM/d19/c03 2/tbmm19032080ss0157.pdf.

———. Ziraat Odaları ve Ziraat Odaları Birliği Kanunu, Pub. L. No. 6964, 3119 (1957). http://www.mevzuat.gov.tr/MevzuatMetin/1.3.6964.pdf.

"TBMM Zabıt Ceridesi, IV. Dönem, 3. Devre (TBMM Journal of Official Report, Period IV, Session 3)" 23 (June 14, 1934).

T.C. Sıhhat ve İçtimai Muavenat Vekaleti, İskan Umum Müdürlüğü. İskan Mevzuatı. Ankara: Köyöğretmeni Basımevi, 1936.

Tekeli, İlhan, and Selim İlkin. Cumhuriyetin Harcı III: Modernitenin Altyapısı Oluşurken. 1. baskı. İstanbul Bilgi Üniversitesi Yayınları; Siyaset Bilimi, 39 4. İstanbul: İstanbul Bilgi Üniversitesi, 2003.

———. "Devletçilik Dönemi Tarım Politikalari (Modernleşme Çabaları)." In 75 Yılda Köylerden Şehirlere, 43–56. Istanbul: Türkiye Ekonomik ve Toplumsal Tarih Vakfı, 1999.

Tekeli, İlhan, and Gencay Şaylan. "Türkiye'de Halkçılık İdeolojisinin Evrimi." Toplum ve Bilim Dergisi 6–7, no. Yaz-Güz (1978): 111–56.

Tekinalp, (Munis). Kemalizm. İstanbul: Cumhuriyet Gazete ve Matbaası, 1936.

Temizer, Raci. Ankara Arkeoloji Müzesi. Ankara: Türk Tarih Kurumu Yayınları, 1966.

Thomas, Lewis, J. "Foreword." In *A Village in Anatolia*, 1. Edition., ix–xii. London: Vallentine, Mitchell & Co. Ltd., 1954.

(Tökin), İsmail Hüsrev. "Milli İktisat Tetkikleri: Anadolu Köyünde Bünye Tahavvülü." *Kadro* 14, no. Şubat (1933): 18–24.

———. "Milli İktisat Tetkikleri: Anadolu'da Zirai İşletme Şekilleri." *Kadro* 24, no. Birinci Kanun (1933): 25–32.

———. "Milli İktisat Tetkikleri: Şark Vilayetlerinde Derebeylik." *Kadro* 11, no. İkinci Teşrin (1932): 22–29.

(Tökin), İsmail Hüsrev. "Milli İktisat Tetkikleri: Türk Köylüsü Bir Toprak Reformu Bekliyor." *Kadro* 21, no. Eylül (1933): 21–24.

(Tökin), İsmail Hüsrev. "Milli İktisat Tetkikleri: Türk Köylüsünü Topraklandırmalı. Fakat Nasıl?" *Kadro* 23, no. İkinci Teşrin (1933): 33–39.

———. "Milli İktisat Tetkikleri: Türkiye'de Toprak Ağalığı." *Kadro* 9, no. Eylül (1932): 23–29.

———. "Türkiye Köy İktisadiyatında Toprak Rantı." *Kadro* 4, no. Nisan (1932): 10–14.

(Tökin), (Tökin), İsmail Hüsrev. "Millet İçinde Sınıf Meselesi II." *Kadro* 26, no. Şubat (1934): 20–26.

Toksoy, Nurcan. *Halkevleri: Bir Kültürel Kalkınma Modeli Olarak*. Kavaklıdere, Ankara: Orion Yayınevi, 2007.

Tonguç, İsmail Hakkı. *Eğitim Yolu Ile Canlandırılacak Köy*. 2. Baskı. İstanbul: Remzi Kitabevi, 1947.

(Tonguç), İsmail Hakkı. "Malik Bey ve Talebesinin Resim Sergisi." *Ülkü* 16, no. Haziran (1934): 296–303.

Tönnies, Ferdinand. *Ferdinand Tönnies: Community and Civil Society*. Edited by Jose Harris. Translated by Margaret Hollis. Cambridge: Cambridge University Press, 2001. https://doi.org/10.1017/CBO9780511816260.

Topçubaşı, Alaettin, Cemil. "Köy Tarım Odaları ve Tarımsal Kredi Kooperatifleri." *Karınca: Türk Kooperatifçilik Cemiyetinin Aylık Mecmuası* 15, no. Temmuz (1935): 16–19.

(Tör), Vedat Nedim. "Millet İktisadiyatı: Köylü Kazanmalıdır." *Kadro* 33, no. Eylül (1934): 11–15.

Cumhuriyet. "Trakya'ya Yerleştirilen Muhacirler (Immigrants Who Are Settled in Trace)." November 16, 1934.

Trigger, Bruce G. "Alternative Archaeologies: Nationalist, Colonialist, Imperialist." *Man* 19, no. 3 (September 1984): 355. https://doi.org/10.2307/2802176

Türkiye Cumhuriyetinin İkinci Sanayi Planı 1936. Vol. 21. XVI. Ankara: Türk Tarih Kurumu Basımevi, 1973.

Uluğ, Naşit Hakkı. *Tunceli Medeniyete Açılıyor*. İstanbul: Cumhuriyet Matbaası, 1939.

Ulusan, Celal. "Şehir İmar Planları Nasıl Tanzim Edilmelidir." *Belediyeler Dergisi* 32 (1939): 37–57.

Umumi Meclisce 937 Yılı Toplantısında Kabul Edilen İzmir İli Köylerinin Kültür Bakımından Beş Yıllık Kalkınma Programı. Vol. 7. İzmir: Cumhuriyet Basımevi, 1937.

Üngör, Uğur Ümit. *The Making of Modern Turkey: Nation and State in Eastern Anatolia, 1913–1950*. Oxford: Oxford University Press, 2011.

Ünsal, Behçet. "Bir Köy Evi Tipi." *Arkitekt* 109–110, no. 1–2 (1940): 17.

———. "Sincan Köyü Planı." *Arkitekt* 109–110, no. 1–2 (1940): 15–16.

Üstel, Füsun. *İmparatorluktan Ulus-Devlete Türk Milliyetçiliği, Türk Ocakları, 1912–1931*. 1. baskı. Araştırma-İnceleme Dizisi 47. Cağaloğlu, İstanbul: İletişim, 1997.

Üstün, Senem. "Turkey and the Marshall Plan: Strive for Aid." *The Turkish Yearbook of International Relations (Milletlerarası Münasebetler Türk Yıllığı)* 27 (1997): 31–52.

Uzer, Umut. *An Intellectual History of Turkish Nationalism: Between Turkish Ethnicity and Islamic Identity*. Salt Lake City: The University of Utah Press, 2016.

V. N. "Köy Kampları." *Kadro* 1, no. 1 (1932): 42–43.

Turan Gazetesi. "Valimizin Mühim Bir Eseri Daha." June 25, 1934.

Varlık, M. Bülent, and Cemil Koçak, eds. *Umumi Müfettişler Konferansı'nda Görüşülen ve Dahiliye Vekâleti'ni İgilendiren İşlere Dair Toplantı Zabıtları ile Rapor ve Hulâsası 1936*. 1. Baskı. Dipnot Yayınları Yakın Tarih, 91 6. Ankara: Dipnot, 2010.

Anadolu. "Vilayetimizde 5260 Göçmen İskan Edilecek." June 2, 1937.

Ward, Stephen V., ed. *The Garden City: Past, Present, and Future*. London: Routledge, 2011.

Whitehorn, Alan, ed. *The Armenian Genocide: The Essential Reference Guide*. Santa Barbara, California: ABC-CLIO, an imprint of ABC-CLIO, LLC, 2015.

Williams, Raymond. *The Country and the City*. New York, USA: Oxford University Press, 1975.

Wolf, Gerhard. "The East as Historical Imagination and the Germanization Policies of the Third Reich." In *Hitler's Geographies: The Spatialities of the Third Reich*, edited by Paolo Giaccaria and Claudio Minca, 93–109. Chicago: University of Chicago Press, 2016.

Wyatt, S. C. "Turkey: The Economic Situation and Five Years Plan." *International Affairs* 13, no. 6 (1934): 826–44.

Yabancı Gözüyle Cumhuriyet Türkiyesi. Ankara: Dahiliye Vekaleti, Matbuat Umum Müdürlüğü, 1938.

Yadirgi, Veli. *The Political Economy of the Kurds of Turkey: From the Ottoman Empire to the Turkish Republic,* 2017.

(Yalnızgil), Samih Rifat. "Birinci Gün, 26 Eylül 1932 Pazartesi, Türk Dili Tetkik Cemiyeti Reisi Samih Rifat Beyin Açma Nutku." İstanbul Devlet Matbaası, 1933.

Yaşar Kemal. *Memed, My Hawk.* Translated by Edouard Roditi. New York Review Books Classics. New York: New York Review Books, 2005.

Anadolu. "Yeni Göçmenler İçin Yer Hazırlandı." July 14, 1937.

Yıldırım, Onur. *Diplomacy and Displacement: Reconsidering the Turco-Greek Exchange of Populations, 1922–1934.* Middle East Studies – History, Politics, and Law. New York: London: Routledge, 2006.

Yıldırmaz, Sinan. *Politics and the Peasantry in Post-War Turkey: Social History, Culture and Modernization.* Library of Ottoman Studies 46. London New York: I.B. Tauris, 2017.

Yılmaz, Niyazi. *Türk Halk Müziğinin Kurucu Hocası Muzaffer Sarısözen.* Ankara: Ocak Yayınları, 1996.

Zandi-Sayek, Sibel. *Ottoman Izmir: The Rise of a Cosmopolitan Port, 1840–1880.* Minneapolis; London: University of Minnesota Press, 2012.

Zirai Kredi Kooperatıfleri Kanunu, Pub. L. No. 1470 (1929). http://www.resmig azete.gov.tr/arsiv/1208.pdf.

Zürcher, Erik Jan. *The Young Turk Legacy and Nation Building: From the Ottoman Empire to Atatürk's Turkey.* Library of Modern Middle East Studies, v. 87. London; New York: New York: I. B. Tauris; Distributed in the United States exclusively by Palgrave Macmillan, 2010.

———. *Turkey: A Modern History.* New rev. ed. London; New York: I.B. Tauris: Distributed by St. Martin's Press, 1998.

———. "Two Young Ottomanists Discover Kemalist Turkey, The Travel Dairies of Robert Anhegger and Andreas Tietze." *Journal of Turkish Studies,* Essays in Honour of Barbara Flamming II, 26, no. I (2002): 359–69.

Demiryollar Mecmuası 85, no. İkinci Teşrin (1932): 78, 92.

Appendix

Village house in Yeniköy, Havuzbaşı and Taşkesik, İzmir (Drawings by the Author according to the field research and archival documents)

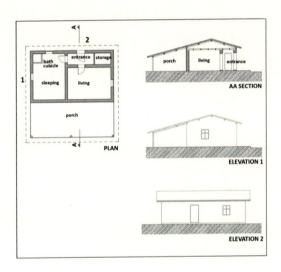

Village house in Kövenk, Elazığ. (Drawings by the Author according to the field research and archival documents)

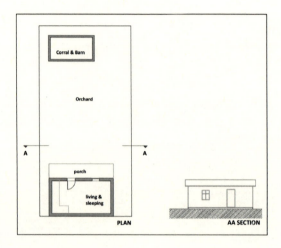

Village House in Etminik, Elazığ. (Drawings by the Author according to the field research and archival documents)

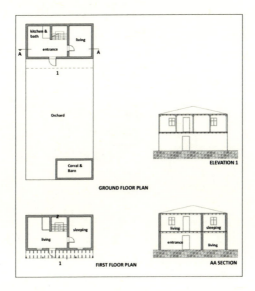

Village House in Vertetil, Elazığ. (Drawings by the Author according to the field research and archival documents)

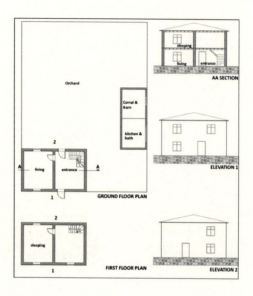

Village House in Perçenç, Elazığ. (Drawings by the Author according to the field research and archival documents)

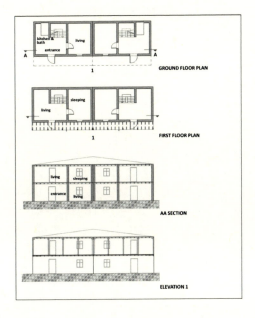

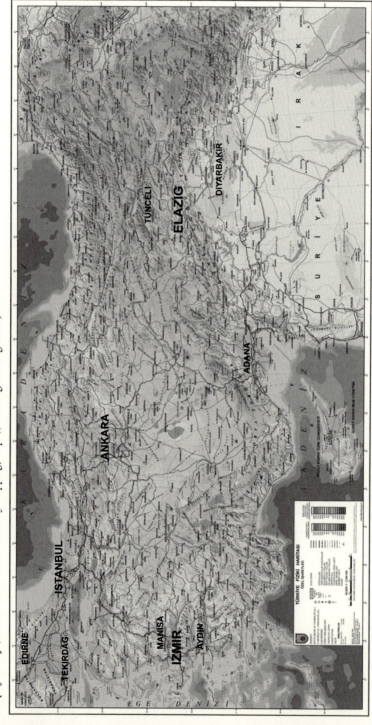

Map of Turkey (Source: General Directorate of Mapping; https://www.hgk.msb.gov.tr.)

Historical Sciences

Sebastian Haumann, Martin Knoll, Detlev Mares (eds.)
Concepts of Urban-Environmental History

2020, 294 p., pb., ill.
29,99 € (DE), 978-3-8376-4375-6
E-Book:
PDF: 26,99 € (DE), ISBN 978-3-8394-4375-0

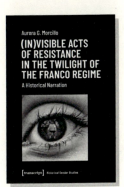

Aurora G. Morcillo
**(In)visible Acts of Resistance
in the Twilight of the Franco Regime**
A Historical Narration

January 2022, 332 p., pb., ill.
50,00 € (DE), 978-3-8376-5257-4
E-Book: available as free open access publication
PDF: ISBN 978-3-8394-5257-8

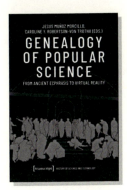

Jesús Muñoz Morcillo, Caroline Y. Robertson-von Trotha (eds.)
Genealogy of Popular Science
From Ancient Ecphrasis to Virtual Reality

2020, 586 p., pb., col. ill.
49,00 € (DE), 978-3-8376-4835-5
E-Book:
PDF: 48,99 € (DE), ISBN 978-3-8394-4835-9

Historical Sciences

Monika Ankele, Benoît Majerus (eds.)
Material Cultures of Psychiatry

2020, 416 p., pb., col. ill.
40,00 € (DE), 978-3-8376-4788-4
E-Book: available as free open access publication
PDF: ISBN 978-3-8394-4788-8

Andreas Kraß, Moshe Sluhovsky, Yuval Yonay (eds.)
Queer Jewish Lives Between Central Europe and Mandatory Palestine
Biographies and Geographies

January 2022, 332 p., pb., ill.
39,99 € (DE), 978-3-8376-5332-8
E-Book:
PDF: 39,99 € (DE), ISBN 978-3-8394-5332-2

Harald Barre
Traditions Can Be Changed
Tanzanian Nationalist Debates
around Decolonizing »Race« and Gender, 1960s-1970s

2021, 274 p., pb.
45,00 € (DE), 978-3-8376-5950-4
E-Book:
PDF: 44,99 € (DE), ISBN 978-3-8394-5950-8

**All print, e-book and open access versions of the titles in our list
are available in our online shop www.transcript-verlag.de/en!**